GRANTA

WHILE WAITING FOR A WAR

D1502091

17

Editor: Bill Buford
Assistant Editor: Graham Coster
Associate Editors: Todd McEwen, Piers Spence
Advertising and Promotion: Monica McStay, Tracy Shaw
Executive Editor: Pete de Bolla
Design: Chris Hyde
Office Manager: Carolyn Harlock
Research: Margaret Costa
US Editor: Jonathan Levi, Granta, 13 White Street, New York, New York 10013

Editorial and Subscription Correspondence in the United States and Canada: Granta, 13 White Street, New York, New York 10013. (212) 864–5644.
All manuscripts are welcome but must be accompanied by a stamped, self-addressed envelope or they cannot be returned.

Granta/0017–3231 is published quarterly for $22 by Granta Publications Ltd, 44a Hobson Street, Cambridge CB1 1NL, England. Second class postage pending at New York, NY. POSTMASTER: send address changes to GRANTA, 13 White Street, New York, NY 10013.

Back Issues: $7.50 each. *Granta* 1,2,3,4 and 9 are no longer available.

Granta is photoset by Lindonprint Typesetters and Hobson Street Studio Ltd, Cambridge, and is printed by Hazell Watson and Viney Ltd, Aylesbury, Bucks, England.

Granta is published by Granta Publications Ltd, 44a Hobson Street, Cambridge CB1 1NL, England, and distributed by Penguin Books Ltd, Harmondsworth, Middlesex, England; Viking Penguin Inc., 40 West 23rd St, New York, New York, USA; Penguin Books Australia Ltd, Ringwood, Victoria, Australia; Penguin Books Canada Ltd, 2801 John Street, Markham, Ontario, Canada L3R 1B4; Penguin Books (NZ) Ltd, 182–90 Wairau Road, Auckland 10, New Zealand. This selection copyright © 1985 by Granta Publications Ltd.

Cover by Chris Hyde

ISSN 0017–3231
ISBN 014–00–8594.7

Published with the assistance of the Eastern Arts Association

CONTENTS

VINTAGE CONTEMPORARIES

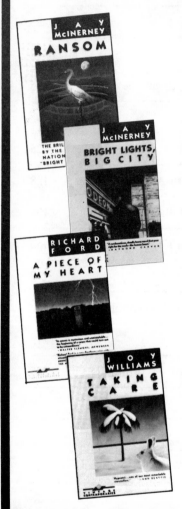

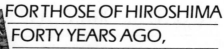

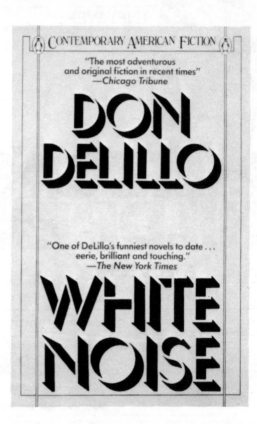

GRAHAM GREENE
WHILE WAITING
FOR A WAR

E velyn Waugh in 1935 went in search of 'the pre-war Georgian era' in the pages of old numbers of *Punch* and the *Illustrated London News*. I find myself in 1985 refreshing my memory of 1937 and 1938 in an old commonplace book and very fragmentary diary of my own: there are verses copied there which I must have chosen for their significance at these moments of my life, and in the diary literary gossip, bizarre crimes and divorces wrenched from newspapers, the sickness of my children (a little girl of five, a boy of two) which seemed more to be feared than the voice of Hitler ranting on the radio, a mysterious arrival at a Channel port of an unknown individual who caused the mobilization of 10,000 police, and then suddenly the digging of trenches on Clapham Common outside our windows, the distribution of gas masks, the evacuation of children, municipal muddle, ending in the temporary peace of Munich—all that period summed up in Stephen Spender's poem written then: 'We who live under the shadow of a war,/What can we do that matters?'

I have cut and selected, but I have altered nothing, and the long distances between dates represent either laziness or in one case absence from England in Mexico, and not self-censorship.

1937

December 26. Discussed film with [John Stuart] Menzies. Two notions for future film. A political situation like that in Spain. A decimation order. Ten men in prison draw lots with matches. A rich man draws the longest match. Offers all his money to anyone who will take his place. One, for the sake of his family, agrees. Later when he is released the former rich man anonymously visits the family who possess his money, he himself now with nothing but his life...

The other idea, a kind of fable: the two young men at the crossroads, penniless. They toss up and separate. One road leads to riches, the other to the scaffold, but both end in the same town on the morning of a public execution.

The hand that signed the treaty bred a fever,
And famine grew, and locusts came;
Great is the hand that holds dominion over
Man by a scribbled name.

13

The five kings count the dead but do not soften
The crusted wound nor pat the brow;
A hand rules pity as a hand rules heaven;
Hands have no tears to flow.

Dylan Thomas

I remember Geoffrey Grigson telling me of the disastrous dinner Cyril Connolly gave to launch this twenty-three-year-old poet. A suave *New Statesman* gathering of patrons: Desmond McCarthy, Peter Quennell. Thomas arrived an hour late, drunk, and all through dinner told McCarthy a series of very stale, old dirty stories, of which he made himself the subject.

December 28. Handed to Menzies the last of the copy for my Korda film [presumably *The Green Cockatoo*].

Henry James in an essay on Crackenthorpe: 'No element assuredly in the artistic temperament of Mr Rudyard Kipling but operates with the ease and exactitude of an alarm clock set to the hour.'

December 29. Ran into Arthur Calder-Marshall and lunched with him at a pub by Leicester Square station. He had been spending the morning joining the Communist Party. Langdon-Davies having lunch in the same pub. About to return to the Spanish Civil War to take moving pictures on sixteen millimetre film which he finally hopes to enlarge for public showing. L.-D. one of those extreme left-wingers who give the impression of a lack of intellectual hardness at the centre. Spender another. They are very pleased with violence and ruthlessness theoretically, but with them it is less a rational policy than a sentimental reaction to their own softness. Like Stevenson playing with pirates.

1938

January 1. Lunch at the Commercio with Oliver Bell and John McMillan. After a bottle and a half of white Orvieta, sherry and brandy, decided to break all engagements for the afternoon. Bought a bottle of brandy and took it back to Bell's roof. A lovely view in the thin rain over Seven Dials and the Great White Lion streets. Nelson's column sticking up out of the mist and the houses on top of the Hippodrome. I had never before realized there *were* houses on the Hippodrome. Climbed recklessly down fire escapes with the brandy and delayed the work on the Queen Mary's sister ship. [A mysterious statement. And were there houses on the Hippodrome?]

Bought *London Life*. Advertisements for men's corsets. All stories and articles deal with corsets, tight lacing and high-heeled shoes. An odd kind of sadistic pleasure over corsets. Completely depraved and completely uncensorable:

> I had not, however, bargained for my friend. After I had worn the corsets for a few days with the lacing loose, she suggested that a general tightening-up was desirable. She gave me lessons in deportment and half an hour of slimming exercises, and my training had begun. The corsets were put around me and laced tight at the back and hips, my stockings pulled up and tightly suspended, and a pair of Court shoes slipped on.
>
> At nights my friend insisted on my wearing a shorter pair of corsets. These were not quite so restrictive, but she saw that I did not tamper with the laces, and I had to bear it.

Correspondence columns full of the same subject.

> *A Mistress and Her Maids.* Very fine black silk stockings are always worn, and our shoes are patent leather Court shoes with tapering 4½ inch heels. An unusual addition to our uniform is that with this costume we wear black kid long gloves, usually of sixteen-button length. This may seem strange for constant wear, but our mistress always attaches great importance to gloves, wearing long gloves of various kinds with nearly all her costumes; and it must be remembered that we are her personal maids for dressing and waiting on her alone, and do not do housework etc. Otherwise, to wear expensive gloves all day would hardly be practical.
>
> As regards another important point, our mistress always insists that we should be well corsetted, and at present we

are wearing rather close-fitting perforated rubber corsets with zip fasteners.

Another subject with obviously sexual appeal: Long Hair.

January 2. Saw the film tests [of *The Green Cockatoo*] at Denham. The excitement of hearing one's own dialogue on the screen for the first time. Good dialogue it sounded too.

Virginia Woolf. Something brought back to mind the story I have heard from two sources of her madness: how she believed she was the Brownings' dog, Flush, and wandered unhappily about the house until Leonard Woolf found her some straw to have her litter of puppies on.

Lunch at Denham with Menzies and Arthur Wimperis. Wimperis one of those faintly arrogant elderly men with the appearance of naval officers whose chaff goes down so well with their mental inferiors who feel complimented at being noticed at all. I found him curiously unbearable. Harrow and hunting in his manner, and nothing in his career to justify his self-confidence. One of those elderly men who take too much care of their bodies.

He spoke of his only trip to America to write a play for Flo Ziegfeld, how unhappy he was, for Z. was surrounded by yes-men who resented an Englishman being introduced to the circle and stuck in their knives as soon as his back was turned. Luckily the play—*Louis Quatorze*—was a success.

Menzies spoke of Ziegfeld's gambling. One night a man—call him S.—lost $20,000 to Z. and paid by cheque. The next night Z. lost $100,000 to S. and also paid by cheque—but Z's cheque was worthless, and S. was never able to get back the 20,000 he had paid.

January 3. Poor little Lucy [my daughter] had a bad night. Vivien now is beginning a cough and Francis is worse [my wife, my son]. It is horrifying how anxious and torn one is by these small creatures' small (I hope to God) sicknesses. How will one feel when the major illnesses come: appendicitis, measles, adolescence? Diphtheria cases at Mitcham, and the lights in the '88' buses which come from there seem unnaturally dim.

Spent the day trying to remove every trace of American influence from the dialogue in my film.

January 4. The first public presentation of television in a cinema [the Dominion, I seem to remember, in Tottenham Court Road]. The screen was eight feet by six, but it looked like a small postage stamp in the corner of the bigger screen. The manager introduced the performers: Lansbury, Bill Bennet, some other comedian who had a back-chat with a performer on the stage, and last Baird [the inventor] gave a short speech. The faces came out with varying clearness. There were times when Lansbury's almost faded out, the outlines were so blurred, presumably by his whiskers. They were like the early telegraphed newspaper pictures; long parallel lines running down the screen took the place of the dots.

Met Tom Harrisson, author of *Savage Civilisations*. A very young, agile-witted man. He has collected £3,000 towards an expedition into the centre of Papua. He plans to stay four years and be fed by aeroplane.

January 5. A note from Harrisson suggesting I might come to New Guinea too. Wrote back that four-year expeditions were impossible for me with a family of three to support.

January 27. F. T. Bason, young man who keeps a bookselling business in Walworth. Mother and father in the old clothes business. B, jumpy and bumptious, writes to authors, actresses etc. Makes up albums of boxing scraps with boxers' autographs collected at the Ring [at Blackfriars] and sells for 10/– an album. Cigarette cards. Complete 'modern' sets of about fifty sell for 3d. Have to be in mint condition. Earliest cards a set of ten Variety Fair about 1896. Worth about £8.10/– mint, 2/6d soiled. Sets double in value in five years. Collectors very fussy. Sent off 1,400 cards to a collector: he could choose any he wanted six a penny. Returned the whole lot. Not in good enough condition. Bason gave me his very ingenuously written bibliography of Maugham. Photo of Maugham taken in a backyard, the dustbin scratched out. Album consisting of picture postcards sent by Maugham from abroad. Signed photograph of Madeleine Carroll. Mrs Bason described tea with Baroness Orczy [creator of the Scarlet

17

Pimpernel]. So badly dressed. 'She was just like the cook when I was in service.' Old Bason pays 52/– a year for his weekly stand in the market. Bought Hueffer's [Ford Madox Ford's] *Fifth Queen Crowned* from B. for 2/6. Had tea in the kitchen. A hint of rather poisoned sexuality in his jumpy and neurotic movements, arms flung out, in his conception of 'shocker' as a book to shock sexually, but above all in his deplorable efforts to paint: a dreadful little crude garish canvas of a woman's torso in flaring yellow, naked with stockings on, stretched on a purple couch, a knife stuck in under one breast: 'Payment'. He retained with pride the rejection slip of the Royal Academy.

Memory of an evening at Violet Hunt's. Good subject for a short story. V.H.'s old anaemic brain reminiscing in circles. Mrs Cecil Chesterton [the widow of G.K. Chesterton's brother], with bright, dyed red hair, the face of a disreputable hard hawky madame, a voice with a grating accent, and a nameless vulgar and mysterious young man in her company. The talk turns on V.'s memoirs, disconnected pages of MSS kept in a box. She has left them to Douglas Goldring. To the hawky madame's disappointment. 'But, my dear Violet, Douglas is a sweet old thing, but you need someone with taste, sympathy, imagination.' The Hawk fishes page after page from the box: memories written with delicious felinity of Mrs G.W. Stevens [wife of the war correspondent who wrote *With Kitchener to Khartoum*], an eighteen-year-old girl's memory of Oscar Wilde. 'You know,' the old brain persisted at intervals, 'he wanted to marry me. He asked my father.' The harsh voice reads on, a hand sawing for silence. At intervals: 'These are priceless. You know, Violet, you are very naughty.' The vulgar man repeats by rote with awful geniality, 'Very naughty.'

February 2. An advertisement for rubber sheaths:

For the connoisseur we recommend the Comac Special Extra-Extra-Thin Transparent.

All sheaths are tested twice, once by the manufacturer and then by us.

Post to us the enclosed postcard and we will forward you seven assorted (with instructions) of which you can use any one, and if you decide to keep the remaining half-dozen, you pay us 3/6 special price; if on the other hand, you decide not to keep them, return the half-dozen to us within fourteen days and the matter will be closed.

What sexual starvation is indicated by a five-year guarantee? The address Bournemouth.

February 18.

Eloquence is the varnish of falsehood; truth has none... Burke is eloquent; I am not. If I write better than he does, it is because I have seen things more distinctly, and have had the courage to turn them up, soft or hard, pretty or ugly, and to turn them on their backs in despite of tooth or claw.

Tom Paine in Landor's *Imaginary Conversations*

'To the Sculptor Chosen to Execute the Statue of Washington'
Take from the mine the coldest, hardest stone,
It needs no fashion: it is Washington.
But if you chisel, let the stroke be rude,
And on his heart engrave—Ingratitude.

Tom Paine

He that would make his own liberty secure must guard even his enemy from oppression.

Tom Paine

Only an author who is aware of the ridiculous and merciless egotism of human beings inspires me with confidence when he does draw attention to the strange intermittent nobility of human nature. When Maupassant melts or admires, I trust him.

Desmond MacCarthy

One must know oneself to the pitch of being horrified.

Bossuet

The French Constitution says, *There shall be no more titles*; and, of consequence, all that class of equivocal generation which in some countries is called *aristocracy* and in others *nobility* is done away, and the *peer* is exalted into MAN. Titles are but nicknames, and every nickname is a title. The thing is perfectly harmless in itself, but it marks a sort of foppery in the human character, which degrades it. It reduces man into the diminutive of man in things which are great, and the counterfeit of women in things which are little. It talks about its fine *blue ribbon* like a girl and shows its new *garter* like a child.

The Rights of Man

March 28. 'It is ignorance which today keeps many from detesting Christ.' François Mauriac.

May 21. The most pornographic—at any rate the most attractively pornographic—magazine to be exported to this country seems to be *Sex Appeal*. Since banned. Flagellation is the stock-in-trade of a series of magazines called *Hollywood so-and-so—Hollywood Revels, Nights* etc. To the man in the know Hollywood is apparently the keyword.

June 4. Bought Cotton's *Poems on Several Occasions* (1689) for 15/– from Storey in Cecil Court.

Martha is not so tall nor yet so fair
As any of the other lovely three,
Her chiefest Grace is poor Simplicity,
Yet were the rest away, she were a Star.

August 28. 'Upon a Gardiner'.

Could he forget his death? that every hour
Was emblem'd to it by the fading flowre:
Should he not mind his end? yes, needs he must,
That still was conversent 'mongst bedds of dust.
Then let no onyon in an handkercher
Tempt your sad eyes into a needlesse feare;
    If he that thinkes on death well lives and dies,
    The gardner sure is gone to Paradise.

Wit Restor'd, 1658

September 12.

Man's like the earth, his hair like grass is grown,
His veins the rivers are, his heart the stone.
                                    Wit's Recreations, 1640.

'Humour is the drunkenness of a Nation which no sleep can cure.'
Davenant, Preface to *Gondibert.*

September 30. '—All the torments and agonies wrought on scaffolds,
in torture chambers, mad houses, operating theatres, under the vaults
of bridges in late autumn...' Rilke, *Notebook of Malte Laurids Brigge.*
    'It is only those who love that draw Him to them; not those who
wait with a small talent for being loved, as with a lamp gone cold.'
Rilke, *Notebook.*
    '—An empty horrible alley, an alley in a foreign town, in a town
where nothing is forgiven.' Rilke, *Notebook.*

Peter Fleming mentioned at lunch that he had been asked by the
Deutsche Lufthansa to look for two men who had been lost in
Sinkiang. He told them they must go cap in hand to the Editor of *The
Times* for permission—a bitter blow considering *The Times*'s
correspondent, Ebbutt, had just been expelled from Germany. Their
face—and Fleming's journey—was saved by the men turning up
safely in an Afghanistan prison.

October 2. At Sherborne. Alec Waugh's *The Loom of Youth* is still
banned in Sherborne in 1938. The booksellers are forbidden to stock
it.
    Story of Earle-Drax fifty years ago who used to be carried daily
to his mausoleum in his coffin, cursing his bearers if they shook him.
    Grave-digger's wise-crack: 'We only bury the deaf and dumb in
this bit.' The same grave-digger remarked to an inn-keeper who drove
us into Cerne Abbas: 'Like a second-hand grave cheap?' The walls of
a newly-dug grave had fallen in and left too little room. 'We can't dig
to the left because there's a policeman buried there and we don't want
to get on the wrong side of the law. And we can't dig to the right
because of the old woman there—she might wake up.'
    Pack Fair at Sherborne. On the Sunday at midnight a procession

21

goes round banging on tin cans—this represents the builders of the Abbey packing up their tools. The fair is on the Monday. Pickpockets, gipsies, drunkenness, reinforcements of police. The gipsies 'they fight like dragons.'

Extract from Newspaper:

Alice Etheridge, aged thirty-nine, was charged with the murder of her husband, Jesse Edward Etheridge, aged forty-three, at Chichester Road, Edmonton, on September 21.

'About five o'clock today he went to bed after dinner and after he had gone I had a feeling that if I did not kill him he would kill me.

'I went upstairs and saw him in bed asleep. I looked at some long daggers in the corner but I thought I could not use them because I would have to stand on the bed springs and the noise of it would wake him up and he would kill me.

'I went downstairs. Oh! I had such a funny feeling. I saw the bread knife. I sharpened it up and thought if only I had the strength I could push it in with one go.

'I went upstairs. My husband was lying on his back. I pulled back the bedclothes, and holding the knife in both hands I made sure to get him in the right place.

'I do not know, but it seemed someone hit my hands down with a mallet. The knife went in as if his body was rotten. He sat up in the bed and hollaed out, "Hi, hi, hi!"

'I took a packet of pepper up with me because I was thinking if he woke up I would throw the pepper in his eyes, and he could not get after me. I flew downstairs out into the street into a neighbour's house.'

October 9. 'The Pleasure in the Act of Venus is the greatest of the Pleasures of the Senses; the Matching of it with the Itch is unproper.' Francis Bacon's *Natural Historie*.

'It hath been observed by the Ancients, and is yet believed, that the Sperme of Drunken Men is Unfruitfull. The Cause is, for that it is Overmoistened and wanteth Spissitude. And wee have a merrie

Saying, that they that goe Drunke to Bed, get Daughters.' Bacon's *Natural Historie.*

October 25. 'I feel my own death will be unworthy because I will go out through the falling-in of walls of clay, whereas I should by the will before this been able to find a secret radiant gateway into the spirit and gone out by my own will, and not been forced out.' A.E. in a letter.

November 18.

All life is but a wandering to find home;
When we're gone we're there. Happy were man
Could here his voyage end; he should not, then,
Answer how well or ill he steered his soul
By Heaven's or by Hell's compass; how he put in—
Losing blessed goodness shore—at such a sin;
Nor how life's dear provision he has spent,
Nor how far he in's navigation went
Beyond commission: this were a fine reign,
To do ill and not hear of it again.

The Witch of Edmonton

[Perhaps it was on this day that I found in the last two lines the epigraph for *Brighton Rock* on which I was working.]

November 28. 'He judges not as the judge judges, but as the sun falling round a helpless thing.' Walt Whitman.

November 30. Herbert Read told me yesterday at the Stage Society's performance of *Queen Christina* (Strindberg) that Heinemann had actually to pay very little in the libel action brought by the Duke of Windsor. The *Daily Mail* had said £10,000, but this was an entirely fictitious figure. Presumably the Duke was glad that a large sum was rumoured.

The loves of the Patmores. The red-haired, amusing, rather bitchy mother of Derek Patmore was formerly Richard Aldington's mistress and now her daughter-in-law has followed her.

1939

January 7. At Mrs Belloc Lowndes's. She told me that the money Thomas Hardy was announced as leaving was an entirely fictitious figure founded on copyrights. The authorities put an absurd price on these and Mrs Hardy had great difficulty in paying the death duties. [Hardy before his death had sold the film rights of *Tess,* and the story goes that the copyrights of all his other novels were calculated on the basis of their value if films were made of them.] She was left so badly off that she found it hard to keep up the small drab villa, Max Gate, at Dorchester. Meanwhile her husband was buried in the Abbey.

January 11. Le Maître, an Admiralty official and my neighbour, told me an odd story about the Duke of Kent's wedding. A foreigner landed from a schooner at Shoreham with a Gladstone bag and a brown-paper parcel and no passport. The local customs officer let him through because he showed a letter from the Lords of the Admiralty saying they would like to have a demonstration of his invention. The 'invention' was contained in the parcel. The letter turned out to be forged and the man had disappeared without trace. The Admiralty feared the man was planning an attempt against the life of the Regent of Yugoslavia (it was not long since the King had been murdered), and they were panic-stricken. 10,000 police were drafted in to line the route from the Palace to the Abbey. No attempt was made, and nothing was ever discovered about the man.

January 12.

> With all the charms of Peace possest,
>   Secure from Life's Tormentor, Pain,
> Sleep and indulge thyself with Rest,
>   Nor dream thou ere shall rise again.
>
> Past is the Fear of future Doubt,
>   The Sun is from the Dial gone,
> The Sands are sunk, the Glass is out,
>   The Folly of the Farce is done.
>
> Thomas D'Urfey

And they say that religion is an escape. The man who believes in eternity must often experience an acute nostalgia for atheism—to indulge himself with rest. There is the real escape.

January 25. At lunch with Denyse Clairouin [then my French agent and translator, who was to die, after working for the British Secret Service, in a German concentration camp.] She tells me that Doctor Freud is staying at—of all places in town—Mount Royal, the cheap palace for the illicit loves of public school boys.

July 2. Stopped outside Gallup's [a second-hand bookshop which bought review copies for a third of the published price—a boon for reviewers] by a square-set dingy woman in black. 'Excuse me. Can you tell me if there are any Book Societies besides the Right and the Left?' Harsh and middle-aged and hungry for what she dreamed of as intellectual companionship. Read Berdyaev. Brought up as a Calvinist. Wildly anti-Catholic. Been on her back for ten years—insomnia for fifteen. If she does sleep, dreams of her father—a hideous nightmare. Out of touch with her family—one brother in America: the other in England, in London probably, never sees him. Owes her £500. 'Would I meet interesting people at Foyle's lunches?'

Impossible to get away from her Ancient Mariner grasp. A basketful of tinned food, greying hair cut in page-boy fashion.

August 2. 'Art nowadays must be the mouthpiece of misery, for misery is the keynote of modern life.' George Gissing.

'"People trifle with love. I deny that love is a strong passion. Fear is the strong passion; it is with fear that you must trifle, if you wish to taste the intensest joy of living. Envy me—envy me, sir," he said with a chuckle, "I am a coward."' Mr Malthus in Robert Louis Stevenson's *The Young Man with Cream Tarts*.

September 14. A curious air of unreality—a rather silent Common—too many strangers talking together in pairs. The papers: CRISIS LATEST, FRENCH WAR CHIEFS HERE, HITLER CALLS HIS GENERALS, THE NEXT FEW HOURS WILL DECIDE PEACE OR WAR.

Francis's birthday [my son, aged two]—a day late. The rocking horses. Thunderstorm in the air and later slow rain. I discover in myself a desire for peace, for just going on. The nursery—everything—looking prettier than I remembered it.

Impossible to work properly—though I somehow got through a review of *The History of the Film*. Who on earth will bother about that? Will reviews be paid for, printed?

Nothing to do but go out and look at the latest posters. This heavy day, one feels, *can't* end in peace. Reading *Scoop*.

'Poverty and lust seek each other out and call to each other in the darkness like two famished beasts.' Bernanos.

'You see, Pity is like an animal. An animal from which one can make great demands—but must not ask too much. Pity is powerful and devouring.' Bernanos.

September 24. 7.15 p.m. Chamberlain's second meeting with Hitler apparently ended in failure. Czech mobilization. Back again where we were on September 14 with war almost certain. Parents called to Notre Dame Convent tomorrow by an urgent notice to discuss what to do with the children. Rain pouring down: a dreadful unreality over everything. But this morning and afternoon, till the doctor had been, the most important thing in the world was a fall Francis had on the stone steps at the back: a war seemed nothing in comparison. Just as last year the Shirley Temple libel action—and possible ruin—seemed unimportant because Lucy was ill.*

September 25. Sunday. The meeting in the gymnasium. A crowd of tradesmen and their wives in their dingy Sunday best or sports clothes. Evacuation plan explained by a small, rather timid-looking man, the headmaster of an L.C.C. school, while an aeroplane droned low overhead. Railways to be taken over, children to be sent to

---

* In 1937, writing for *Night and Day,* the short-lived weekly magazine he then co-edited, Graham Greene described Shirley Temple, in a review of *Wee Willie Winkie,* in the terms of a pre-adolescent Marlene Dietrich. Twentieth Century Fox sued, claiming that Graham Greene had accused the film company of procuring Shirley Temple for immoral purposes, and was awarded £3,500 in damages, £500 of which—equal roughly to £15,000 today—was to be paid by Graham Greene himself.

THE FILMS BY GRAHAM GREENE

Wee Willie Winkie—The Life of Emile Zola

THE owners of a child star are like leaseholders—their property diminishes in value every year. Time's chariot is at their back; before them acres of anonymity. What is Jackie Coogan now but a matrimonial squabble? Miss Shirley Temple's case, though, has peculiar interest: infancy with her is a disguise, her appeal is more secret and more adult. Already two years ago she was a fancy little piece (real childhood, I think, went out after *The Littlest Rebel*). In *Captain January* she wore trousers with the mature suggestiveness of a Dietrich: her neat and well-developed rump twisted in the tap-dance: her eyes had a sidelong searching coquetry. Now in *Wee Willie Winkie*, wearing short kilts, she is a complete totsy. Watch her swaggering stride across the Indian barrack-square: hear the gasp of excited expectation from her antique audience when the sergeant's palm is raised: watch the way she measures a man with agile studio eyes, with dimpled depravity. Adult emotions of love and grief glissade across the mask of childhood, a childhood skin-deep.

It is clever, but it cannot last. Her admirers — middle-aged men and clergymen—respond to her dubious coquetry, to the sight of her well-shaped and desirable little body, packed with enormous vitality, only because the safety curtain of story and dialogue drops between their intelligence and their desire. "Why are you making my Mummy cry?"—what could be purer than that? And the scene when dressed in a white nightdress she begs grandpa to take Mummy to a dance— what could be more virginal? On those lines her new picture, made by John Ford, who directed *The Informer*, is horrifyingly competent. It isn't hard to stay to the last prattle and the last sob. The story—about an Afghan robber converted by Wee Willie Winkie to the British Raj—is a long way after Kipling. But we needn't

be sour about that. Both stories are awful, but on the whole Hollywood's is the better.

It's better cinema anyway than *The Life of Emile Zola*. More pompous than *Pasteur* and far more false, this picture's theme is supposed to be truth—but truth to the film mind is the word you see on news posters. We begin in 1862 with Zola starving in a garret with Cézanne who keeps on popping up irrelevantly from then on. Zola meets Nana, and soon she is giving him her diaries and her letters, but not—what apparently Zola particularly wants—a baby's vest. ("Take all, all but this"). Then Cézanne pokes his head round the door, and Zola writes *Nana* which is an enormous success. (He had really, of course, been a successful writer for about eighteen years before he wrote *Nana*). Then suddenly—everything in this picture happens suddenly including Cézanne—comes war. Soldiers in the street;

a woman says "Where are they all going?" and a man says "Haven't you heard? War's been declared." Zola says "Never did I think I should live to see France grovelling in the dust under the German heel." Cézanne pokes his head round the door—or doesn't he? Anyway the war's over. Zola's middle-aged at Meudon, though his wife's not changed at all. Cézanne looks round the door again. "The old struggling carefree days." He takes an ugly look at the majolica and starts away. "Paul, will you write?" "No, but I will remember." Then the Dreyfus case, and on the night before Dreyfus's rehabilitation Zola—he's an old man now—dies (it's more than un-American to live another two years). Paul Muni acts Zola—quaintly, and lots of old friends turn up in fancy dress but quite themselves as the Governor of Paris, Clemenceau, Colonel Piquart, Count Esterhazy.

His LORDSHIP.–Who is the author of this article?

Mr. HOLMES.–Mr. Graham Greene.

His LORDSHIP.–Is he within the jurisdiction?

Mr. HOLMES.–I am afraid I do not know, my Lord.

Mr. THEOBALD MATHEW, on behalf of the printers, said that they recognized that the article was one which ought never to have been published. The fact that the film had already been licensed for universal exhibition refuted the charges which had been made in the article. The printers welcomed the opportunity of making any amends in their power.

His LORDSHIP.–Can you tell me where Mr. Greene is?

Mr. MATHEW.–I have no information on the subject.

His LORDSHIP.–This libel is simply a gross outrage, and I will take care to see that suitable attention is directed to it. In the meantime I assent to the settlement on the terms which have been disclosed, and the record will be withdrawn.

Reprinted from the Law Reports of *The Times*, 23 May 1938.

unknown destinations—the parents informed later by telegram. The Mother Superior, an old lady with a bone-white face and a twitching upper lip, sat taking notes. One woman sat crying silently but rather melodramatically. Questions afterwards—avid women put them on a too-personal basis—can Philip go with James and so on. The men better at the general questions. Most of the London boroughs fitting gas masks; in some cases, as in Chelsea, distributing them. Not Wandsworth [our borough].

September 26. Monday. No notices anywhere about gas masks, but when I rang up the council I was told fitting was in progress at Clapham baths. Not even a notice at the public library. Went in the afternoon. Almost had to drag our old cook.

'Oh, I'm much too busy washing up.'

'Will you go with Mrs Greene tomorrow?'

'Oh no, that's my day off. I'll tell you what. I'll go on Friday.'

Queued up for an hour. An unpleasant thing!

Had to pack a bag for Lucy to take to school in case of evacuation. Blanket, one change of underclothes, food for one day. Marked H 105, the mark of the school.

A grim wet night. Elisabeth [my sister] came to dinner and we played poker dice for pennies and Hitler spoke in Berlin. A notice on the radio warned ships that in certain waters owing to 'obstructions', they must proceed at their own risk if without a pilot.

September 27. Vivien, Lucy and Frieda [our maid] stood for an hour-and-three-quarters before being told there was to be no fitting. Masks were to come to houses. Absolutely exhausted. No co-ordination between councils. Chelsea, for instance, distributed from the first. Brixton didn't fit, but took measurements.

All the Macaulay telephone exchange not working (deliberate?). Anti-aircraft guns set up on Common and trenches apparently being dug.

Have planned to evacuate family by car with Eleanor [my brother Raymond's wife] tomorrow afternoon.

This is the desert, this the solitude:
How populous, how vital is the grave.
Young's Night Thoughts

Life being what it is, one dreams of revenge. Gauguin.

The best of what we do and are,
   Just God, forgive!

Wordsworth

I take it that no man is educated who has never dallied with the thought of suicide. William James in a letter.

The wife, in letters written to her husband in a tone of justifiable bitterness, had said she thought he might have kept their home and yacht a little sacred.
Newspaper report of a divorce case.

2 PLUS 2

Fiction · Poetry · Translations · Drama · Essays

2PLUS2 will now appear every Autumn. It will continue to provide an unusual forum where new works of established and promising writers are given an opportunity to be appreciated beyond their own borders.

The current 480 page volume features the 1984 Nobel Laureate Jaroslav Seifert in an exclusive and major selection of his poetry and prose, translated by Ewald Osers.

Some of the contributors to this 1985 edition:

Ajñeya
Octavio Armand
Kenneth Bernard
Paul Bowles
Victor Brombert
Margaret Browne
Dino Buzzati
Nancy Cardozo
E.M. Cioran
H. Díaz-Casanueva
Stephen Dixon
Russell Edson
Gabriel Fitzmaurice
André Frénaud
Paavo Haavikko
Eleanor Hakim
John Hollander
Magda Isanos
Vladimir Kazakov
Herbert Lomas

Izaak Mansk
J.D. McClatchy
Eugenio Montale
Les Murray
Naomi Shihab Nye
Michael O'Loughlin
Philip O'Connor
Heberto Padilla
Sheenagh Pugh
Jean-Claude Renard
Mark Rudman
Jaroslav Seifert
Osten Sjöstrand
Gustaf Sobin
R.S. Thomas
Fred Urquhart
Sidney Wade
Ania Walwicz
W. Wilde-Menozzi
Peter Wortsman

Mylabris Presse S.A., Case Postale 171, 1018 Lausanne, Switzerland.
Mylabris Press Ltd., P.O. Box 20725, New York, N.Y. 10025

Please send me ____ copies of the 1985 Edition of 2PLUS2

I enclose check   USA $ 16.00 + $ 1.50   postage and handling
                   UK   £ 13.00 + £ .90
                   Payable to Mylabris Press

TERESA TORANSKA
'THEY'

Julia Minc

Between 1981 and 1984, Teresa Toranska, a pro-Solidarity journalist, interviewed seven aged and, for the most part, disgraced Communist leaders who had been instrumental in establishing the first communist government in Poland under Stalin's supervision. In her interviews, Toranska has, in effect, clarified a time in history that has been famously murky: the three year period between 1945 when, months before the end of World War Two, Poland, virtually in ruins, was already occupied by Russian troops, and 1947, the year when purportedly democratic elections were held establishing the Moscow-educated government in power. Some indication of just how democratic those elections were is evident in the remarks about them made by Jakub Berman (quoted last October in *Time*): 'The results were not rigged—only corrected. Either we win and stay or we lose and we hand over power to someone else . . . I suppose you're going to tell me it would be democratic if we did. So what? Who needs that kind of democracy? We can't have free elections now any more than we could ten or twenty years ago because we'd lose, I've no doubt as to that. So what's the point of such an election?'

Toranska's interviews have been clandestinely published in Poland under the title of *Oni* (*They*). Edited extracts from two of the interviews are presented here, the first of which is with Julia Minc, head of the Polish Press Agency in the forties and fifties, and wife of Hilary Minc, the Minister of Industry and one of the four or five most influential people in the postwar government in Poland.

Teresa Toranska: Mrs Minc, Mr Berman told me that—

Julia Minc: How can you talk like that?

Toranska: Have I said something offensive?

Minc: Yes. You referred to a comrade as 'Mister'. That's offensive.

Toranska: But surely, Mr Berman is no longer a Party member.

Minc: He may not be a Party member, but he is a comrade. Before the war, even if someone paid only his Red Aid dues without belonging to the Party, he was still a different person, and you addressed him as 'Comrade'. And if at any time you began addressing him as 'Mister', that meant he'd done something wrong. As one woman comrade talking to another we ought to respect our old habits.

Toranska: But Mrs Minc, I'm not—

Minc: There you go again!

Toranska: Because we're in Poland. Anyhow. Berman—is that all right?—told me that there was a void in his place after he'd left.

Minc: There's a Soviet novel where the main character describes how, after her husband had been put in prison, the house suddenly became very quiet. The phone stopped ringing and their friends stopped coming round.

Toranska: Was your house suddenly quiet too?

Minc: I made noise.

Toranska: And your friends? Didn't they call?

Minc: No political friendship lasts forever. I didn't blame them.

Toranska: What about your private friends?

Minc: We didn't have any. There wasn't time. Minc was at the Planning Commission every day until midnight or one in the morning, and I was usually at the Polish Press Agency until ten o'clock at night, putting together the day's bulletin. I'd go to bed at three, get up at eleven and drive back to the Press Agency. That was what my day looked like. We all worked hard; people don't appreciate that nowadays.

Toranska: And on Sundays?

Minc: I slept the whole day. So did Minc, unless he had a meeting. Everyone was exhausted.

Toranska: Didn't you have any time to enjoy yourself?

Minc: Work was our enjoyment. It's a marvellous feeling to be building a new country from the very beginning, and it's satisfying to see the results.

Toranska: You're pleased with them?

Minc: Of course. We're going through a difficult stage now, and there are some complications: the 'Solidarity' revolt, the American restrictions, and maybe the Gierek government made some mistakes as well, but the Party said quite clearly at the Ninth Congress that it would put them right, and that's just what it's doing. Anyway, no one has ever claimed that socialism could be built in a few years. This is a struggle for socialism, and it will always go on, because that is what our communist song says: 'All our life is a struggle.'

Toranska: Did you ever go to the theatre?

Minc: Of course not! There wasn't time.

Toranska: What about the cinema?

Minc: The cinema came to us. We'd ring them up and they'd screen films for us at home. There was another cinema at the club. Our estate had a club, a canteen, and a cook who was crazy about dogs. I had three myself (I love dogs, have always had them, and take them in even from the street).

Toranska: Who ate in the canteen?

Minc: I don't know; someone must have. My dinner was cooked at home and brought up to the Polish Press Agency for me.

Toranska: Who went to the club, then?

Minc: Witek did. Witek was my charge. The son of a good comrade who died at the battle of Lenino. His mother died after the war, when he was twelve. He was a smart little boy. He knew all our 'nannies' [the security men] as well as those from the Soviet embassy. Every morning he'd stand out on the road, and he always found a car to take him to school. It is, after all, twenty kilometres to Warsaw, from Constantin, where we lived.

Toranska: Couldn't you or your husband give him a lift in your 'democrats on wheels', as Warsaw people used to call them?

Minc: He had to be in school by eight. Anyway, he didn't want us to give him lifts. I once came to pick him up from school on my way back from the Polish Press Agency, and he said, 'Mrs Minc, please don't come to pick me up any more, because I don't want my friends to see.'

Toranska: He called you Mrs Minc?

Minc: What was he supposed to call me? I wasn't his mother.

Toranska: Is he a Party member?

Minc: No, he's an engineer and never joined the Party.

Toranska: And your nephew, the son of the famous activist Ewelina Sawicka?

Minc: No, he's not in the Party, and what of it? Others belong and that's enough. It's not important.

Toranska: It's curious that almost none of the children of old communists belong to the Party, and most of them have emigrated to the West.

Minc: So what? Socialist ideology doesn't forbid people to go to the West.

Toranska: You were under constant security surveillance. Did it ever bother you?

Minc: It's true: they always had a couple of their adjutants around, but after a while you get used to being protected and you stop noticing them.

Toranska: But someone like Bierut, for instance, wouldn't have been able to slip out to pick up some girls.*

Minc: Why should he slip out? They would have been brought to him if he'd wanted them, or they would have come themselves. But Bierut certainly had neither the time nor the inclination for that sort of thing. He was very hard working, like all of us. I don't

---

* Boleslaw Bierut assumed Party leadership in 1948.

want to make too much of my own work, but do you imagine that building up a huge agency like the Polish Press Agency could have been easy? We started off in Lublin with just a handful of people who were still directly reponsible to the Minister of Information. A year later we moved to Warsaw and were allotted first one floor of a building, then another, and finally the whole building. The agency started to grow and people flowed in.

Toranska: What kind of people did you take?

Minc: Anyone who was any good, knew how to write, was intelligent, and knew what was what: socialism, trade unions, a political party.

Toranska: Would I have done?

Minc: Certainly not. You haven't grasped basic things and you ask too many questions. But you wouldn't have asked questions then. In those times we had order and discipline and people worked instead of gabbling on to no purpose.

Toranska: What about people who'd been in the Home Army? Would they have done?

Minc: If they wrote what was necessary and according to the Party line, I left them alone. Anyway, I asked them all at the start: do you agree with us, do you want a socialist Poland? If they said yes, they could stay.

Toranska: They didn't lie?

Minc: No. You can always tell what someone's attitude is. In general, the team we put together at the Agency was really good in every respect. They only arrested one of my people—Glowacki.

Toranska: Did you intervene on his behalf?

Minc: Why on earth should I? After all, it's not as if he was family or anything. And I only knew him from work, so I couldn't have done anything anyway. But I did take him back after they let him out.

Our team was a good one because we used the right method of selection, especially in picking out young people. We would collect all the candidates and then see what they could do. I thought up funny names for them: 'frelks' and 'nittlers'. The 'nittlers' were the stupid ones who scurried around collecting bits of totally useless information, and the 'frelks' (I called them after Richard Frelk, who was training with me then, and later became a head of department in the Central Committee) were the ones who knew what to look for and where to go to find it.

Toranska: What did they find at political trials?

Minc: They were usually covered by the social section. We'd send out a reporter and he wrote down what went on. After all, they weren't secret trials.

Toranska: What about prison trials? Weren't they secret either?

Minc: There weren't any trials in prisons. You've been picking up some peculiar information.

Toranska: What kind of people were tried, then?

Minc: Traitors and enemies.

Toranska: What were Party comrades tried for?

Minc: Well, if one of them stole something, or tried to abuse his position, he had to be locked up—that's normal.

Toranska: And what did Comrade General Kuropieska steal?

Minc: But he's alive. Efforts were made to protect him.

Toranska: And Comrade General Spychalski?

Minc: Spychalski died a natural death a few years ago.

Toranska: What about Gecow? You must have known him.

Minc: I did know him, indirectly. He is indeed dead: a sentencing error.

Toranska: And Gomulka? Was that a sentencing error as well?

Minc: Don't be ridiculous, Gomulka was never in prison! He was only under house arrest, and he stayed at his villa in Miedzeszyn.

Toranska: What about Slansky?

Minc: A very decent sort. We worked together at Moscow Radio.

Toranska: But he was a spy!

Minc: Rubbish!

Toranska: Really? He was sentenced to death for espionage.

Minc: So what?

Toranska: Nothing, except that the Polish Press Agency, where you were chief editor, said he was a spy, and now you say he was a decent sort.

Minc: Well, he was.

Toranska: Did you tell your husband what you thought?

Minc: There was no point. And they couldn't have done anything about it anyway. You're such a child: what do you think Bierut or Minc could have said to Stalin? What arguments could they have used? They had to come up with something, and Stalin could always say, quite truthfully, that Czechoslovakia was an independent country, that Slansky's trial was the Czechs' own affair, and that he, Stalin, wasn't officially involved.*

---

* Rudolf Slansky, sworn in as Deputy Prime Minister of Czechoslovakia in September 1951, was arrested two months later, and after nearly a year of interrogation and torture was tried and executed for high treason, espionage, sabotage and betrayal of military secrets in a case that, lasting for eight days, was accompanied by hysterical abuse from *Rude Pravo,* the state newspaper. Wladyslaw Gomulka, First Secretary of the Polish Party, fell from power in 1948, but his defeat was largely cushioned by other members of the politburo: he was never tried or handed over to Soviet authorities.

Toranska: That's what Stalin would have said. But what about you? What do you think?

Minc: Look, in banking you have assets and you have losses. We waged a victorious war against fascism, and there were some bad things. But the victorious war compensated for all the bad. And anyhow, if you have to choose between the Party and an individual, you choose the Party, because the Party has a general aim, the good of many people, but one person is just one person.

Toranska: Can he be killed?

Minc: The questions you ask! The Party isn't a Christian sect that takes pity on every individual, with a vision of a heavenly tsardom; the Party struggles for a better life for all mankind.

Toranska: Can you rebel against the Party?

Minc: You can rebel against particular people, but not against the Party, because that would mean you were rebelling against socialism, which aims to better the living standards of the working class.

Toranska: What exactly is this working class?

Minc: The working class is a class which owns the means of production and has its own party, which acts, and its actions represent the workers' participation in government.

Toranska: Isn't it the whole working class that governs?

Minc: How could it possibly govern! We're not anarchists. It's the workers' avant-garde that governs, the most militant, select core: workers who are Party members, representatives of trades unions and workers' councils. They are the ones who set the Party's tone and represent the interests of the working class.

Toranska: So the worker Walesa doesn't?

Minc: A worker isn't an iron-clad figure with a sign that reads, 'Creed: Communism.' Walesa is a worker who didn't follow the path that Poland is taking.

Toranska: And what path is Poland taking?

Minc: The road to socialism. But Walesa was against this, and he was punished for it. Rakowski clearly said at the meeting in the Gdansk shipyards that he'd got his Ph.D. through hard work, whereas Walesa had done it by agitating against the good of Poland.

Toranska: What is the good of Poland?

Minc: Work, building socialism and defence against imperialist war.

Toranska: Who is going to declare this war?

Minc: You want me to explain *that* to you? It's quite clear who. And it won't be the Soviet Union, because if the Soviet Union declared war, it wouldn't be a socialist state.

Toranska: But surely the Soviet Union has declared war more than once in the past. In 1939, for instance, against Poland.

Minc: Nonsense! In 1939 the Soviet Union took a stand in defence of the Belorussian and Ukrainian people, and if it took possession of a bit too much, it was given back later.

Toranska: What about the war against Afghanistan?

Minc: The Soviet Union is helping Afghanistan towards a revolutionary victory, and it isn't helping on its own initiative, but on the wish of the legal Afghan government, which is trying to build socialism.

Toranska: What is socialism?

Minc: A higher standard of living for everyone, free education and social security.

Toranska: As in the West?

Minc: I know all about what it's like in the West.

Toranska: Have you been there?

Minc: Not after the war, but I know, I see it on TV. It's very bad there. The shops are full, but people haven't got the money to buy anything: they go hungry and sleep under bridges.

Toranska: And here?

Minc: Here we have no poverty, and we have social care, which anyone can take advantage of if they've suffered an accident of fate. We have child benefits, benefits for non-working mothers, what more do you want?

Toranska: In the West mothers don't have to work at all.

Minc: Women who don't work are degraded. Before the war they used to sit at home and rot, and gossip about clothes. It's only in People's Poland that they've been able to flourish. They go to meetings, develop, widen their horizons and raise their consciousness.

Toranska: In the textile factory in Lodz that I went to see, none of the mothers I met go to the cinema, watch television or read books. They get up at three or four in the morning to be at work by six; when they finish their day's work they spend several hours scouring the shops for a pair of socks, a piece of elastic, a shirt, or a pair of children's shoes, as well, of course, as queuing for meat; then they make dinner, clean the house and do the laundry; and very often, too often, after that they do a night shift at the factory, because eight hours' work spent on their feet amid the stink and din earns them half as much as your retirement pension, and in the end, counting the privileges which you have but which aren't available to them, they get one third of that. That's exploitation.

Minc: That's not exploitation; those are difficult work conditions. Think about it: who could be exploiting them?

Toranska: The state.

Minc: That's ridiculous: the state doesn't exploit, the state provides. It provides pensions, it provides benefits, it pays for education and, most important, it has got rid of unemployment.

Toranska: Officially, yes—because it's hidden.

Minc: Rubbish. We don't have any hidden unemployment; all we have is a perfectly visible reluctance to work. If everyone pulled their socks up and got down to it, things would be better. But they don't want to. There's nothing I can do about that. They've got guaranteed employment, everyone in Poland has: that's a lot. Do you have any idea how humiliating it is not to be able to find work? I remember Poland in 1933—it was full of unemployed lining up for their free rations of soup. We had a woman who came in to do the washing. She got fifteen zlotys a month—next to nothing.

Toranska: Couldn't you have given her more?

Minc: What do you mean, 'given'? That's what people were paid for that kind of work, and she thought herself lucky to have it at all. There was unemployment, after all.

Toranska: So there was unemployment in capitalist Poland. What about the Soviet Union at that time?

Minc: They were building socialism.

Toranska: And concentration camps?

Minc: There weren't any.

Toranska: And did seven million peasants starve to death during collectivization, or didn't they?

Minc: I don't know where you get that kind of information. No one starved to death, and if they sent kulaks to Siberia, well, so much the better for them, because they got what they wanted: more land to cultivate.

Toranska: Why, then, didn't the collectives work?

Minc: Because the peasants didn't want them, and it's quite clear why: they like to look after their own interests. But it's because the countryside wasn't collectivized that we now have a food crisis. Anyway when they were decollectivizing in Poland, I was no longer at the Polish Press Agency; I'd left two years before that, in 1954.

Toranska: As a result of the struggle with cosmopolitanism? Along with Starewicz, Kasman and Staszewski?

Minc: I don't know what you're talking about. I left shortly after they'd gone. [President] Bierut told me I had to leave, because that was the way it had to be, and I didn't ask him why.

Toranska: You didn't ask your husband either?

Minc: I didn't ask anyone. I became vice-president of the State Commission for Employment.

Toranska: And after the State Commission for Employment was closed down, you retired?

Minc: I felt fine, so I tried to find other work. It was suggested that I work on the military paper, *Armed Poland*, but I didn't want to.

Toranska: You didn't try at the employment office?

Minc: Me? At the employment office? They don't find jobs for chief editors and no one like me would ever go there.

Toranska: But workers have to.

Minc: The difference between a worker and a chief editor is that if a chief editor makes a mess of things, it takes years to correct his mistakes—

Toranska: And when a worker damages an expensive piece of machinery, it doesn't?

Minc: If a worker damages a piece of machinery then he's a saboteur and he'll be locked up.

Toranska: And what did your husband do?

Minc: Nothing. He retired.

Toranska: He retired on a pension fourteen years before the normal age; you retired five years before you were due to, and Berman ten.

Minc: It was all according to the law. There are legal provisions for such privileges for activists. After all, socialism is built on the principle of equality before the law, not total equality for everyone. And the law clearly states that those who have rendered services to the Polish People's Republic have certain privileges. They used to be certified by special ID cards; those have gone out of use now, but the custom has been retained. A very appropriate rule.

Toranska: Rendered services? But surely they left because they'd made mistakes?

Minc: They made mistakes, yes, but they also did a lot of good; that should be taken into account, and it is. Individuals whose lives prove that they have worked for the good of People's Poland ought to be treated differently. Just as a person who works more ought to have better living and resting conditions. Bierut had villas in Constantin and Warsaw—

Toranska: And in Lansk and Sopot, as well as other villas at his disposal in Natolin, Jurat, Miedzywodzie, Krynica and Karpacz. I didn't do the counting: Swiatlo did.*

Minc: Well, was he supposed to stifle in three rooms? Everyone has to have guaranteed living conditions appropriate to his rank and burden of responsibility. The time of total equality may come, but not until communism; under socialism you can't have a minister earning and living like a shopkeeper. Mainly because then no one would want to be a minister. In socialism everyone should be given not an equal share, but a share according to his deserts.

Toranska: I see. So that's why the woman doctor I met out in the hall rents a cubicle behind the kitchen in your three-room flat.

Minc: She's not being treated unfairly. She had a flat in Torun, but she gave it to her son and moved to Warsaw. She's trying to get a flat of her own and she will, eventually.

Toranska: But when!

Minc: Dziunka [addressing the dog], bark at the lady, she's pretending to be a Solidarity fan.

---

* Josef Swiatlo, an early Party defector to the West, whose disclosures of Polish political affairs in 1955 created a public scandal that resulted in, among other things, the abolishing of the Ministry of Security.

46

Jakub Berman

Communism in Poland has always assumed one of two forms, being either nationalist in outlook or 'internationalist'. The more nationalist movements have their roots in the early trade unions and are dedicated to an independent Poland, free from foreign domination. The more international communist movements— ideological and anti-nationalist—develop from the early activism of Rosa Luxemburg, and are dedicated to world revolution: their allegiance is with the Soviet Union. And between these two extremes, every Polish communist movement has had to work, negotiating on the one hand the potential hostility of popular opinion if policy deferred too much to Moscow, and on the other hand the suspicions of its Soviet patron if policy deferred too much to Warsaw. This juggling act was especially apparent in the make-up of the provisional government set up after the war.

Wladyslaw Gomulka—a nationalist who had spent the war years in Poland—was the First Secretary of the new Polish Workers' Party, reconstructed from the remains of various communist movements in the thirties. Most of the actual reconstructing, however, had been done in Moscow, and when the first Polish Workers' Party Congress convened in December 1945, Gomulka was surrounded by members of the Soviet Secret Police and Party members from Russia. Of the Russian Party members, three were to assume important responsibilities: Hilary Minc, Boleslaw Bierut and Jakub Berman.

An academic by training, Berman was the principal ideologist of the Polish Politburo. He was in Moscow during the War, where he ran a training course for activists, preparing them for future government. He returned to Poland in 1945 and was appointed Undersecretary of State in the Ministry of Public Security. Arthur Bliss Lane, the United States Ambassador to Poland from 1945 to 1947, described Berman as the most powerful figure in the Polish politburo.

Jakub Berman: Whenever we went to Moscow after the war, Stalin would invite us to supper, followed by a film. It became a custom, and our visits never ended without a meal together. Dinner would start late in the evening and last until morning. The food and drink were exquisite. I particularly remember a delicious roast of bear meat. Bierut always sat next to Stalin, and I sat next to Bierut. Stalin proposed toasts: the first one to 'comrade Bierut', then to 'comrade Berman', and although the toast to Bierut was friendly, both were very brief and clearly formal. Then Stalin would put on a record, mostly Georgian music, which he loved. Once, I think it was in 1948, I danced with Molotov [laughter].

Teresa Toranska: You mean with Mrs Molotov?

Berman: No, she wasn't there; she'd been sent to a labour camp. I danced with Molotov—it must have been a waltz, or at any rate something simple, because I haven't a clue about how to dance— and I just moved my feet to the rhythm.

Toranska: As the woman?

Berman: Molotov led; I wouldn't know how. He wasn't a bad dancer, actually, and I tried to keep in step with him, but for my part it was more like clowning than dancing.

Toranska: What about Stalin, whom did he dance with?

Berman: Oh, no, Stalin didn't dance. Stalin turned the gramophone: he treated that as his duty. He never left it. He would put on records and watch.

Toranska: He watched you?

Berman: He watched us dance.

Toranska: So you had a good time.

Berman: Yes, it was pleasant, but with an inner tension.

Toranska: You didn't really have fun?

Berman: Stalin really had fun. But for us those dancing sessions were good opportunities to say things to each other which we wouldn't have been able to say out loud. That was when Molotov warned me about being infiltrated by various hostile organisations.

Toranska: Did he threaten you?

Berman: No, it was called a friendly warning. Molotov took the opportunity—or perhaps he'd even arranged it himself, since after all he was the one who asked me to dance—to mention a few things which he thought would be useful to me. I made it clear that I understood, and I didn't say anything in response.

Toranska: Were there any women?

Berman: No, never. There were never any women to be seen around Stalin. All that was arranged very discreetly, and no one except the people in his closest circle knew about it. Stalin was always very careful that there shouldn't be any gossip about him; he knew gossip could be dangerous, and he wanted to have the image of someone pure and uncorrupted.

Toranska: Who were the servants? Soldiers?

Berman: When I was there we were always served by normal waitresses. Once one of them—she was quite a tall girl—was serving us tea, and she stood next to us for a moment as she was setting out the dishes. There were three of us around the table, and suddenly Stalin burst out: 'What's she listening to?' It gave me a shock, because for the first time I saw Stalin in a different light, as a person who could react with such violent distrust to a waitress: someone who'd been checked thousands of times before being brought into direct contact with him, totally reliable. I thought then that he must be bordering on a pathological state.

I remember another occasion, also very typical of him. It took place near the end of the forties. Bierut and I were in Moscow, and in the interval between talks I told Stalin that we wanted to put out an album about the activists in the Polish Communist Party, and include in it the names of Kostrzewa and Warski. Stalin accepted the project, and then suddenly started to talk about Vera Kostrzewa in glowing terms: how she had been such a good communist, so wise and so dedicated to the Party. Both Bierut and I were completely taken aback; we couldn't reconcile what Stalin was saying with her death ten years before.*

Toranska: And what did you feel in 1937 and 1938, when thousands of communists were being murdered in the Soviet Union?

Berman: I didn't try to justify what was happening. I accepted it as a tragic turn of events that involved the sacrifice of an enormous number of people. I tried desperately to cling to the thought that you can't make omelettes without breaking eggs—not a profound saying, but one that made its rounds among us then. The trials that took place cast a terrible cloud over the history of the communist movement. Many Party members began to have doubts.

The Polish Communist Party asked me to attend various 'meetings'—mainly those concerned with the intelligentsia. The arguments that the Party hacks produced at these meetings were difficult to refute because of the clumsy and artificial way in which the Moscow trials were constructed. Old communists with a long record of service to the Party were put in the dock and accused of spying for the Japanese, for the Turks, and for who the hell knows who else. It simply wasn't acceptable. I thought that if there were any doubts about these people then they ought to be dismissed from their posts or transferred elsewhere, not sentenced. And it was a mystery to me that Bukharin, for example, or Kamenev, should have presented such absurd self condemnations at their trials, confessing to crimes they hadn't

---

* Vera Koszutska (pseudonym, Kostrzewa) and Adolf Warszawski (pseudonym, Warski). In 1938 and 1939, Stalin, believing that the Communist Party of Poland (the KPP) had betrayed its socialist ideals, liquidated it: the KPP disappeared from the list of Comintern's affiliated parties, and members who found themselves in the Soviet Union at the time—at the height of the Purges—also disappeared. In all, 5,000 lifelong devotees of communism were killed, including 'Kostrzewa' and 'Warski'.

committed.* At that point the accused may not yet have known
that he would be killed—it was only a question of a trial, a public
confession—and so, often, he agreed to perform a service for the
Party if the Party demanded, or expected, such a sacrifice,
because serving the Party was, for the old communists, not just a
goal in life but also an inner need. And while other methods were
probably also used—such as hunger or threats to harm the
family—I suspect these only played a subsidiary role. Many an
old Bolshevik may have suffered, struggled and even have been
afraid, but he wouldn't have gone through with a self-
condemnation unless he had found what he took to be higher
grounds to justify his decision.

I don't want to go into the rights and wrongs of the ideological
conflicts that took place in the Soviet Union; they were, after all,
unavoidable. I could see how there might have been individual,
isolated acts of treason, but I couldn't believe that everyone was
a traitor, which was how the situation was portrayed at the time.
I found it hard to believe in the guilt of the Polish Communist
Party leaders, whom I knew and who were now sentenced to
death. So I found consolation in the thought that some day,
perhaps, in the years to come, people would arrive at the truth,
and the injuries done would be made good.

Toranska: How?

Berman: People would be rehabilitated.

Toranska: Did you bring in Soviet advisors [into Poland] from the
start?

Berman: We didn't bring anyone in; they came by themselves.

Toranska: But you agreed to have them there.

Berman: But, my dear lady, we couldn't refuse to have them. We

---

* Nikolay Ivanovich Bukharin and Lev Borisovich Kamenev.
Bukharin, described by Lenin as the Party's most valuable
theoretician, spoke out against Trotsky's exile, was put on trial in
1938 during the Purges and executed. Kamenev, a member of the
1923 triumvirate with Zinoviev and Stalin, also sided with Trotsky,
and, after a five year sentence, was tried in 1936.

could after Stalin's death, and then, as you know, we did limit their role. But that wasn't possible earlier; Stalin thought they were helping, not hindering us.

Toranska: Did you talk to him about it?

Berman: We couldn't: Stalin would never have agreed to any discussion on the subject, he thought it was too touchy. And anyhow, the advisors were supposed to save us.

Toranska: How many of them were there?

Berman: It's not a question of numbers; what's important is that they were there. It could have been just one person in the department, but that would have been enough for a considerable influence on decision-making.

Toranska: What about blocking their access to information? Couldn't you have done that?

Berman: That kind of thing is just childish and silly and doesn't work. These people are quite cunning and experienced: after all, they are not just 'advisors', they are security men. They can smell deceit. It's far better to discuss everything with them openly and honestly and to try to oppose particular decisions.

Toranska: With what results?

Berman: Mixed. But it's still not true to say that they reigned supreme among us. I personally saw little of them. I myself was Undersecretary of State for foreign affairs at the time and I had no influence on the selection of security personnel. It's a myth invented later that I was the lord and master who, in charge of everything, kept a telephone with a line to Beria on his desk, consulted him on all matters and took instructions from him.* That's ridiculous. It's true that certain matters did come to me, and I would cautiously assess them positively or negatively—I don't deny any of that—but I had no contact with Beria. I didn't telephone anyone, and even when I went to Moscow to see

---

* Lavrenty Beria, in charge of the Soviet secret police and one of the principal organizers of the Purges.

JAKUB BERMAN: Minister of Public Security during the first year of provisional government, when security forces, mainly the Soviet secret police, were killing, arresting or deporting anyone seen as a representative of the opposition. After 1948, he was officially responsible for Party ideology and propaganda, education and culture, foreign affairs and matters of security. After the death of Stalin, Berman, discredited by the stories of tens of thousands returning from the Soviet camps, was expelled from the Party, having been judged responsible for the 'period of errors and perversions'.

WLADYSLAW GOMULKA: First-Secretary of the Polish Workers' Party. A disciplined, orthodox, and patriotic communist, Gomulka was devoted to the twin goals of social revolution *and* national independence, and is famous for his anti-Soviet policy of following the 'Polish Road to Socialism'. At the June 1948 Plenum of the Party's Central Committee, he openly defied Soviet policy—in a speech that managed to praise not only national independence but both Luxemberg and Trotsky—and was placed under house arrest. Following Stalin's death in 1956, he was reinstated as Party Secretary.

BOLESLAW BIERUT: Elected President in 1947. Following the arrest of Gomulka, he was made the Party's General Secretary preparing the way for the imposition of a Stalinist government from 1948 to 1956. Described as a stool-pigeon and a puppet, he was seen to represent the 'Moscow line'. In 1956, following Stalin's death, Bierut was in Moscow when Krushchev attacked Stalin, and died the following month, apparently by suicide.

HILARY MINC: Member of Politburo, having spent war years in the Soviet Union. Minister of Industry, responsible for all financial planning that was, ultimately, a slavish imitation of Soviet economic methods. Oversaw the controversial forced collectivization of farms, directed mainly at peasants. Resigned in 1956 shortly after Bierut's death.

Stalin, which happened two or three times a year, I rarely spoke to him.

Toranska: So who formed your security apparatus?

Berman: Until 1947 the Ministry of Public Security was controlled by Gomulka, who from the beginning took a great interest in it and even, one could say, looked after it. So everyone brought reports to him. After Gomulka left, Bierut asked me to take charge of the Ministry along with him and I agreed, foolishly as it turned out, because later I ended up with all the blame. Until then I'd been in charge of culture, schooling, higher education, the Polish Academy of Sciences, propaganda and ideology. I took general charge of Security while Bierut controlled the Military Information Bureau—espionage and counter-espionage—and the division between Public Security and Military Information was respected by both them and us.

Toranska: You didn't have any contacts with the heads of Soviet Military Intelligence?

Berman: I took care of the smaller, day-to-day matters; the more important decisions were made by Bierut or at conferences of the 'Three' (Berman, Bierut and Minc). Nevertheless I think I was able to protect a large number of people from harm. When trials took place on a large scale, I tried either to defer them all together or else keep death sentences from being passed. I did this in all cases to which I had access; this was difficult, because many of them were matters of military intelligence, not security, and also because the influence of Soviet advisors on trials and sentences was definitely significant. So there were, I'm sorry to say, quite a few cases which fell outside my scope or which, despite my attempts at persuasion, I wasn't able to bring to a positive outcome: it turned out my arms weren't long enough.

Toranska: Nevertheless, [it was as Minister of Security that] you in August 1949 arrested Herman Field, who had come to Poland to look for his brother Noel, believed to have disappeared but in fact already arrested.

Berman: The Field affair—the Fields were American fellow-travellers—came to a head when other trials here were in full swing, and all the Soviet bloc countries were enmeshed in a web of suspicion. Mass arrests took place in all the people's democracies. And everyone who had ever come into contact with the Fields was arrested: the Field brothers had been in touch with a large number of communists; the net of arrests was cast very wide.

I was in Moscow then, with Bierut. Stalin, when the three of us were standing together during a break between meetings, suddenly asked me about my secretary, Anna Duracz. I knew at once what he was getting at. Anna had been in the Home Army and as a member of the Warsaw Uprising ended up in a Nazi camp; from there she went to Switzerland for medical treatment, along with many other Polish communists. They were looked after by Noel Field. Some time in 1946 or 1947 Field came to Warsaw and tried, on the basis of his acquaintance with Anna, to arrange to see me. He told her that he wanted to ask for my help in explaining his situation. I didn't think I ought to see him, but I agreed to accept a letter. Naturally, I showed the letter to Bierut, but Field's inquiries about his situation remained unanswered. That was where my part in the whole affair ended. But once he was arrested and charged with treason, espionage, Trotskyism, cosmopolitanism and any number of other things— once he'd been connected and even made to stand trial with Laszlo Rajk—his case assumed new proportions.*

---

* Noel Field, an agent from the Office of Strategic Services based in Switzerland, met Laszlo Rajk shortly after the Spanish Civil War. The association with Field was used against Rajk, when in 1948 he was accused of trying to break from Moscow, colluding with Tito and being a spy.

The Home Army, of which Berman's secretary had been a member, was the main armed resistance of Polish nationalists during the war with diplomatic links with the Polish Government-in-Exile in London. It was the Home Army that led the disastrous Warsaw Uprising against the Germans in July 1944, assuming armed support from the Soviet Union—support that Stalin, at the last minute, apparently withheld.

I told Stalin about Anna Duracz but he remained unconvinced by my explanations. This, as it later transpired, was to be my last conversation with Stalin. Soon afterwards Anna was arrested.

Toranska: Your people arrested her, did they not?

Berman: The decision was Stalin's; there was nothing I could do about it, since the move was aimed against me personally and that, indeed, was how everyone viewed it.

Toranska: Why against you?

Berman: Stalin had evidently come to the conclusion that I had disappointed him. It's hard to say why exactly. A number of things I'd done could have displeased him, and thus, to his mind, I could then be suspected of anything, even of being an American spy. At that point any little thing is enough—for instance the fact that my secretary had been in contact with Field—and given the right interpretation my case becomes crystal clear.

Toranska: Did Stalin think this up himself?

Berman: I don't know; perhaps someone suggested it to him. It could have been someone eager for his favour. In Stalin's mind, you know, everything had to be connected, and I was the right kind of person, in his view, to be guilty of cosmopolitanism.

Toranska: Of what?

Berman: Cosmopolitanism. Stalin had launched the struggle against cosmopolitanism in 1948. That was when the Soviet papers began to include people's real names in parentheses—

Toranska: What, how?

Berman: When the papers cited a Jewish activist who had a Russian pseudonym, they would also give his real name in parentheses, and this was a sign that the person was destined to be removed and his position to be taken over by someone else.

Toranska: In other words, anti-Semitism?

Berman: Indeed, but Stalin called it cosmopolitanism.

Toranska: Was he an anti-Semite?

Berman: That's putting it a bit too simply, but Stalin certainly wasn't free of anti-Semitism. After 1945, Stalin's suspicion increased; he began to see enemies everywhere and he imagined that the Jewish minority would be an excellent base of support for American aggression. At about that same time, some activists had come up with the idea of expanding the Jewish settlement in Crimea, which had been abandoned by the Tartars, and this made him all the more wary. He got the idea that Crimea could become a base for a possible American invasion, owing to the international family connections among Jews. Stalin used the slogan of 'the struggle against cosmopolitanism' as an instrument to remove Jews from various positions. Jews were fired *en masse*; there were arrests and trials and widespread suspicion. One of the victims was Molotov's wife. She'd been interested in the Crimean settlement and her interest was, of course, sufficient proof to justify dealing with her and sending her off to a labour camp.

Toranska: Yes, but what about Molotov himself?

Berman: He was very fortunate; he managed to retain his position.

Toranska: He didn't try to help her?

Berman: He helped her in the sense that she was sent to a camp, whereas she could have been killed, couldn't she? They must have forced him to divorce her, because that was what he did, but after Stalin's death, when she returned to Moscow, they lived together again until the end of her life.
Stalin also dealt quite gently with Michoels, a distinguished actor and a director of the Jewish theatre, and very popular with the public. He died in a rigged car accident. For appearances' sake he was even given a grand funeral. But his case was exceptional. Others received plainer treatment; they were simply executed by a firing squad after being sentenced by a military court. The flower of Jewish culture and Yiddish literature was razed to the ground.

Toranska: Let's just name a few of the 238 writers, 106 actors, nineteen musicians and eighty-seven painters and sculptors who were shot or murdered in labour camps: Fefer, Bergelson, Markish. Only Ilia Ehrenburg remained.

Berman: Ehrenburg never belonged to that circle and never discussed a Jewish republic in the Crimea. He was, first and foremost, a Russian journalist, and very popular because of the articles he wrote during the war. Stalin was partial to him, perhaps because Ehrenburg had emigrated for a time and then come back, or perhaps for no particular reason: from time to time Stalin enjoyed helping or showing kindness towards a gifted intellectual or a talented writer. He might suddenly ring up such a person to say an encouraging word, or summon him and do something for him; he did this for Bulghakov, suddenly finding work for him after years of unemployment, and for Pasternak, whom he rang up on the spur of the moment to encourage him when he was having difficulty publishing his books. It's true the books didn't get published, but nevertheless a myth, widely repeated, grew up around these gestures of Stalin's, and gained him many adherents. Stalin knew how to do these things.

But he was brutal with the Jewish writers, heedless of the consequences his actions would have abroad. Because here they were, all these people in the West who thought the Soviet Union was nurturing a flowering Jewish culture that produced its own literature and had excellent theatre, and they would never believe that a writer whom they read was also a spy.

Toranska: Did you?

Berman: No, of course I didn't believe it. It was all rubbish, complete rubbish.

Toranska: And?

Berman: My dear lady, surely you can see that all this was happening in an aura of victory and saving the Jews from the Nazis. Our protests would have been useless.

Toranska: Did you try?

Berman: No, never. We never discussed the struggle against cosmopolitanism with them and they didn't put pressure on us to wage it in Poland. Or if they did, it was a very discreet kind of pressure.

1938: Stalin orders the Comintern to dissolve the Communist Party of Poland, and over 5,000 members of it are killed in the Purges.

1939: Warsaw falls. Nazi-Soviet Pact: Poland partitioned by Germany and the Soviet Union.

1940: The Katyn Massacre: 15,000 Polish army officers taken into Soviet detention and killed in the Katyn Forest in the Soviet Union.

1941: Germany invades the Soviet Union. Soviet Union re-establishes diplomatic relations with the Polish Government in exile in London.

First concentration camp using *Cyclon B* gas cylinders established at Kulm. -

1942: The Polish Workers' Party (PPR) established in Moscow.

1943: Soviet Union severs diplomatic relations with Polish Government-in-Exile.

1944: Soviet armies invade Polish territory. Warsaw Uprising against the Germans: 225,000 died; Hitler orders the city razed. Soviet Union recognizes the largely Soviet-created Polish Committee of National Liberation as the 'sole legal Polish executive power'.

1945: Soviet Army arrives in Warsaw.

Yalta Conference: Roosevelt and Churchill recognize the Provisional Polish Government of National Unity instead of the Polish Government-in-Exile.

Provisional Government established with Gomulka as Party's First Secretary. Ministry of Public Security established, followed by mass killings, deportations and civil war.

1946: Rigged national referendum demonstrates support of Provisional Government.

1947: Rigged election consolidates Party's position in government. Protests that the terms of the Yalta agreement have not been met are ignored.

1948: Gomulka expelled. The Polish United Workers' Party established with Bierut as General Secretary.

Toranska: Did you hear anything about the building of a prison for 'cosmopolites' in Poland?

Berman: That's not true, I don't believe it. It's a pack of lies invented later.

Toranska: Could you not have known about it?

Berman: Certainly, it's possible I might not have known. After all, I was already suspect by then. My secretary had known Field, I was a Jew, and to top it all I'd met with a group from the Jewish Anti-Fascist Committee just before its trip to America at the end of the war. I became the perfect candidate for another Slansky trial; that was the way everything was pointing and may have turned out if Stalin hadn't died. But the direct accusation against me was the Field affair.

That was the time when Bierut displayed real determination and strength of character and loyalty towards me. He defended me against the accusations until the end, although Stalin tried to break him. Bierut was subjected to brutal forms of pressure.

Toranska: Like what?

Berman: I won't tell you.

Toranska: Threats to do with his family?

Berman: No, no, Stalin wasn't as much of a bastard as all that. Let's not exaggerate. He could get away with some fairly mild insults, but if he knew he had someone's co-operation—and Bierut's was guaranteed—he had to maintain certain standards of behaviour, and he never exceeded the limits of the permissible.

Toranska: Was Bierut afraid?

Berman: There were such moments, yes, but I don't want to discuss it.

Toranska: You mean he gave in, broke under pressure?

Berman: Not in all cases, no, I wouldn't say that. At least not in mine, although everyone thought he was mad to defend me the way he did against charges of cosmopolitanism, with the possibility of my dismissal or even trial. It can't have been an easy choice for him, but somehow he found the resolve to make it, and resisted all forms of pressure.

Toranska: You mean there was no struggle against cosmopolitanism in Poland?

Berman: No, there was, because we had to follow the Soviet model in everything; so even though I was always on about it to Bierut, and he himself was of course against it, it did seep into Poland, regardless. The problem itself was so acute in the Soviet Union that we even noticed certain signs of it emerge in Gomulka's speech at the Congress of Unity in 1948. When Gomulka fell from power, we began to see the struggle against cosmopolitanism in our propaganda. We tried to moderate it, tone it down, so that it never assumed the proportions it had in the Soviet Union, but the fact is that it was there.

[Gomulka's fall began] a year earlier, in 1947, when the Soviet Union wanted to establish a Communist Information Bureau— an attempt to co-ordinate the activities of the various communist parties [throughout the bloc countries] on principles of unanimity and not, as before, through majority decisions.

First Gomulka went to see Stalin, and then, afterwards, I was summoned to the Kremlin. Tea was served. It was obvious from the first that this was not to be just a friendly chat, although Stalin was unusually polite and solicitous. He spoke in a very subdued way about what he wanted, although he never explained exactly what this Information Bureau was supposed to do. He merely stressed that with the international situation being what it was and America trying to squeeze everyone, we needed to concentrate our forces. This kind of reasoning could strike quite a responsive chord, because America had indeed become extremely pushy and determined, and we needed to pool our resources to defend against her. The Bureau was our chance to consolidate the Communist parties and protect the entire socialist bloc from enemy aggression.

After the meeting in the Kremlin, I wrote a letter to Gomulka, telling him how matters stood. I knew Gomulka suspected that other, further reaching aims, unknown to us, might be lurking behind the idea of the Information Bureau. This was admittedly something we also suspected, but you can't base your actions on suspicions.

A secret council of the European Communist parties was then held in Szklarska Poreba [in Poland]. The Polish Party was represented by Gomulka and Minc, and I was there as an advisor. But the meeting unfolded along lines that were totally different from the way Stalin had initially described it to Gomulka and me, and Gomulka began to get agitated. He said Stalin had deceived him; we would vote against the formation of the Bureau of Information. I was appalled. I knew what the consequences would be if Poland voted against it. I kept telling Gomulka that this was unacceptable; it would mean we were trying to break away, to crack the entire unity of the bloc; surely you can see what the consequences would be. It would mean Poland was betraying, endangering the Soviet Union . . . I don't have to spell out for you what would happen to us then.*

Toranska: What?

Berman: We would all be got rid of, naturally, and whoever came to power after us would be horrendous, absolutely unthinkable. But none of this had any effect on Gomulka. He behaved like a child. I called a meeting of the Polish Politburo and presented the situation. We all realized that we were bound by certain canons and allegiances: so we took up a firm stand against Gomulka and

---

* In 1947, Marshall Aid was offered to both Poland and Czechoslovakia, at a time when Stalin was made more and more uneasy both by the increased American presence in Europe and by the spirit of independence that characterized the bloc countries— both Gomulka and Tito were referred to as 'rightist nationalist deviationists'. The Communist Information Bureau (Cominform) was set up to co-ordinate the activities of communist parties in the eastern bloc and ensure ideological solidarity. It was in the following year that all frontiers were closed and the economy was governed by military priorities.

passed a motion binding him to a solidarity vote in favour of the Information Bureau and of any resolution the Soviet Union would propose. He had to submit to our decision.

After the meeting, someone proposed that the Bureau should have its headquarters in Warsaw. That was when we summoned up all our courage and dissented, pleading some rather indirect economic reasons: we said that we were in the middle of negotiations with America, applying for loans, trying to retrieve the gold held by the Polish government in London, and that it would be strategically unwise to complicate these talks.

Toranska: If the Bureau had its headquarters in Warsaw, wouldn't that give you some influence over its decisions?

Berman: That wasn't something we could count on. The Soviet delegation would always be able to force its view on us. We didn't have our heads in the clouds, you know. In sum, we wanted to participate, but as a member of the collective, not as the leading party. We anticipated—rightly, as it turned out—that the Bureau's activities would be limited to anti-American propaganda (which wasn't all that effective), discussions and resolutions. As a project it was, quite simply, stillborn.

Toranska: Not quite. In June 1948 the Bureau condemned Yugoslavia and the nationalist right wing in the Polish Party. It also passed a resolution binding all the parties in the bloc to collectivize their countryside. All this was further lent dramatic flavour by the fact that T. Kostov, who did the condemning for Bulgaria, was got rid of a year later; A. Pauker, who did the condemning for Romania, suffered the same fate two years later; and R. Slansky, condemning for Czechoslovakia, followed their example four years later.*

---

*Triacho Kostov, the nationalistic Deputy Prime Minister of Bulgaria at the time, was tried and executed in 1949. Ana Pauker was expelled from the Romanian Communist Party and put under house arrest in 1949. Her arrest was not, it seems, because she was a nationalist but because she was Jewish.

Berman: One source of the conflict with Yugoslavia was the desire to put Central Europe in order. A number of ideas emerged to form federations, so that the bloc would consist of strong, united elements. Poland was supposed to form a federation with Czechoslovakia. Yugoslavia and Bulgaria, or possibly Albania, were marked out as another pair for a federation. Hungary was by itself. Stalin was in favour of the Polish-Czech federation but against the Yugoslav-Bulgarian project. He must have made his own calculations and had his reasons. Dymitrov, who had been pro-Yugoslavia from the beginning, found himself in trouble.

Toranska: Did he die?

Berman: Yes, a year later.

Toranska: Like Kostov?

Berman: Kostov had supported the union and was shot, but I don't know whether that was the reason. There could have been many pretexts. Dymitrov, on the other hand, died normally. You shouldn't accept at their face value the myths created to embarrass the Soviets. They have enough sins; there's no need to go to absurd lengths to magnify them.

Quite frankly, I hesitated with the condemnation of Yugoslavia. I hoped that some kind of compromise could be reached, and scandal avoided.

Toranska: And? Did you condemn Yugoslavia?

Berman: What else were we supposed to do? Re-enact Gomulka's scene in Szklarska Poreba?

Gomulka couldn't be made to see things from our point of view. He couldn't grasp that the Bureau should be treated as a necessary evil, with patience; that we had to sit it out and in the meantime look after our own affairs. He still suspected that the Polish Party's autonomy would be undercut. So he came up with another idea. After the meeting at Szklarska Poreba, he suggested that we go to see Stalin and get his signature on a document guaranteeing our Western border, not realizing that this would only offend Stalin. And in June 1948, at the Party Plenum, he decided to make a speech without first getting its content approved by the Politburo. I warned him not to do it, but he'd always been stubborn.

After this it was more than ever clear that Gomulka was refusing to toe the Party line. The conflict was growing, and signalled the beginning of what was to be a crisis in the Party leadership. At the Plenum I stood up and said so. In the transcripts of the Plenum, I also deleted from this speech the part concerning Gomulka's proposal to see Stalin and ask for a guarantee of our border; I thought it was too compromising.

Toranska: What did Gomulka say that was so terrible?

Berman: He said that we should respect the tradition of independence fostered by the Polish Socialist Party.

Toranska: Well, shouldn't we?

Berman: That depends. The conflict with Gomulka hinged on a serious issue of principle: should Poland's independence be linked with the tradition of the Polish Socialist Party, or with the victory of the revolution.

Toranska: For ten years you were the second most important person in Poland after Bierut. You were the brain behind the Party; you were its highest authority. Then they accused you of the gravest crimes, the worst acts of treason a man can commit. After that, you were crossed off, finished. They even crossed you out of the general encyclopaedia.

Berman: Of course. When you're cast out, you don't exist. When I was in power, they included me even in the Soviet encyclopaedia, but later they deleted all that. But then, they've always manipulated their history; the Poles are doing the same. My expulsion, though, did come as a shock. I felt that a great injury had been done to me.

Jakub Berman died in April 1984, shortly after granting this interview.

Stefan Staszewski—until 1958, editor-in-chief at the Polish Press Agency—was dismissed from the Party in 1968, and is now a KOR and Solidarity sympathizer: 'When I saw Bierut again after the war, our relations were still friendly. I told him everything I knew about the fate of my friends and his, most of whom had been murdered in Russia. There were two or three he was particularly interested in, because Stalin and Beria were always telling him how they must have got lost somewhere in that vast country and how no one could find them. I told him exactly what had happened to them. But he said that it was a tragedy, and that perhaps a few of them might still be alive, so he would go on looking for them, asking about them and pressing for their release. He mentioned the subject to Stalin on a number of occasions. Beria was always present at these meetings. Bierut would ask, "What's happening to those Polish Communists? Where are they?" And Stalin would turn to Beria and say, "Lavrenti Pavlovich, don't you know where they are? I told you to look for them, why haven't you found them yet?" He played out this scene every time.

Once, at the beginning of 1950, or maybe near the end of 1949, Bierut returned completely shattered from one of his trips to Moscow; he was so shaken that he came back and described it. He'd gone to see Stalin, asked once again about the Polish communists, and once again watched Stalin act out his little game with Lavrenti Pavlovich. Then he left, along with Beria, and that was when Beria said to him (please forgive the roughness of this Party language): "Why do you keep fucking around with Josif Vissarionovich? Why don't you fuck off from him? That's my advice to you. You'll regret it if you don't." Bierut took the hint—no longer a hint now, but a final warning—and never again alluded to his friends in front of Stalin.'

Translated from the Polish by Agnieszka Kolakowska

PATRICK MARNHAM
IN SEARCH OF
AMIN

The journey started uneventfully with an application to the appropriate Ministry. The earliest letter is dated 5 October 1973. 'Dear Permanent Secretary,' it begins.

> On the advice of the press officer at the Uganda High Commission here in London I am writing to you directly to request an interview with the President of Uganda, His Excellency General Idi Amin Dada. I have been commissioned by *Esquire*, one of the most prominent and influential magazines in America, to seek this interview. I found on a recent visit to New York that there was a great deal of interest among Americans, especially the young people . . .

Extraordinary what one will say in order to earn a living.

Something went wrong with my plans after that. In November there was a letter from an editor at *Esquire*. 'I regret terribly that after I talked to you I was informed that we already *have* an Amin assignment out to Auberon Waugh.' Unknown to the editor, I shared an office with Auberon Waugh at that time and it did not take very long to establish that Mr Waugh had long since told *Esquire* that he had no further interest in this project. For some reason I continued with it.

Before Christmas I set out for Africa having heard nothing from the President, who was preoccupied at that time with a purge of opponents in the northern tribal areas. I wrote three further letters from Nairobi and made several telephone calls, without success. During the next three months it was not difficult to forget about Uganda. I travelled all over Kenya and Tanzania and flew to Zaire, the Ivory Coast, Senegal, Mauritania, Mali, Upper Volta and Ghana before preparing to return to London. In those days the English papers were richer and more interested in abroad. They were happy to pay the expenses of travelling correspondents. Before returning to London, I called for the last time at my post office box in Nairobi. There was one letter in it from Economy Tours and Travel, *'re Visitors Pass IM/2128/71'*: 'We have been requested by the Uganda Tourist Development Corporation to arrange for your transport. We would like to request you to contact us as soon as you arrive. Assuring you of our attention . . .' Still, I was perfectly safe. I didn't have a commission, so I couldn't afford to go. But in due course another letter reached me. It was from *Oui* magazine of Chicago, Illinois, offering £500 for an interview with President Amin. I think I may have been a little overwrought after three months of travelling around Africa because these courteous invitations now read to me like a judgement.

At Entebbe airport, two weeks later, there was a banner over the building saying 'Uganda Welcomes Tourists' just where Courtney Fitch had tied it up. Courtney Fitch had, until the previous year, been the Englishman responsible for running the country's tourist industry. On the instructions of General Amin he had arranged for a large party of East African travel agents to go to Uganda for a reconnaissance. As they disembarked, in some trepidation, they saw Courtney Fitch being escorted to the plane they had just left. He was being deported. Since then the Immigration Office had virtually closed down. None of the ministries wanted to take responsibility for admitting a foreigner. At the airport I had to surrender my passport.

In those days Kampala seemed like a model city. Laid out around its seven hills it possessed one of everything, like Toytown. There was a scenic golf course and a park, a bandstand, a sports stadium, a Salvation Army hostel, the RSPCA dog kennels, the Animal Clinic, the caravan site, the Police Sports Club, the Masonic Hall, the campus of Makerere University and the leafy grounds of Mulago Teaching Hospital. There was a Vehicle Testing Centre and a Domestic Science College. Perhaps they are still there; such details tend to survive even civil wars.

By February 1974 Amin had completed his massacres of the Lango and Acholi tribes, who were Christian and thought to be faithful to Obote, and had started to move against the Lugbara army officers. The tribal killings in the countryside had stopped for the time being; the murder squads—called the 'Public Safety Unit' and the 'Bureau of State Research'—were concentrating on Amin's other main enemy, the educated people of Uganda. But Kampala appeared reasonably quiet. After looking round for a day or so I set out to contact those who had so mysteriously provided me with the means of entering Uganda. The Immigration Department knew nothing about it so I went to the Uganda Tourist Development Corporation. It seemed sensible to do everything as conspicuously as possible. There was less chance, then, of being accused of spying and more chance of somebody noticing if I went missing. I don't know what I thought anyone could do in either case. I telephoned the managing director of the Uganda Tourist Development Corporation, who was astute enough to require me to make an appointment. When I kept it he was out. This meant that his deputy had to sign the letter of introduction which I was to carry. Neither of them, however, had my Visitor's Pass. That was still with Economy Tours and Travel. They sent the document, via an elderly messenger, to my hotel. On reading the letter of introduction I found that I was now travelling under a false identity. Although I had entered the country as an emissary of *Oui* magazine, this letter stated that I was a travel writer with *African Encounter*. I had never heard of this publication.

The next person to call on was the man who had proved more evasive than anyone else, the man who was supposed to have provided me with a special visa in the first place, the Permanent Secretary. When I walked into his office he was clearly surprised to see me. 'How did you get in to the country?' he asked. Not very polite. When I told him, he said that there must have been some mistake. Still, deportations were not his responsibility. He certainly wasn't going to do anything about it. He had never heard of *Oui* magazine so I told him that it was owned by *Playboy*. He looked appalled. He himself was a Christian and unphased by the First World's obsession with saucy photographs, but the President was a Moslem. The possible juxtapositions worried him. I told him that *Oui* was actually quite different from *Playboy*. I described a paper that was somewhere between the *New York Review of Books* and *Encounter*. Then I asked the Permanent Secretary why he had failed to answer all my letters. He said that there was no point in replying if one had nothing to say. He asked me why I wanted to see the President. Why did I not interview Kenyatta or Nyerere? Weren't they also well-known in North America? He was completely unimpressed by my explanation—'a new style of leadership, question of the Middle East' and so on. He was confident that he knew what I was going to write.

The Permanent Secretary was a threatened species in Uganda: a serious, highly-educated and efficient civil servant trying to run a government ministry. He was rude to me because I had complicated his life and possibly placed him at some risk merely by my arrival. In the circumstances, rudeness was a moderate response.

I suppose I must have realized that it was tactless to go on pressing him, and I met him only once more: in the hallway of the Ministry, late on a Friday afternoon. He was in a bad-tempered hurry. We smiled at each other with our teeth. The next day's headlines explained his bad temper. He had been rebuked before his assembled staff by the Minister, an upstart illiterate from Amin's 'home district'. Men like Amin were much easier to understand than men like the Permanent Secretary. Ambition might have explained why he stayed on, or the chance to earn an unofficial fortune. But he did not seem a corrupt man, and it needed more than ambition to explain why an intelligent person should risk his life and the lives of his family for some short-term advantage. Men like him were killed every week.

The next official I saw was an under-secretary who left me alone in his room for some time. 'Have you been reading the papers on my desk?' he asked when he came back.

'No'.

'You should. Some of them are marked *confidential*. I haven't read them either. There are so many and I can't find anything interesting. Go out and do some research. And then some sight-seeing. You will have the place to yourself. Don't forget to count the dead bodies you will see on the street corners.' Very dry.

There were then various theories about 'the General'. The English expatriates offered the first clear view, although in this, as in much else, they were behind the times. You find the expatriates in several places. One was the Kampala Rugby Club, with its white members and black caddies—it was actually on the golf course. The members were a curious assortment of unidealistic teachers who had chosen the wrong African country, old colonials and slightly dubious businessmen. The atmosphere in the club was deteriorating with the African members picking quarrels for no reason, resentful perhaps that the club's protective aura, the white aura, had begun to disperse. The whole place was a bit threadbare. There was another British club which had been turned into a hotel, but there was something colonial, paramilitary, about it still: the bare flagpole, the neat white lines on the tarmac outside, the bougainvillaea hedge, now out of control. Inside, the old clock with its brass pendulum still occupied the stained wooden case on the wall; the breeze crept through the open French window and rustled the faded chintz curtains; and a businessman told me that Amin was 'Not nearly as black as he is painted . . . Always found him quite charming, terribly pro-Scottish, loves the bagpipes and plays the accordion himself quite well. Twice played rugby for Uganda . . . extremely brave . . . terrific energy . . . natural leader . . . stopped all the freelance armed robbery . . . tourists have gone but so have the beggars.' Such men, of course, had lost virtually everything they had. They wanted it to be true, they were shipwrecked, washed up. They were reassured when Amin played the big buffoon.

This picture of the bluff, black Highlander, an over-promoted pipe-major, was not assisted by the true story of how Amin had come to power. About that there had been nothing essentially African at all. Before Obote was overthrown, his regime had been accused of gold-smuggling across the Zairean border. One of the leading participants in this activity was Colonel Amin. Later Brigadier Amin came under suspicion of stealing £1.2 million from the Defence budget and of murdering a fellow Brigadier. On the night of 25 January 1971, Amin was due to be arrested and charged with these crimes. But the telephone call issuing the order to loyal officers was connected by an *effendi* of Amin's tribe, Sergeant Musa. Amin was duck shooting. Musa seized the armoury and sent for 'the Boss'. By the time of my visit Sergeant Musa had become Colonel Musa, officer commanding the Fifth Mechanized Regiment.

These facts did not illuminate the Palestinian view of Amin either. Their representative was living in an abandoned colonial villa, too dilapidated to be suburban. He told me: 'No matter what people might say about the General, he is a true friend of the Palestinian people.' Nor did gold-smuggling square with the Libyan picture of Amin as a devout Moslem, nor with the Second World's view of Amin as an effective African ally. The Russians, who supplied Amin with tanks and planes, saw their protégés dumped in the Nile with everyone else. The coffee crop continued to go to the United States. East Germany sent one of their best men to Uganda, Gottfried Lessing, unusual among Second-Worlders in being an experienced Africa-hand. His name adorns hundreds of thousands of books all over the world because his former wife writes under it. There is a memorable picture of a young man like him in her early African books, an ideologue living in a colony, a hardliner. This man, who should have been famous, was killed during the 'liberation' of Kampala by the Tanzanian army when Amin was overthrown. He and his family died when their car was set alight by a flame-thrower; an obscure death during a political non-event. Palestinians, Russians, East Germans, British—all were eventually made to look foolish by Amin, all were as thoroughly duped as the sodden, shifty expats in their run-down club.

One day I took a taxi over the pot-holes and under the trees and up the hill to the former palace of the Kabakas of Uganda, now a deserted tourist resort. There was a recent name in the Visitors' book, 'Stokely Carmichael, Conakry, Guinea'. Mr Carmichael had just completed a triumphal visit to Uganda in his capacity as leader of the All African People's Party in the United States. On leaving he had assured Amin that 'what he had seen in Uganda had encouraged him very much and that he was going to do everything possible to represent Uganda very well'. The reports of his speech appeared under a photograph of Mrs Kay Amin clasping the hand of the wife of the Yugoslav ambassador. Mrs Amin died later that year. Her dismembered body was taken to the city mortuary. Amin, by then divorced from her, took their children to visit her and abused their mother's corpse. 'Your mother was a bad woman,' he shouted, 'see what has happened to her.' These children, like Svetlana Stalin, were brought up with a privileged insight into the brutal use of power. Unlike Svetlana, they were also trained as future rulers. When Amin attended the Pan-Moslem conference in Pakistan he took one of his sons with him. The entire conference, packed with heads of state, and locked behind impenetrable security, sat there listening to the burblings of little Mwanga.

In order to discover what was really happening in Toytown I sought out 'the Opposition'. They didn't have an office of course, not even an underground newspaper, but they weren't hard to find.

I applied for an interview with the Archbishop of Kampala, E.K. Nsubuga, now a Cardinal. He refused to see me. He is a very canny man, a skilful politician, a protector of the various Catholic tribes of Uganda, and a survivor. He was reported at that time to have had an unusually frank exchange with the General. While thanking Amin for donating 50,000 shillings for the completion of a shrine to Uganda's early Christian martyrs, the Archbishop asked him to stop opening his incoming and outgoing letters. The exchange took place on the site of the Martyrs' shrine. The previous time the Archbishop visited it the General had not been there but an army patrol had: four members of the Archbishop's family were abducted. Today, Cardinal Nsubuga is still in his palace and has become one of the most influential political leaders in Uganda, a mediator between the guerrillas and the government. He has the right stuff, whatever that is, to survive as a prominent, unarmed Ugandan under Amin, the Tanzanians, Obote (twice) and Okello. His Anglican counterpart, a brave but less subtle man whom I spoke to at length, was eventually shot in the back of the head, and mourned by Amin as 'the victim of a road accident'.

The sites of such atrocities were not always remote. From my hotel it was only a stroll down the Queen's Road to the High Court. Down these steps the Lord Chief Justice of Uganda, Benedicto Kiwanuka, was dragged to his death in his socks one working morning by unidentified men. Incredibly, the High Court continued to function, and while I was there an army corporal, Bahemuka from the West Nile region, Amin's homeland, was sentenced to six years prison for encouraging cannibalism. He had cut off the ears of a man suspected of witchcraft and forced the poor fellow to eat them. On the same day, another known cannibal, Lieutenant Colonel Isaac Malyamungu, was reported merely to have harangued Magamaga shopkeepers for overcharging. The High Court was at the mercy of some of the most brutal men in the county and yet continued to condemn them, and yet not all of them. It was easy to parody this reality from London, easy to simplify it even in Kampala. At times it *was* simple enough. When Amin seized the armoury, then the barracks, then the capital, he needed to show that he had support. The Inspector-General of Police, Wilson Oryema, was photographed with him, posed in a friendly handshake. In due course Oryema joined Amin's cabinet as Minister of Mineral and Water Resources. His son was selected for training as a military pilot in West Germany. On the day that this

77

pilot returned to his country, trained to fight for it, he was abducted and shot. That was during my visit. Oryema's usefulness was exhausted in 1977. He was taken from a meeting of diplomats and Ugandan notables, with the Anglican Archbishop and the Minister for Internal Affairs, by Malyamungu, the same Lieutenant Colonel; all three were murdered. Amin no longer cared who saw his men at work. He needed to frighten everyone and the more prominent the witnesses were the better.

For most Kampalans life continued to run its familiar, haphazard course. Setting out on one visit to the Ministry, near a corner on Speke Road, I came across a man lying on the pavement. He was having a fit. He was an old man, his hair was grey and he was wearing a brown suit. His shirt had ridden up and as he rolled and jerked across the pavement one could see that underneath his trousers he was wearing tight, elasticated, nylon bathing shorts. They did not look comfortable. This man was in danger of swallowing his tongue. He was experiencing muscular contractions which caused his back to arc up in a curve, lifting his torso five or six inches into the air. His suit was soon covered in dust, there was dust on his face and the black grit on the ground was mixed with the bubbling foam from his mouth. His eyelids were open, his eyeballs immobile, rolled up beneath his brow, just the bulging whites exposed. One wondered, as he jerked over onto his face, that his eyes were not crushed by the weight of his head as it banged onto the pavement. A girl picked up his brown trilby hat, other people stepped out of his way. There was a feeling among those watching him that might shortly express itself in laughter. They were nervous. The girls put their hands up to cover their mouths. One could use the listless reaction to illustrate the general fear of Amin—the fear of making oneself prominent by taking the initiative—but it would not be true. Such scenes and such reactions can be seen in all the cities of Africa. The particular effects of Amin's rule were not usually so public.

There was a consultant surgeon at Mulago Teaching Hospital, a Scotsman, who invited me into his house and gave me a list of prominent men who had recently been murdered. He had good Scotch whisky and plenty of ice, but he had to check both the door and the window for eavesdroppers; he didn't trust his own 'houseboy'. I took notes of our conversation which omitted all the names and then posted the names, without notes, to my post office box in Nairobi. It was melodramatic but essential. Two years before there had been another reporter from London who had taken notes in the usual way, with names. He had been arrested on his way out to Entebbe airport, his notebooks had been examined and several of the Ugandans he had spoken to had subsequently been murdered. In all this, the curious visitor to Toytown had one excellent camouflage; the routine confusion of life in Africa. In a country which could admit a foreign journalist by mistake, where even a Permanent Secretary was too cautious to implement a deportation order, it was more than likely that the visitor would have left before any hostile inquiry had been organized. So often in Africa the danger arises not by intention but by chance; the drunken sentry at the road block, the once faithful servant who has been denied a bag of old clothes.

And so, I am convinced, was it by chance that I was denied my interview with His Excellency General Idi Amin Dada. I had been to see another 'permanent' secretary, Peter Ucanda, who ran the President's office, and who was subsequently to flee the country. I was also on speaking terms with Juma, the illiterate minister, who happened to be Amin's current favourite. They told me that it was just a matter of the president 'fitting me into his schedule'. And then something quite unexpected occurred.

The news-stand on Speke Road received a consignment of *Oui* magazine. A city which was short of bread, beer, sugar, and a country which no longer had the foreign currency to buy toothpaste or shoes, had managed to import about one hundred copies of a not very recent issue and display them along the pavement. There was the usual cover picture, not the sort favoured by either *Encounter* or the *New York Review of Books*.

After that, my interview became less and less likely. The President was reported to be taking spiritual instruction from the Chief Kadhi before attending the Pan-Moslem conference. The ministry adopted a much friendlier attitude to my visits; they were no longer worried about me.

In the time left to me in Uganda there was a crowded official schedule to cover. I never met the Archbishop's future murderer, the cannibal Malyamungu, but I did met Ali Towelli, the head of the

Public Safety Unit at a diplomatic cocktail party. This was followed
by an International Medical Conference, which Amin addressed.
His speech was devoted to the problems of 'disabled children in
rural areas' to which he intended to devote the President's charity
fund. One of the administrators of the conference disappeared on
the morning that it opened. Then there was the downfall of the
foreign minister, Lieutenant Colonel Ondoga: it started with a
newspaper report that Amin thought his ministry 'the most
inefficient he had ever seen'; then came the announcement that
Ondoga had been 'assigned to other duties', then the appointment
of his successor, Princess Elizabeth of Toro—'Miss Bagaya' as
Amin called her. The Princess accepted my congratulations with a
trill in her voice. Two weeks later Ondoga's body was found in the
Nile, by members of the Public Safety Unit. Miss Bagaya's good
fortune was made public on the campus of Makerere University.
Everyone was there, students and faculty. Amin was frightened of
this audience; he felt ignorant and foolish. The professors sucked
their pipes and looked at the ground. There is a special horror for
people who think clearly in the realization that they are living in a
country where to think clearly is to risk your life. Looking back on
the Amin days it was his fear and hatred of educated people that
were both the most characteristic and unpredictable aspects of his
tyranny. He was not the only African leader who carried out tribal
massacres; the advantage of such behaviour is that it identifies those
at risk. They may be able to avoid the danger. But Amin also
attacked people for being good at their jobs. The better you served
him the more likely you were to attract his resentment.

At my last meeting with Juma, the General's favourite son, he
said: 'Do not worry that you have not seen the Head of State. You
just came at the wrong time.' Then he chuckled, 'Heh, heh, heh.'
But he was wrong about that. I *had* seen Amin. I had seen him in the
way Juma fingered the telephone receiver and opened his eyes wide
while he listened to the 'Effendi' on the telephone. I had seen Amin
in the fear shown by those who were queueing in the corridor
outside Juma's office. This was a fear which men who were
frightened of Amin instilled in men who could be made dependent
on *them*; fear in this way becoming a burden to be more equally
shared. I had seen Amin in the clumsy buffoonery of the leader, as
imitated by anyone who wished to evade an inquisitive question.

'Not quite as black as he's painted!' Oh very good, a joke from the sergeant's mess, appropriate in a country which was being drilled by an evil-tempered sergeant. And I had watched Amin himself, sweating with fear into his Savile Row suit, before starting a speech to an educated audience; the almost hapless victim of Uganda's post-colonial plight, a man trained to kill by the King's African Rifles, who used his single professional skill to keep himself in power.

'You just came at the wrong time,' Juma said. 'Anyway I hope you will come back. Anyway you have seen a lot. I think you will go away quickly. Oh yes.' Yes. I went away quickly—on the flight before the one I said I was going on, to be exact. No one had violated my notebooks, no one would be blamed for admitting me. Almost all the evidence of my visit disappeared with my departure. From Nairobi, in delighted relief, I sent a long telex to the *Sunday Times* dealing with the topical information. It was prominently used in that week's issue. Then I set out for London, looking forward to writing the real story, the complicated truth about Uganda, for *Oui* magazine. Sabena had a flight from Nairobi to Brussels, with connections to London. Nobody mentioned that it called at Entebbe.

And so it was that, with my completed records, names and all, and a copy of my telex to the *Sunday Times*, and my all-too-familiar appearance, I found myself back in Uganda, sitting in a Sabena plane in the middle of the night and refusing to join the other passengers in the transit lounge of Entebbe airport. A hard-faced Belgian stewardess told me that it was a rule at Entebbe that *all* passengers had to leave the plane. I told her that in my case that would be inadvisable. She said that Ugandan security men always boarded the plane to enforce the rule. I told her that I had a high fever and must not be moved. She looked extremely irritated but brought me a blanket. It was not difficult to look ill, running with sweat, teeth chattering, grey skin, when the security men passed down the plane. The stewardess explained. The security men passed on.

In due course *Oui* magazine rejected my article, on the grounds that it was not an interview, and declined to pay most of my expenses. It had turned out to be rather a costly adventure. The

African correspondents of Fleet Street continued to write about Uganda as one more piece on the world chessboard, and to press for the return of the legitimate ruler, the moderate Dr Obote. Today, when the appalling Obote has been overthrown for the second time, they continue to report Uganda in terms of ideologies and 'spheres of East-West influence'; the word 'tribalism' rarely appears in their copy, and they don't seem to have noticed that *they* may have got Dr Obote wrong.

They got Field-Marshall Amin wrong too. The Western view of Uganda, the view which is formed by 'interviews', makes no sense at all. It fails to explain how a 'simple buffoon' could rule so many sophisticated men for so long. Nor does it explain how such a man could dominate Uganda's complicated mixture of tribal and religious groups, Muslim and Christian, Catholic and Protestant, Bantu and Nilotic, Bantu and Bantu. Perhaps the truth was that nobody in the West wanted to read that Amin was more than a buffoon, or that he was extremely popular in parts of Uganda, or that the return of Obote would be a disaster. In Chicago and London the men who had never been to Amin's Uganda already knew what they thought. An eye-witness account only served to confuse them.

They preferred the *Punch* view of an illiterate oaf, straight down from the trees, who spoke in phrases like 'Who am dat?' *Punch* ran a highly successful parody along those lines for several years. If you had been to Uganda it read like a weekly lesson in the limitations of popular humour.

Amin was a shrewd man who played an old trick on those who opposed him. He encouraged them to underestimate him. He knew what expatriates thought of him so he fed their prejudices and clowned about. He had another role to play for Gadaffi, another for the Yugoslavs, another for Kenyatta. To have interviewed a man who could disguise himself so successfully would have been interesting, but it was not essential. There was more to be learned by watching him sweating with fear before he spoke to a room full of unarmed doctors.

MILAN KUNDERA
PRAGUE:
A DISAPPEARING
POEM

1

Prague, this dramatic and suffering centre of Western destiny, is gradually fading away into the mists of Eastern Europe, to which it has never really belonged. This city—the first university town east of the Rhine, the scene in the fifteenth century of the first great European revolution, the cradle of the Reformation, the city where the Thirty Years War broke out, the capital of the Baroque and its excesses—this city tried in vain in 1968 to westernize a socialism 'that came in from the cold.'

The picture of Atlantis comes to mind. And it's not just the relatively recent political annexation of Prague which has made this city seem so far away and vague. The Czech language, so inaccessible to foreigners, has always stood as an opaque glass between Prague and the rest of Europe.

Everything known about my country, outside the borders of Bohemia, has been known at second hand. Czech history has been based on German sources. The work of Antonin Dvořák and Leoš Janáček has been discussed without a knowledge of their correspondence, their theoretical writings, their milieu. And even now people are looking at the relationship between Prague and Kafka without knowing anything about Czech culture. And 'brilliant' speculations have been advanced about the Prague Spring without any knowledge of the newspapers and magazines of those days. The great wave of structuralism that has swept over the entire world originated in Prague, but most of the work of the founder of that school has not been translated because it analyses Czech novels and poetry which are unknown abroad.

It often strikes me that the known European culture harbours within it another unknown culture made up of little nations with peculiar languages, such as the culture of the Poles, the Czechs, the Catalans and the Danes. People suppose that the little countries necessarily imitate the big ones, but that is an illusion. In fact they're quite different. A little guy's outlook is different from a big man's. The Europe made up of little countries is *another Europe*; it offers another perspective and its culture is often completely at odds with the Europe of big countries.

2

It's noon and I'm sitting under a gaudy parasol
Prague is stretched out at my feet

I see it as I've imagined enchanted cities
I see it as the dream of capricious builders

I see it as a throne, as the home town of magic
I see it as a volcanic citadel carved into the rock by a
feverish madman
Vitězslav Nezval

If one wanted to make a distinction among the various cultural
periods in Europe, between those influenced by the spirit of
rationalism and those inspired by the irrational, one could say that
the latter have dominated the history of Prague: the Gothic, the
mannerism of the late Renaissance and especially the Baroque.

During the decline of the Renaissance, the court of Emperor
Rudolf II became the European centre of esoteric knowledge and
fantastic art. At that time Kepler, the astrologer and astronomer,
worked in Prague, as did Archimboldo, the Salvador Dalí of the
sixteenth century, and the great Jewish humanist Rabbi Loew, who
according to legend created the first artificial man, the golem.

The Thirty Years War, which ended Rudolf's reign, was a
catastrophe during which the Czech people nearly vanished, because
the country was forcefully reconverted to Catholicism and
Germanicized. The hypnotic spell of Baroque art assisted in the
gigantic brainwashing used to change a Protestant Slavic nation into
a German Catholic one. All these statues, expressive and theatrical,
all these churches, fascinating and exuberant, are just the 'flowers of
evil', the fruits of oppression. (This complicity between beauty and
evil is typical of Prague, and we have all been initiated into it since our
childhood.)

Not only did the Baroque era bring about the full flush of
architectural and musical beauty, but it also stifled free thought,
literature, the novel and philosophy—all of which, for the next two
centuries, the sixteenth and seventeenth, were nearly non-existent.
The absence of rationality and realism was made up for by an over-

development of the irrational and the fantastic—legends, fairy-tales, ecstasy, the morbid imagination. The extraordinary one-sidedness of our literature, whether written in Czech or in German, developed at this time. From then on the magical was always to be immeasurably more important than the realistic. Quoting a poem by Nezval, André Breton rightly called Prague 'the magical capital of Europe'.

In the streets of Prague Franz Kafka could have met only one great German writer of the preceding generation: Gustav Meyrink, an author of tall tales. In 1902 Meyrink published in *Simplicissimus* his first tale, 'The Burning Soldier', the story of a military man who suddenly comes down with a fever that keeps rising, first to a temperature of 200 degrees, then to 220, until everything around him begins to burn and everyone flees from him. This is a metamorphosis— unexplained, unjustified—of a man into a monster. Ten years later, Franz Kafka would write his first famous story: a tale in which Gregor Samsa, in a manner equally unexplained and unjustified, turns himself into a beetle.

Prague's magical heritage, then, was at once preserved and perfected in the work of Kafka: his great innovation did not consist of instilling the novel with an imagination of the fantastic. He was completely faithful to the tradition of the magical capital. But he went radically beyond all his predecessors (and this is what distinguishes his 'Metamorphosis' from the writing of Meyrink) by filling the fantastic with the real (the reality of minuscule observations, but also of social vision), so that his dream-ridden imagination did not become, after the romantic fashion, a kind of escapism or pure subjectivity, but rather a delving into real life and a way of unmasking it, of taking it by surprise.

He was the first writer to bring about (before the Surrealists proposed it) an alchemical blending of dream and reality, and to create an autonomous universe in which the real seems to be fantastic and the fantastic unmasks the real. Modern art owes the discovery of this alchemy to the Prague heritage of Franz Kafka.

3

Jaroslav Hašek was born in the same year as Kafka and died one year
earlier. Both remained faithful to their home town and, according to
legend, they met at the same Czech anarchist meetings.
It would be hard to find two writers more fundamentally
different. Kafka was a vegetarian, Hašek a drunk; one was proper,
the other eccentric; Kafka's work is considered difficult, coded,
hermetic, while Hašek's has become very popular, though it is not
considered to be 'serious' literature.

Though seemingly so different, these two artists were children of
the same society, the same period, the same climate, and they spoke
about the same thing: humanity facing a society transformed (in
Kafka) into a gigantic bureaucratic machine, or (in Hašek) a military
machine: K. facing the trial or the castle, Schweik facing the totalitarianism of the Austro-Hungarian army.

About the same time, in 1920, another Prague writer, Karel
Čapek, told in his play *RUR* the story of robots (it's from his play that
the newly-coined Czech word *robot* was derived, and it soon became
international). These robots, made by man, begin to fight against
him. Because of their insensitivity and their self-discipline, they
eventually eliminate mankind from the earth and establish their own
empire of order. This picture of humanity disappearing under the
wave of fantastic totalitarianism runs through all of Čapek's works
like an obsession, a nightmare.

Right after World War I, when the rest of European literature
succumbed to a radiant vision of the future and to the eschatology of
revolution, these writers in Prague, by contrast, were the first to
disclose the hidden face of progress—its dark face, menacing and
morbid.

Indeed, these writers are the best representatives of their
country: what they have in common is the disabused outlook of this
other Europe of little countries and minorities. They have always been
the victims rather than the initiators of events: the Jewish minority
(Kafka), surrounded by other peoples but isolated from them by its
own solitude and anxiety; the Czech minority (Hašek), annexed to an
Austrian Empire whose politics and wars were meaningless to it; the

newly-born Czech state (Čapek), also a minority, lost amid a Europe of big nations rushing towards the next catastrophe, and never being consulted.

To write a great *comic* novel about *war,* as Hašek did in *The Good Soldier Schweik,* is something that would be hard to imagine happening in either France or Russia. Such a book presupposes a particular notion of comedy (one which concedes nothing, which undermines seriousness everywhere), and a particular way of looking at the world. Jews or Czechs have not usually identified themselves with history or thought that its events were either serious or intelligible. Their age-old experience has taught them to stop worshipping this goddess History and eulogizing her wisdom. Thus the Europe of little countries, insulated against the demagogy of hope, has had a more clear-sighted picture of the future than has the Europe of big countries, always so ready to become intoxicated with their glorious sense of historical destiny.

4

What makes the books of Kafka and Hašek immortal is not their description of the totalitarian machine, but the two great Josephs (Joseph K and Joseph Schweik) who embody two basic human responses to this machine.

What is Joseph K's attitude? At all costs he wants to understand the court, which is as opaque as the will of God in Calvin; he wants to understand it and to make himself understood. In this way he becomes an *eager culprit*: he rushes to the interrogation in order to arrive on time although no one has ever set the time of the meeting. When the two executioners lead him to his death, he shelters them from the regard of the municipal police. The court is no longer an enemy to him but an inaccessible truth which he is pursuing. He wants to confer meaning on a meaningless world, and this effort costs him his life.

What is Schweik's attitude? At the beginning of World War I, which started with the invasion of Serbia, a completely healthy Joseph Schweik has himself pushed right across Prague in a wheelchair to report to the draft board. He lifts his two borrowed crutches and shouts with warlike enthusiasm, 'To Serbia! To Belgrade!' All the citizens of Prague who see him are greatly amused and laugh at him, but the state cannot do anything against Schweik. He apes perfectly the gestures of the people in power around him; he repeats their slogans; he participates in their ceremonies. But since he doesn't take them seriously at all, he turns them into an enormous joke.

During a military mass, attended even by the soldiers in the prison, the chaplain Katz, who's always drunk, delivers a long sermon against the soldiers' sins. Schweik, in his long prison underwear, begins to sob noisily. He pretends to be so moved by the chaplain's words that he makes his companions snicker. The spirit of buffoonery protects the integrity of Schweik's humanity, even when he is totally manipulated by an army at war. Schweik has managed to live and to survive in a meaningless world because, unlike Joseph K, he refuses to look for any meaning in it.

It's fascinating to see the continuity that connects the fictional and real Prague: these great figures of the imagination, Schweik and K merge with life itself. Although it's true that the novels of Kafka have been taken off public library shelves, today's Prague keeps re-enacting them. That's why they are so well-known there and why they are quoted in daily conversations in Prague—just as often as are the deliberately more accessible works of Hašek.

We saw thousands of Joseph Ks during and after the famous trial of Slansky in 1951. At that time there were innumerable trials of every kind—condemnations, dismissals, reprimands, persecutions— and all this occurred while the guilt-ridden victims, engaged in ceaseless self-criticism, wanted dearly to understand the court and make themselves understood by it. Even up to the last minute they did their best to find some sense in the workings of the senseless machine that was crushing them. *Eager culprits* as they were, they were ready to help their executioners all the way to the stake, and kept crying, 'Long live the Party!' (They saw moral grandeur in their own grotesque dedication. The poet Laco Novomeský after he came out of a Communist prison, wrote a cycle of poems to the glory of this fidelity. The people of Prague nicknamed these poems 'Joseph K.'s Gratitude'.)

92

Schweik's ghost is just as alive in the streets of Prague. Sometime after the Russian invasion in 1968 I went to a big student meeting. The students were waiting for Husák, the new party leader, who had been appointed by the Russians and was supposed to speak. He could not utter a single word, because everyone started shouting, 'Long Live Husák! Long Live the Party!' The shouting went on for five minutes, then ten minutes, a quarter of an hour, until, finally, Husák, getting redder and redder, was forced to leave. Surely it was Schweik's genius which suggested this unforgettable tactic to the students.

In these two cries of 'Long Live the Party!'—the cry of those condemned to the stake and the cry of the students facing Husák—I see two extreme attitudes towards totalitarianism. But it was the literature of Prague that had defined those extremes some thirty years earlier.

'Enough psychology!' Kafka wrote in his diary, a remark that Jaroslav Hašek could have written just as easily. Who is this Schweik who acts like an imbecile and who, regardless of the situation, comes out with the most inappropriate speeches? What is he really thinking? What does he feel? What could prod him towards such inexplicable behaviour? The popular and seemingly easy flow of the novel should not obscure the unusual and unconventional way in which the character of Schweik is actually constructed.

The anti-psychological attitude of the Prague authors preceded by ten or twenty years the famous example set by those American novelists who stripped their tales of all introspection. The Americans did so in the interest of action and events, trying to seize the world from the outside, by its visible and tangible aspect. The Prague approach was somewhat different: it did not consist of a love of manly adventure or of external description, but of a new way of looking at humanity.

This new look at humanity can be seen in a striking fact: *the two Josephs have no past.* What is their family background? What was their childhood like? Did they like their father, their mother? What were their past stages of development? We know nothing, and it's this *nothing* that constitutes a break with past literature. For what had always excited writers above all was their search for psychological motivation, their reconstruction of the mysterious link between past and present actions, and their pursuit of 'Things Past', in whose web is held the astonishing infinity of the soul.

Kafka does not renounce introspection, but no matter how much we pursue K's reasoning from one chapter to another, it's never the richness of his soul which dazzles us. K's reasoning is strictly defined by the authoritarian and tyrannical situation in which he is completely absorbed. The novel as written by Prague authors does not ask: What is the hidden treasure of the human psyche? But rather: What are the possibilities for humanity in the trap that the world has become? The spotlight is focused on just one situation and on the human being who confronts it. It is this situation alone which yields the 'infinite' that must be explored to the end.

It was during the very period when Marcel Proust and James Joyce were reaching the limits of mastering introspection that this declaration, 'Enough psychology'—expressed in Prague by Kafka and Hašek—marked another artistic direction for fiction. Twenty or thirty years later Sartre was to speak of his intention to concentrate no longer on *characters* but on *situations*—'all the elementary situations of human life'—and to try to grasp their metaphysical nature. In the artistic climate existing after World War II, the direction Prague novelists had taken much earlier became more familiar. But it is in their work that we can discover the original meaning of this change in orientation: *inner* motives no longer mean much in a world where *outer* forces are gaining more and more power over man.

This new orientation of the novel, which rejects the conventions of the psychological novel, is therefore linked historically to a foreboding about totalitarianism. This coincidence is charged with meaning.

5

In his well-known biography of Kafka, Klaus Wagenbach expatiates on Prague and its culture without knowing Czech and really without knowing what he's talking about. It's easy to understand, then, why he sees Prague as nothing but a provincial city—cut off from the world, a little old-fashioned—into which the work of this great solitary figure fell like a meteor off course.

At the time of Kafka, Prague was anything but provincial. First, being the capital of the Czech people, Prague was enjoying a lively and challenging new sense of national identity.

Secondly, because the Czechs had an international orientation in fending off a German influence, they had become very cosmopolitan: pro-English, pro-Russian, but (in the realm of the arts) especially pro-French.

Finally, this dynamic and modernist Czech culture was living on intimate terms with the culture of the German minority in a competitive and fruitful manner.

Yes, there was the Prague of the Czech minority (450,000 people at the beginning of the century) and there was the Prague of the German minority (33,000 people, mostly middle-class and intellectual) but there was also the *integrated* Prague, where the bilingual Kafka lived. And not just him but all his friends—Jewish writers such as Max Brod, Franz Werfel, Egon Erwin Kisch and Oscar Baum— who, because they were above nationalistic quarrels between the Czechs and the Germans, could draw upon and integrate the traditions of both peoples.

In his diary in 1911 Kafka describes his encounter with the painter Wili Nowak, who had just finished a series of portraits of Max Brod. In the manner of Picasso, the first drawing was a faithful likeness, whereas the others moved further and further away from the original model until they reached a terse degree of abstraction. This was the first (but not the last) experience Kafka had with Cubism. The diary reveals Kafka's interest and understanding, which contrasts amusingly with Brod's discomfort; Kafka recounts it all in a tone of friendly irony.

People love to speculate endlessly about the relationship that Kafka may have had with the Czech anarchists (a relationship that has never been proved), but they forget about his much more obvious and important contacts with modern Czech art.

From the beginning of the century, Czech Prague participated passionately in the adventure of modern art. It was at that time that the ties between Paris and Prague became intricate: the Czechs Alfons Mucha and František Kupka heavily influenced French painting, and the impetus of Parisian Cubism found no response that was richer than, or as original as, that in Prague before the war.

Max Brod nicknamed the group of Jewish writers around him and Kafka *der Prager Kreis*—the Prague Circle. After 1925 people began to speak about another Prague circle, one of linguists and aestheticians (Vilém Mathesius, Jan Mukařovský, Roman Jakobson, and others) who created the term 'Structuralism' and proclaimed themselves to be 'Structuralists'. Before the outbreak of World War II, Roman Jakobson left Prague and went to America, where Structuralism was to become the dominant way of thought in the decades to follow.

All of which did not happen by chance: Prague was one of the most dynamic centres of modern thought and artistic sensibility.

6

Several factors can account for why Prague became the cradle and the first centre of Structuralism: the moral prestige of the young Republic and President Masaryk, a great defender of democracy admired by all of Europe and the author of an impressive philosophical work which left its mark on structural linguistics; the welcoming and cosmopolitan climate, so open to foreign influences, which allowed Czech, German, Russian and Polish linguists to pursue the same investigations; the native tradition of Czech Formalist aesthetics (the Aesthetic School of Prague at the end of the nineteenth century) and intense linguistic investigations (centring around Vilém Mathesius, Masaryk's student, before the war); and finally, and especially, the dynamic Czech avant-garde, which found its best friend and ally in Structuralism.

The work of Czech Structuralists can be characterized by its taste for concrete analysis, the breadth of its scope (encompassing everything from modern poetry to medieval texts, from Čapek's prose to folkloric and ethnographic research), a love of clarity and an eagerness to get to the bottom of things. The fussiness and dogmatism that marked the later stages of Structuralism were unknown to these pioneers.

The alliance of Structuralist theory and modernism after World War I constituted a unique phenomenon. Usually the theories that are spun around modernist movements are mere apologies. That was not at all the case with Structuralism in Prague. What linked it to the avant-garde was a more general goal: the urge to grasp and defend art in all its particularity.

If a novel (or a poem or film) is just content poured into a form, then it is nothing but a disguised ideological message; its artistic nature falls apart. An ideological interpretation of a novel—which is constantly and everywhere being urged on us—is as simplistic, as much a mindless flattening-out of things, as is the ideological reduction of reality itself. If we insist on the particularity of art, we do so not to escape reality. Far from it. This insistence is because we want to see a tree in a tree, a painting in a painting; it's a resistance against the reductionist forces that maim humanity and art.

The Prague Structuralists, in treating the work of art as an organism in which everything is both content and form, and in which nothing can be reduced to the terms of another language, (language of ideological explication) served to defend the irreducibility of man himself. It's as though they shared with Kafka, Capek and the others a typically Prague-anxiety in the face of the *reductive forces* that were drawing relentlessly closer out of the depths of the future.

French Surrealism is often explained as a revolt against Western rationality, against Cartesian coldness. But strangely enough this counter-rational revolt was quickly transformed into a new rationalistic wave of theoretical manifestos which have left far deeper marks on French consciousness than did the fascinating irrationality of Surrealist art.

Czech Surrealism had no reason to revolt against Czech rationalism, which simply didn't exist; Surrealism represented, on the contrary, the organic fulfillment of the artistic tradition of Prague, the confirmation of its irrational nature.

Because it is steeped in Czech cultural history, this so-called Czech Surrealism (which is nothing but an outgrowth of native avant-garde tendencies, especially 'Poetism') had, in the context of the national literature, an influence incomparably larger than had French Surrealism on the whole of French culture. Nearly all of the important figures in modern Czech culture have been influenced by Surrealist enchantment, imagination, possibilities. Even the public at large in Czechoslovakia is surprisingly open to its brand of beauty. The first time I ever heard the poetry of Vítězslav Nezval, the greatest

Czech Surrealist, I was a boy of ten spending the summer in a Moravian village. In those days students who spent their vacations with their peasant relatives would recite Nezval's poems as though bewitched. During evening strolls out across wheat fields, they taught me all the verses in his *Woman in the Plural.*

Because there were no aristocracy and upper classes in Czech society, the Prague avant-garde was much closer to ordinary people and to the working world and nature. This situation influenced Nezval's imagination. In my memory I can still see Nezval, with his wild red face, as he keeps repeating the word *concrete,* an adjective that for him embodied the basic quality of modern imagination, that he wanted charged as fully as possible with feelings, felt life and recollections.

'Instead of the lily, the symbol of chastity,' he said, 'I prefer the actual one I broke one morning when I was a kid playing hide-and-seek.' Another time he said to me: 'Isn't it surprising to come across a distinguished man who can't understand modern poetry simply because he's always looking for allegories in it?' Nezval hated the 'ideologues of art' who did their best to reduce poetry or painting to the clichés of meaning, to the poverty of message. In the thirties, along with the other Czech Surrealists, he discovered and espoused Kafka, and he would make fun of all those who saw in *The Castle* the state of grace, or hell, or God, instead of recognizing in it the concrete absurdity of our times.

To understand the magic of the imagination not as an *ersatz* version of life but as an 'intoxication with the concrete'—that's what strikes me as the deepest direction of Czech Modernism. This outlook linked the Surrealist Nezval to his opposite, Vladimír Holan, whose poetry has often been compared to that of Rilke or Valéry. And yet Holan's poetry—peopled with peasants, maids, drunks and criminals—collapses under the 'weight of the concrete' and in that way is radically distinct from the poetry of Rilke and Valéry.

7

What other work could better demonstrate the originality of Czech modernism, its hunger for the concrete, its plebian flavour, than the music of composer Leoš Janáček? Along with Kafka, he is the greatest personality in modern art in his country. Nobody knew this better than Max Brod, who not only preserved and championed the work of Kafka but (and this is less well-known) defended the work of Janáček with the same fervour. He wrote marvellous analyses of his musical compositions, translated his operas into German and published in 1924 the first biography of him. Brod's struggle for this neglected though brilliant composer was so passionate and so important that Kafka did not hesitate to compare it with that of the French intellectuals on behalf of Dreyfus.

What is astonishing about this music (and the greatest drawback in popularizing it) is that it cannot be categorized. In the last symphonies of Mahler and in the first works of Schoenberg, musical Romanticism had exhausted all of its possibilities. The young generation buried Romanticism with glee, and with it a whole era that had thought of music as the mirror of the soul, as a form of confession and self-expression. At this crucial moment, Janáček decided he could give music another direction. Nobody else saw that direction. And he pursued it all alone.

He, too, was opposed to Romantic music, but his argument against it took another form: he criticized it not for expressing the soul and its moods, but for failing to do so; for having cheated; instead of revealing naked feelings, Romanticism had offered us clichés, empty gestures, mere posturing. He wanted to rip off the masks that concealed the truth. That's why he didn't reject music because it was expressive. On the contrary, he wanted to eliminate every note that would not be an expression of pure and naked feeling. He therefore arrived at a musical language of an amazing economy and eloquence.

But to talk about the truth of feeling—isn't that just harping on a cliché devoid of all meaning? No. Before Olivier Messiaen, before Edgar Varèse, Janáček was enthralled by concrete music, by the noises of nature, by bird songs; but above all (and in this realm he stands alone and is without followers) Janáček studied spoken language and its intonations, its melodies, its difficult rhythms; he snatched fragments of words overheard in the streets, in the markets, among the crowds at the railway station, indeed everywhere—as though he were a nosy photographer (even the groans of his dying daughter did not elude him)—and he transcribed them all into his notebook. There exist thousands of these musical jottings, now kept in a museum, which bear witness to how serious his research was: it was a search after a musical semantics. It's as though he wanted to set up an emotional vocabulary of melodic formula, as though he wanted to grasp the mysterious link between music and psychology.

Whatever may be the objective value of this work, it typifies the direction of this composer's mind. He wanted to free himself from music made out of other music (a little like a writer who might want to avoid just making 'literature'), and he looked for new sources of musical utterance that would be closer to psychology and more tightly connected with life. He wanted to end up not only with a new form of beauty—a new sonority, a new form of melody, a new construction—but also with a greater accuracy (psychological accuracy) of the musical unit, convinced as he was that music belongs to the humanities.

His efforts were neither utopian nor quixotic. He succeeded in creating in the last two decades of his life, between fifty and seventy-four (he's certainly the greatest old man in the history of music), a marvellous *oeuvre*: incomparable choruses, and a new concept of the opera—he wrote five that are masterpieces.

8

In the year of his death, Janáček wrote his last, and most beautiful and astonishing, opera, his true musical legacy: *The House of the Dead,* based on the novel by Dostoevsky. How did it come to him, this impossible subject, designed to offend the public, this dry report of prison life, without plot or intrigue? Why did he choose this grim setting which had no link whatsoever with his own life?

Of course it's true that the music, violently modern, instantly changes this nineteenth-century penal colony into a concentration camp, and that audiences are bewildered by a drama that could not possibly be more up to date. But in 1928, in those peaceful years? Which of our latterday evil nights transmitted this bleak picture to Janáček?

I don't know how to explain this phenomenon: there are no

fewer than three great artistic monuments in this century that my country has built, which are the three panels of a triptych portraying the hell that was to come: the bureaucratic maze of Kafka, the military idiocy of Hašek, the concentration camp despair of Janáček. Indeed, between the creating of *The Trial* in 1917 and *The House of the Dead* in 1928, everything had already been said in Prague, and History had only to make its entrance in order to mime what fiction had already imagined.

The famous 1948 coup in Prague not only brought about trials *à la* Kafka or idiocy *à la* Hašek and prisons *à la* Janáček but also annihilated a culture that had foreseen these very developments. We still can't grasp exactly what happened then. After a thousand years of a history that had been western European, Czechoslovakia became an Eastern European country. It became the site where the West— which traditionally stands for the very image of the colonizer—would henceforth be colonized. It was also where Western culture—which everyone regards as possessive and aggressive—was destined to lose its identity. What a historical irony it is that this 'colonization of the West' should have taken place in a country that never colonized anyone.

Immediately after the Prague coup, a major campaign was organized 'against cosmopolitanism'—by which the Communists meant Western culture. Instantly, the entire modern intellectual heritage of my country was blacklisted. It was then that Jan Mukařovský committed intellectual suicide and renounced all of his great Structuralist work. It was then that Vladimír Holan shut himself up in his Prague apartment as though voluntarily in solitary confinement; he still hasn't come out.

And yet that wasn't the end of it. The nation's cultural vitality held out and gradually regained the ground it had lost, thanks to the stubbornness, the common assent and the cunning of the people: what had been banned returned to the stage in the 1960s. And that was the real war, the war of a culture fighting for its life, for its survival.

One of the biggest battles in this war was waged over Franz Kafka. In 1963 Czech intellectuals organized an international conference in a Bohemian castle where the reputation of this tabooed writer was rehabilitated. Russian ideologues will never forget such

101

disobedience. In the official Russian documents that were used to justify the invasion of Czechoslovakia in 1968, it was duly noted that the first sign of Czech counter-revolution had been Kafka's rehabilitation.

This argument looks absurd, but it is less stupid than it is revealing: the invasion was not only the victory of 'dogmatic Communism' over 'liberal Communism' (the current explanation of the event) but also—an aspect that will in the long run loom larger— the definitive annexation of a Western country by the civilization of Russian totalitarianism. And I do mean *civilization,* not the Russian political system nor the state. It is not because he would have been anti-Communist, nor because he would have opposed the military interests of Russia, that Kafka provoked this outburst of rage in Moscow. No, rather it's because Kafka embodies another culture, foreign to the colonizers, and one they cannot absorb. At the same time that the Russians are politically advancing against the whole world, they are regressing culturally towards their own Byzantine past.

9

Like a burning leaf of paper on which a poem is disappearing...

Vitězslav Nezval

The culture of Prague is a thousand years old. It was at its peak between 1910 and 1940. After a bloody intermission, the sixties ushered in the last echo of a long history. It was then that this culture woke up into a world where its own darkest dreams had become reality. Although swallowed up by the night of totalitarianism, Czech culture has still known how to reflect upon totalitarianism, to judge it, to be ironic about it, to analyse it and finally to transform it into an object of its own intellectual experience. The ingenuity of the little country has been able to penetrate the arrogance of the big country. The Czech spirit of buffoonery has undermined the horror of serious ideology. Its sense of the concrete has been a way of resisting the greatest reductive forces that History has ever unleashed. Out of this multiple collision was born a whole group of works, a new theatre, cinema, literature, a whole way of thinking, along with a new sense of humour, an entirely unique and irreplaceable intellectual experience. For, as Vladimír Holan said:

Only Christ would know how to portray
Pontius Pilate's wife.

The West was never able to understand at the right time the meaning of this creative explosion, blinded as it was by its own politicized (and also reductive) vision of things: on the one hand (the stupidity of the Western left), it could only see in this explosion a confirmation of the vitality of socialism; or on the other hand (the stupidity of the Western right), it refused to grant any value to anyone standing behind the façade of a Communist regime. A curtain of Western misunderstanding was added to the Russian Iron Curtain.

The Russian invation of 1968 swept away the generation of the 1960s and with it all preceding modern culture. Our books are buried away in the same cellars containing those of Kafka and the Czech Surrealists. The living who have been killed are now lying side by side with the dead, who are thereby doubly dead.

Let it be known: it is not just human rights, democracy, justice, which no longer exist in Prague. It is an entire great culture that today is

Like a burning leaf of paper on which a poem is disappearing...

Translated from the French by Edmund White

A shortlist of our own

The only criterion for their selection is excellence. Six leading British novelists conjure up a procession of lovers and madmen, artists and dreamers, murderers and ghosts for your entertainment. To inspire, provoke and move you. What more could you want from a novel?

■ **FICTION FROM HAMISH HAMILTON** ■

BRUCE CHATWIN
A COUP

The coup began at seven on Sunday morning. It was a grey and windless dawn and the grey Atlantic rollers broke in long even lines along the beach. The palms above the tide-mark shivered in a current of cooler air that blew in off the breakers. Out at sea—beyond the surf—there were several black fishing canoes. Buzzards were spiralling above the market, swooping now and then to snatch up scraps of offal. The butchers were slaughtering, even on a Sunday.

We were in a taxi when the coup began, on our way to another country. We had passed the Hôtel de la Plage, passed the Sûreté Nationale, and then we drove under a limply-flapping banner which said, in red letters, that Marxist-Leninism was the one and only guide. In front of the Presidential Palace was a road-block. A soldier waved us to a halt, and then waved us on.

'Pourriture!' said my friend, Domingo, and grinned.

Domingo was a young, honey-coloured mulatto with a flat and friendly face, a curly moustache and a set of dazzling teeth. He was the direct descendant of Francisco-Félix de Souza, the Chacha of Ouidah, a Brazilian slaver who lived and died in Dahomey, and about whom I was writing a book.

Domingo had two wives. The first wife was old and the skin hung in loose folds off her back. The second wife was hardly more than a child. We were on our way to Togo, to watch a football game, and visit his great-uncle who knew a lot of old stories about the Chacha.

The taxi was jammed with football-fans. On my right sat a very black old man wrapped in green and orange cotton. His teeth were also orange from chewing cola nuts, and from time to time he spat.

Outside the Presidential Palace hung an overblown poster of the Head of State, and two much smaller posters of Lenin and Kim Il-Sung. Beyond the road-block, we took a right fork, on through the old European section where there were bungalows and balks of bougainvillaea by the gates. Along the sides of the tarmac, market-women walked in single file with basins and baskets balanced on their head.

'What's that?' I asked. I could see some kind of commotion, up ahead, towards the airport.

'Accident!' Domingo shrugged, and grinned again.

Then all the women were screaming, and scattering their yams and pineapples, and rushing for the shelter of the gardens. A white Peugeot shot down the middle of the road, swerving right and left to miss the women. The driver waved for us to turn back, and just then, we heard the crack of gunfire.

'C'est la guerre!' our driver shouted, and spun the taxi round.

'I knew it.' Domingo grabbed my arm. 'I knew it.'

The sun was up by the time we got to downtown Cotonou. In the taxi-park the crowd had panicked and overturned a brazier, and a stack of crates had caught fire. A policeman blew his whistle and bawled for water. Above the rooftops, there was a column of black smoke, rising.

'They're burning the Palace,' said Domingo. 'Quick! Run!'

We ran, bumped into other running figures, and ran on. A man shouted 'Mercenary!' and lunged for my shoulder. I ducked and we dodged down a sidestreet. A boy in a red shirt beckoned me into a bar. It was dark inside. People were clustered round a radio. Then the bartender screamed, wildly, in African, at me, and at the boy. And then I was out again on the dusty red street, shielding my head with my arms, pushed and pummelled against the corrugated building by four hard, acridly-sweating men until the gendarmes came to fetch me in a jeep.

'For your own proper protection,' their officer said, as the handcuffs snapped around my wrists.

The last I ever saw of Domingo he was standing in the street, crying, as the jeep drove off, and he vanished in a clash of coloured cottons.

In the barracks guardroom a skinny boy, stripped to a pair of purple underpants, sat hunched against the wall. His hands and feet were bound with rope, and he had the greyish look Africans get when they are truly frightened. A gecko hung motionless on the dirty whitewash. Outside the door there was a papaya with a tall scaly trunk and yellowish fruit. A mud-wall ran along the far side of the compound. Beyond the wall the noise of gunfire continued, and the high-pitched wailing of women.

A corporal came in and searched me. He was small, wiry, angular, and his cheekbones shone. He took my watch, wallet, passport and notebook.

'Mercenary!' he said, pointing to the patch-pocket on the leg of my khaki trousers. His gums were spongy and his breath was foul.

'No,' I said, submissively. 'I'm a tourist.'

'Mercenary!' he shrieked, and slapped my face—not hard, but hard enough to hurt.

He held up my fountain-pen. 'What?'

'A pen,' I said. It was a black Mont-Blanc.

'What for?'

'To write with.'

'A gun?'

'Not a gun.'

'Yes, a gun!'

I sat on a bench, staring at the skinny boy who continued to stare at his toes. The corporal sat cross-legged in the doorway with his sub-machine-gun trained on me. Outside in the yard, two sergeants were distributing rifles, and a truck was loading with troops. The troops sat down with the barrels sticking up from their crotches. The colonel came out of his office and took the salute. The truck lurched off, and he came over, lumpily, towards the guardroom.

The corporal snapped to attention and said, 'Mercenary, Comrade Colonel!'

'From today,' said the colonel, 'there are no more comrades in our country.'

'Yes, Comrade Colonel,' the man nodded; but checked himself and added, 'Yes, my Colonel.'

The colonel waved him aside and surveyed me gloomily. He wore an exquisitely-pressed pair of paratrooper fatigues, a red star on his cap, and another red star in his lapel. A roll of fat stood out around the back of his neck; his thick lips drooped at the corners; his eyes were hooded. He looked, I thought, so like a sad hippopotamus. I told myself I mustn't think he looks like a sad hippopotamus. Whatever happens, he mustn't think I think he looks like a sad hippopotamus.

'Ah, monsieur!' he said, in a quiet dispirited voice. 'What are you doing in this poor country of ours?'

'I came here as a tourist.'

'You are English?'

'Yes.'

'But you speak an excellent French.'

'Passable,' I said.

'With a Parisian accent I should have said.'

'I have lived in Paris.'

'I, also, have visited Paris. A wonderful city!'

'The most wonderful city.'

'But you have mistimed your visit to Benin.'

'Yes,' I faltered. 'I seem to have run into trouble.'

'You have been here before?'

'Once,' I said. 'Five years ago.'

'When Benin was Dahomey.'

'Yes,' I said. 'I used to think Benin was in Nigeria.'

'Benin is in Nigeria and now we have it here.'

'I think I understand.'

'Calm yourself, monsieur.' His fingers reached to unlock my handcuffs. 'We are having another little change of politics. Nothing more! In these situations one must keep calm. You understand? Calm!'

Some boys had come through the barracks' gate and were creeping forward to peer at the prisoner. The colonel appeared in the doorway, and they scampered off.

'Come,' he said. 'You will be safer if you stay with me. Come, let us listen to the Head of State.'

We walked across the parade-ground to his office where he sat me in a chair and reached for a portable radio. Above his desk hung a photo of the Head of State, in a Fidel Castro cap. His cheeks were a basketwork of scarifications.

'The Head of State,' said the colonel, 'is always speaking over the radio. We call it the *journal parlé*. It is a crime in this country *not* to listen to the *journal parlé*.'

He turned the knob. The military music came in cracking bursts.

Citizens of Benin . . . the hour is grave. At seven hours this morning, an unidentified DC-8 jet aircraft landed at our International Airport of Cotonou, carrying a crapulous crowd of mercenaries. . . black and white. . .

financed by the lackeys of international imperialism. . . .
A vile plot to destroy our democratic and operational
regime.

The colonel laid his jowls on his hands and sighed, 'The Sombas! The Sombas!'

The Sombas came from the far north-west of the country. They
filed their teeth to points and once, not so long ago, were cannibals.

'. . . launched a vicious attack on our Presidential Palace. . .'

I glanced up again at the wall. The Head of State was a
Somba — and the colonel was a Fon.

'. . . the population is requested to arm itself with stones and
knives to kill this crapulous. . .'

'A recorded message,' said the colonel, and turned the volume
down. 'It was recorded yesterday.'

'You mean. . .'

'Calm yourself, monsieur. You do not understand. In this
country one understands nothing.'

Certainly, as this morning wore on, the colonel understood less
and less. He did not, for example, understand why, on the nine
o'clock communiqué, the mercenaries had landed in a DC-8 jet,
while at ten the plane had changed to a DC-7 turbo-prop. Around
eleven the music cut off again and the Head of State announced a
victory for the Government Forces. The enemy, he said, were
retreating en catastrophe for the marshes of Ouidah.

'There has been a mistake,' said the colonel, looking very
shaken. 'Excuse me, monsieur. I must leave you.'

He hesitated on the threshold and then stepped out into the
sunlight. The hawks made swift spiralling shadows on the ground. I
helped myself to a drink from his water-flask. The shooting sounded
further off now, and the town was quieter. Ten minutes later, the
corporal marched into the office. I put my hands above my head,
and he escorted me back to the guardroom.

It was very hot. The skinny boy had been taken away and, on the
bench at the back, sat a Frenchman.

Outside, tied to the papaya, a springer spaniel was panting
and straining at its leash. A pair of soldiers squatted on their hams
and were trying to dismantle the Frenchman's shotgun. A third sol-

dier, rummaging in his game-bag, was laying out a few brace of partridge and a guinea-fowl.

'Will you please give that dog some water?' the Frenchman asked.

'Eh?' The corporal bared his gums.

'The dog,' he pointed. 'Water!'

'No.'

'What's going on?' I asked.

'The monkeys are wrecking my gun and killing my dog.'

'Out there, I mean.'

'Coup monté.'

'Which means?'

'You hire a plane-load of mercenaries to shoot up the town. See who your friends are and who are your enemies. Shoot the enemies. Simple!'

'Clever.'

'Very.'

'And us?'

'They might need a corpse or two. As proof!'

'Thank you,' I said.

'I was joking.'

'Thanks all the same.'

The Frenchman was a water-engineer. He worked up-country, on artesian wells, and was down in the capital on leave. He was a short, muscular man, tending to paunch, with cropped grey hair and a web of white laugh-lines over his leathery cheeks. He had dressed himself en mercenaire, in fake python-skin camouflage, to shoot a few game-birds in the forest on the outskirts of town.

'What do you think of my costume?' he asked.

'Suitable,' I said.

'Thank you.'

The sun was vertical. The colour of the parade-ground had bleached to a pinkish orange, and the soldiers strutted back and forth in their own pools of shade. Along the wall the vultures flexed their wings.

'Waiting,' joked the Frenchman.

'Thank you.'

'Don't mention it.'

Our view of the morning's entertainment was restricted by the width of the doorframe. We were, however, able to witness a group of soldiers treating their ex-colonel in a most shabby fashion. We wondered how he could still be alive as they dragged him out and bundled him into the back of a jeep. The corporal had taken the colonel's radio, and was cradling it on his knee. The Head of State was baying for blood—'Mort aux mercenaires soit qu'ils sont noirs ou blancs. . . .' The urchins, too, were back in force, jumping up and down, drawing their fingers across their throats, and chanting in unison, 'Mort-aux-mercenaires! . . . Mort-aux-mercenaires! . . .'

Around noon, the jeep came back. A lithe young woman jumped out and started screeching orders at an infantry platoon. She was wearing a mud-stained battledress. A nest of plaits curled, like snakes, from under her beret.

'So,' said my companion. 'The new colonel.'

'An Amazon colonel,' I said.

'I always said it,' he said. 'Never trust a teenage Amazon colonel.'

He passed me a cigarette. There were two in the packet and I took one of them.

'Thanks,' I said. 'I don't smoke.'

He lit mine, and then his, and blew a smoke-ring at the rafters. The gecko on the wall hadn't budged.

'My name's Jacques,' he said.

I told him my own name and he said, 'I don't like the look of this.'

'Nor I,' I said.

'No,' he said. 'There are no rules in this country.'

Nor were there any rules, none that one could think of, when the corporal came back from conferring with the Amazon and ordered us, also, to strip to our underpants. I hesitated. I was unsure whether I was wearing underpants. But a barrel in the small of my back convinced me, underpants or no, that my trousers would have to come down—only to find that I did, after all, have on a pair of pink-and-white boxer shorts from Brooks Brothers.

Jacques was wearing green string pants. We must have looked a pretty couple—my back welted all over with mosquito bites, he with his paunch flopping over the elastic, as the corporal marched us

113

out, barefoot over the burning ground, and stood us, hands up, against the wall which the vultures had fouled with their ash-white, ammonia-smelling droppings.

'Merde!' said Jacques. 'Now what?'

What indeed? I was not frightened. I was tired and hot. My arms ached, my knees sagged, my tongue felt like leather, and my temples throbbed. But this was not frightening. It was too like a B-grade movie to be frightening. I began to count the flecks of millet-chaff embedded in the mud-plaster wall. . . .

I remembered the morning, five years earlier, my first morning in Dahomey, under the tall trees in Parakou. I'd had a rough night, coming down from the desert in the back of a crowded truck, and at breakfast-time, at the café-routier, I'd asked the waiter what there was to see in town.

'Patrice.'

'Patrice?'

'That's me,' he grinned. 'And, monsieur, there are hundreds of other beautiful young girls and boys who walk, all the time, up and down the streets of Parakou.'

I remembered, too, the girl who sold pineapples at Dassa-Zoumbé station. It had been a stifling day, the train slow and the country burnt. I had been reading Gide's *Nourritures terrestres* and, as we drew into Dassa, had come to the line, 'Ô cafés—où notre démence s'est continuée très avant dans la nuit. . . .' No, I thought, this will never do, and looked out of the carriage window. A basket of pineapples had halted outside. The girl underneath the basket smiled and, when I gave her the Gide, gasped, lobbed all six pineapples into the carriage, and ran off to show her friends—who in turn came skipping down the tracks, clamouring, 'A book, please? A book? A book!' So *out* went a dog-eared thriller and Saint-Exupéry's *Vol de nuit,* and *in* came the 'Fruits of the Earth'—the real ones—pawpaws, guavas, more pineapples, a raunch of grilled swamp-rat, and a palm-leaf hat.

'Those girls,' I remember scribbling in my notebook, 'are the ultimate products of the lycée system.'

114

And now what?
The Amazon was squawking at the platoon and we strained our ears for the click of safety catches.

'I think they're playing games,' Jacques said, squinting sideways.

'I should hope so,' I muttered. I liked Jacques. It was good, if one had to be here, to be here with him. He was an old Africa hand and had been through coups before.

'That is,' he added glumly, 'if they don't get drunk.'

'Thank you,' I said, and looked over my shoulder at the drill-squad.

'No look!' the corporal barked. He was standing beside us, his shirt-front open to the navel. Obviously, he was anxious to cut a fine figure.

'Stick your belly-button in,' I muttered in English.

'No speak!' he threatened.

'I won't speak.' I held the words within my teeth. 'But stay there. Don't leave me. I need you.'

Maddened by the heat and excitement, the crowds who had come to gawp were clamouring, 'Mort-aux-mercenaires! . . . Mort-aux-mercenaires!' and my mind went racing back over the horrors of Old Dahomey, before the French came. I thought, the slave-wars, the human sacrifices, the piles of broken skulls. I thought of Domingo's other uncle, 'The Brazilian', who received us on his rocking-chair dressed in white ducks and a topee. 'Yes,' he sighed, 'the Dahomeans are a charming and intelligent people. Their only weakness is a certain nostalgia for taking heads.'

No. This was not my Africa. Not this rainy, rotten-fruit Africa. Not this Africa of blood and laughter. The Africa I loved was the long undulating savannah country to the north, the 'leopard-spotted land', where flat-topped acacias stretched as far as the eye could see, and there were black-and-white hornbills and tall red termitaries. For whenever I went back to that Africa, and saw a camel caravan, a view of white tents, or a single blue turban far off in the heat haze, I knew that, no matter what the Persians said, Paradise never was a garden but a waste of white thorns.

'I am dreaming,' said Jacques, suddenly, 'of perdrix aux choux.'

'I'd take a dozen Belons and a bottle of Krug.'

'No speak!' The corporal waved his gun, and I braced myself, half-expecting the butt to crash down on my skull.

And so what? What would it matter when already I felt as if my skull were split clean open? Was this, I wondered, sunstroke? How strange, too, as I tried to focus on the wall, that each bit of chaff should bring back some clear specific memory of food or drink?

There was a lake in Central Sweden and, in the lake, there was an island where the ospreys nested. On the first day of the crayfish season we rowed to the fisherman's hut and rowed back towing twelve dozen crayfish in a live-net. That evening, they came in from the kitchen, a scarlet mountain smothered in dill. The northern sunlight bounced off the lake into the bright white room. We drank akvavit from thimble-sized glasses and we ended the meal with a tart made of cloudberries. I could taste again the grilled sardines we ate on the quay at Douarnenez and see my father demonstrating how his father ate sardines à la mordecai: you took a live sardine by the tail and swallowed it. Or the elvers we had in Madrid, fried in oil with garlic and half a red pepper. It had been a cold spring morning, and we'd spent two hours in the Prado, gazing at the Velasquezes, hugging one another it was so good to be alive: we had cancelled our bookings on a plane that had crashed. Or the lobsters we bought at Cape Split Harbour, Maine. There was a notice-board in the shack on the jetty and, pinned to it, a card on which a widow thanked her husband's friends for their contributions, and prayed, prayed to the Lord, that they lashed themselves to the boat when hauling in the pots.

How long, O Lord, how long? How long, when all the world was wheeling, could I stay on my feet. . . ?

How long I shall never know, because the next thing I remember I was staggering groggily across the parade-ground, with one arm over the corporal's shoulder and the other over Jacques's. Jacques then gave me a glass of water and, after that, he helped me into my clothes.

'You passed out,' he said.

'Thank you,' I said.

I kept off the streets to avoid the vigilante groups that roamed the town making citizens' arrests. My toenail was turning black and my head still ached. I ate in the room, and read, and tried to sleep. All the other guests were either Guinean or Algerian.

Around eleven next morning, I was reading the sad story of Mrs Marmeladov in *Crime and Punishment*, and heard the thud of gunfire coming from the Gezo Barracks. I looked from the window at the palms, the hawks, a woman selling mangoes, and a nun coming out of the convent.

Seconds later, the fruit-stall had overturned, the nun bolted, and two armoured cars went roaring up the street.

There was a knock on the door. It was the manager.

'Please, monsieur. You must not look.'

'What's happening?'

'Please,' he pleaded, 'you must shut the window.'

I closed the shutter. The electricity had cut off. A few bars of sunlight squeezed through the slats, but it was too dark to read, so I lay back and listened to the salvoes. There must have been a lot of people dying.

There was another knock.

'Come in.'

A soldier came into the room. He was very young and smartly turned out. His fatigues were criss-crossed with ammunition belts and his teeth shone. He seemed extremely nervous. His finger quivered round the trigger-guard. I raised my hands and got up off the bed.

'In there!' He pointed the barrel at the bathroom door.

The walls of the bathroom were covered with blue tiles and, on the blue plastic shower-curtain, was a design of tropical fish.

'Money,' said the soldier.

'Sure!' I said. 'How much?'

He said nothing. I glanced at the mirror and saw the gaping whites of his eyes. He was breathing heavily.

I eased my fingers down my trouser pocket: my impulse was to give him all I had. Then I separated one banknote from the rest, and put it in his outstretched palm.

'Merci, monsieur!' His lips expanded in an astonished smile. 'Merci,' he repeated, and unlocked the bathroom door. 'Merci,' he kept repeating, as he bowed and pointed his own way out into the passage.

That young man, it struck me, really had very nice manners.

The Algerians and Guineans were men in brown suits who sat all day in the bar, sucking soft drinks through straws and giving me dirty looks whenever I went in. I decided to move to the Hôtel de la Plage where there were other Europeans, and a swimming-pool. I took a towel to go swimming and went into the garden. The pool had been drained: on the morning of the coup, a sniper had taken a pot-shot at a Canadian boy who happened to be swimming his lengths.

The frontiers of the country were closed, and the airport.

That evening I ate with a Norwegian oil-man, who insisted that the coup had been a fake. He had seen the mercenaries shelling the palace. He had watched them drinking opposite in the bar of the Hotel de Cocotiers.

'All of it I saw,' he said, his neck reddening with indignation. The palace had been deserted. The army had been in the barracks. The mercenaries had shot innocent people. Then they all went back to the airport and flew away.

'All of it,' he said, 'was fake.'

'Well,' I said, 'if it was a fake, it certainly took me in.'

It took another day for the airport to open, and another two before I got a seat on the Abidjan plane. I had a mild attack of bronchitis and was aching to leave the country.

On my last morning I looked in at the 'Paris-Snack', which, in the old days when Dahomey was Dahomey, was owned by a Corsican called Guerini. He had gone back to Corsica while the going was good. The bar-stools were covered in red leather, and the barman wore a solid gold bracelet round his wrist.

Two Nigerian businessmen were seated at lunch with a pair of whores. At a table in the corner I saw Jacques.

'Tiens?' he said, grinning. 'Still alive?'

'Thanks to you,' I said, 'and the Germans.'

'*Braves* Bosches!' He beckoned me to the banquette. 'Very intelligent people.'

'*Braves* Bosches!' I agreed.

'Let's have a bottle of champagne.'

'I haven't got much money.'

'Lunch is on me,' he insisted. 'Pierrot!'

The barman tilted his head, coquettishly, and tittered.

'Yes, Monsieur Jacques.'

'This is an English gentleman and we must find him a very special bottle of champagne. You have Krug?'

'No, Monsieur Jacques. We have Roerderer. We have Bollinger, and we have Mumm.'

'Bollinger,' I said.

Jacques pulled a face: 'And in Guerini's time you could have had your oysters. Flown in twice a week from Paris. . . Belons. . . Claires. . . Portugaises. . . .'

'I remember him.'

'He was a character.'

'Tell me,' I leaned over. 'What *was* going on?'

'Sssh!' his lips tightened. 'There are two theories and, if I think anyone's listening, I shall change the subject.'

I nodded and looked at the menu.

'In the official version,' Jacques said, 'the mercenaries were recruited by Dahomean emigrés in Paris. The plane took off from a military airfield in Morocco, refuelled in Abidjan. . .'

One of the whores got up from her table and lurched down the restaurant towards the Ladies.

' '66 was a wonderful year,' said Jacques, decisively.

'I like it even older,' I said, as the whore brushed past, 'dark and almost flat. . . .'

'The plane flew to Gabon to pick up the commander. . . who is supposed to be an adviser to President Bongo. . . .' He then explained how, at Libreville, the pilot of the chartered DC-8 refused to go on, and the mercenaries had to switch to a DC-7.

'So their arrival was expected at the airport?'

'Precisely,' Jacques agreed. 'Now the second scenario . . .'

The door of the Ladies swung open. The whore winked at us. Jacques puushed his face up to the menu.

'What'll you have?' he asked.

'Stuffed crab,' I said.

'The second scenario,' he continued quietly, 'calls for Czech and East German mercenaries. The plane, a DC-7, takes off from a military airfield in Algeria, refuels at Conakry. . . you understand?'

'Yes,' I said, when he'd finished. 'I think I get it. And which one do you believe?'

'Both,' he said.

'That,' I said, 'is a very sophisticated analysis.'

'This,' he said, 'is a very sophisticated country.'

'I know it.'

'You heard the shooting at Camp Gezo?'

'What was that?'

'Settling old scores,' he shrugged. 'And now the Guineans have taken over the Secret Police.'

'Clever.'

'This is Africa.'

'I know and I'm leaving.'

'For England?'

'No,' I said. 'For Brazil. I've a book to write.'

'Beautiful country, Brazil.'

'I hope so.'

'Beautiful women.'

'So I'm told.'

'So what is this book?'

'It's about the slave-trade.'

'In Benin?'

'Also in Brazil.'

'Eh bien!' The champagne had come and he filled my glass. 'You have material!'

'Yes,' I agreed. 'I do have material.'

NADINE GORDIMER
DAVID GOLDBLATT: SO FAR

Out of the language of photography in South Africa can be made *dompas* photographs, beauty-spot photographs for *Flying Springbok*, the South African Airways magazine, a smuggled photograph of the body of Steve Biko after he had died in detention, happy Polaroids of crowds at Sun City and news photographs of families being evicted from their homes. Because of this drama of environmental association, photography has become the most emotive language of the several dozen spoken by us South Africans. It has at the same time tended to make enormities and beauties equally commonplace, less and less capable of rousing differentiated response. Because of the immediacy with which photographs rouse an emotional response and the concommitant blunting of response that follows over-exposure to that immediacy, what makes a work of art, in the language of photography, is a quality that neither depends upon associative sensationalism nor can be blocked by blunted sensibility. The art of David Goldblatt's photographs lies in finding a visual way to touch a nerve of sensibility that has not been reached by the bang-on impact of a thousand similar images. The photographer is popularly seen as a being turned into a huge single eye. But David Goldblatt is no Cyclops; he is the photographer as a whole man. In his work here, you will see that he has put not only a great talent but all he knows—as a human being, as a man, as a South African, as a white African, with a vision constantly subject to his own unflinching self-criticism—into his photographs. He has given them literally all he has got.

'I needed to grasp something of what a man is and is becoming in all the particularity of himself and his bricks and bit of earth and of this place, and to contain all this in a photograph. To do this, and to discover the shapes and shades of his loves and fears and my own, would be enough.' This is David Goldblatt, speaking in 1975. In grasping that 'something of what man is and is becoming,' Goldblatt has become the most important influence on contemporary South African photography; widely imitated, he has thus, both directly and indirectly, influenced our perception of ourselves and our world. our world.

One of the ways in which his work finds its way to our sensibilities is, in the words of Satyajit Ray, 'in the presence of the essential thing in a very small detail which one must catch in order to express larger things.' Catching detail is, of course, first of all a matter of highly-sensitized observation. I have worked as a writer in tandem with David Goldblatt and I know that with him this concentrated observation passes over almost into meditation—not on any next world, but on the concrete manifestations of this one. You cannot convey what you do not seek to know for yourself. He does not snatch at the world with a camera. He seeks to strip away preconceptions of what he is seeing before he goes into it still further with his chosen instrument—the photographic image. The 'essential thing' in Goldblatt's photographs is never a piece of visual shorthand for a life; it is informed by this desire for a knowledge and understanding of the entire context of that life to be conveyed, in which that detail above all others has meaning. And it is the *presence* of the 'essential thing'—not the detail itself—that holds the balance between the generality of what has been seen many times and what is being seen uniquely. This is as demonstrable in an amusing photograph—like that of a ballroom dancing lesson, where the framing discreetly includes the picture of General Smuts on the wall, and under a chair the pair of everyday shoes the woman has exchanged for high-heeled sandals—as in his famous photograph, 'Boss Boy' where the insignia, the 'essential small things', almost parasitically become the identity of the man.

I think I could, without exaggeration, speak of Goldblatt's South Africa, but I know he would repudiate such an appropriation. It would go against the grain. A photograph can fix a moment of someone's life like a butterfly pierced by a pin. The subject becomes a species. An exhibition a taxonomy. If you look at these photographs, you will not find any such. Goldblatt does not sum up and take possession of South Africa, here; he leads us into it. His photographs are a beginning, not a fixed moment. The more you look at them, the more you follow them into yourself, supply the holographic dimension they imply.

In praising works of art in South Africa, it is usual to pay lip service if not obeisance to the moral role of the maker in creating 'understanding' of our society. Goldblatt's photographs, in their beauty and honesty, offer the very reverse of the easy panacea of 'understanding'. They cause us to face the ultimate implications of what we understand very well.

Greaser, Number 2 North Winder, Randfontein Estates Gold
Mines, Soweto.

GRANTA
SUBSCRIBE · TO · GRANTA

MOST OF OUR READERS are subscribers. They enjoy savings, special offers and regular delivery to their homes.

If you would like to subscribe (and receive the first US edition free), or if you are already a subscriber and want to *renew, give a gift subscription or change your address*, please use this order form.

Tear out and return this business reply card, or, if you are enclosing a cheque, put this form in an envelope and send it to *Granta*, 13 White Street, New York, NY 10013.

1 NEW SUBSCRIPTION OR RENEWAL
Please enter/renew my subscription for
1 year (4 issues) at $12 ☐   2 years (8 issues) at $22 ☐
3 years (12 issues) at $30 ☐

Name

Address

City   State   Zip

(renewals please attach postage label below)
Payment by
Cheque enclosed   ☐
I will pay later; please invoice me   ☐

2 CHANGE OF ADDRESS
Please enter your new address above, and attach your current postage label here. Please allow us four weeks to correct our records.

3 FOREIGN SUBSCRIPTIONS
Please add $3 per year for foreign (including Canadian) subscriptions. Airmail rates on application.

4 GIFT SUBSCRIPTIONS
Please send a year's subscription for $12 to

▶ Name

Address

City   State   Zip
Gift card to read from

▶ Name

Address

City   State   Zip
Gift card to read from

▶ Name

Address

City   State   Zip
Gift card to read from

(send additional names on separate sheet of paper)

GRANTA

SUBSCRIBE ▸ TO ▸ GRANTA

MOST OF OUR READERS are subscribers. They enjoy savings, special offers and regular delivery to their homes.

If you would like to subscribe (and receive the first US edition free), or if you are already a subscriber and want to *renew, give a gift subscription or change your address*, please use this order form.

Tear out and return this business reply card, or, if you are enclosing a cheque, put this form in an envelope and send it to *Granta*, 13 White Street, New York, NY 10013.

Shaftsinker, President Steyn Gold Mines, Welkom.

Leader of the Viking Gang, Orlando East, Soweto.

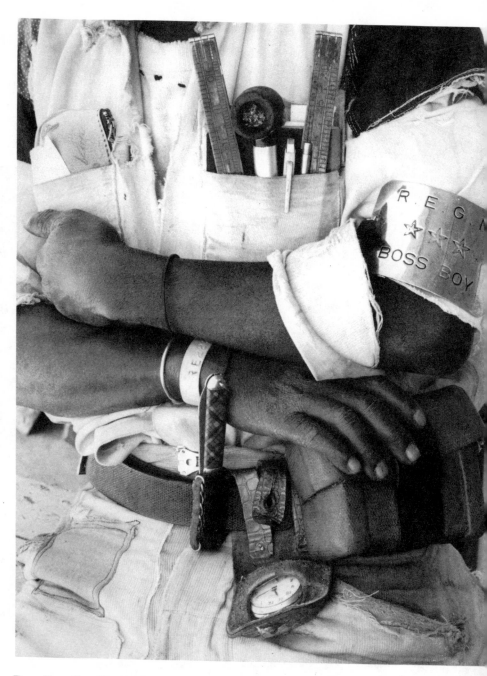

Boss Boy, Randfontein Estates Gold Mines, Soweto.

Peasant woman at home.

The peasant woman's lamp, Coffee Bay, Transkei.

In the Jabulani
'Single' Men's
Hostel, Soweto.

The playing fields of Tladi, Soweto.
New Year's day picnic, Hartebeespoort Dam.

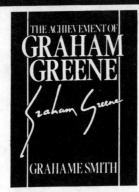

HANIF KUREISHI
EROTIC POLITICIANS
AND MULLAHS

T he man had heard that I was interested in talking about his country, Pakistan, and that this was my first visit. He kindly kept trying to take me aside to talk. But I was already being talked at.

I was at another Karachi party, in a huge house, with a glass of whisky in one hand and a paper plate in the other. Casually I'd mentioned to a woman friend of the family that I wasn't against marriage. Now this friend was earnestly recommending to me a young woman who wanted to move to Britain with a husband. To my discomfort this go-between was trying to fix a time for the three of us to meet and negotiate.

I went to three parties a week in Karachi. This time I was with landowners, diplomats, businessmen and politicians: powerful people. This pleased me. They were people I wouldn't have been able to get at in England and I wanted to write about them. They were drinking heavily. Every liberal in England knows you can be lashed for drinking in Pakistan. But as far as I could tell, none of this English-speaking international bourgeoisie would be lashed for anything. They all had their trusted bootleggers who negotiated the pot-holes of Karachi at high speed on disintegrating motorcycles, the hooch stashed on the back. Bad bootleggers passed a hot needle through the neck of your bottle and drew your whisky out. I once walked into a host's bathroom to see the bath full of floating whisky bottles being soaked to remove the labels, a servant sitting on a stool serenely poking at them with a stick.

It was all as tricky and expensive as buying cocaine in London, with the advantage that as the hooch market was so competitive, the 'leggers delivered video tapes at the same time, dashing into the room towards the TV with hot copies of 'The Jewel In The Crown', 'The Far Pavilions' and an especially popular programme called 'Mind Your Language' which represented Indians and Pakistanis as ludicrous caricatures.

Everyone (except of course the mass of the population) had videos. And I could see why, since Pakistan TV was so peculiar. On my first day I turned it on and a cricket match was taking place. I settled in my chair. But the English players, who were on tour in Pakistan, were leaving the pitch. In fact Bob Willis and Ian Botham were running towards the dressing rooms surrounded by armed

Photo: Hussein Shehadeh (MEPhA)

141

police, and this wasn't because Botham had made derogatory remarks about Pakistan. (He'd said it was a country to which he'd like to send his mother-in-law.) In the background a section of the crowd was being tear-gassed. Then the screen went black.

Stranger still and more significant, was the fact that the news was now being read in Arabic, a language few people in Pakistan understood. Someone explained to me that this was because the Koran was in Arabic, but everyone else said it was because General Zia wanted to kiss the arses of the Arabs.

I was having a little identity crisis. I'd been greeted so warmly in Pakistan, I felt so excited by what I saw and so at home with all my uncles, I wondered if I were not better off here than there. And when I said, with a little unnoticed irony, that I was an Englishman, people fell about laughing. Why would anyone with a brown face, Muslim name and large well-known family in Pakistan want to lay claim to that cold decrepit little island off Europe where you always had to spell your name? Strangely, anti-British remarks made me feel patriotic, though I only felt patriotic when I was away from England.

But I couldn't allow myself to feel too Pakistani. I didn't want to give in to that falsity, that sentimentality. As someone said to me, provoked by the fact I was wearing jeans: we are Pakistanis, but you, you will always be a Paki—emphasizing the derogatory name the English used against Pakistanis, and therefore the fact that I couldn't rightfully lay claim to either place.

In England I was a playwright. In Karachi this meant little. There were no theatres; the arts were discouraged by the state—music and dancing are un-Islamic—and ignored by practically everyone else. As I wasn't a doctor, or businessman or military person, people suspected that this writing business I talked about was a complicated excuse for idleness, uselessness and general bumming around. In fact, as I proclaimed an interest in the entertainment business, and talked loudly about how integral the arts were to a society, moves were being made to set me up in the amusement arcade business, in Shepherd's Bush.

Finally the man got me on my own. His name was Rahman. He

was a friend of my intellectual uncle. I had many uncles but Rahman preferred the intellectual one who understood Rahman's particular sorrow and like him considered himself to be a marginal man. In his fifties, a former Air Force officer, Rahman was liberal, well-travelled and married to an Englishwoman who now had a Pakistani accent.

He said to me: 'I tell you, this country is being sodomized by religion. It is even beginning to interfere with the making of money. And now we are embarked on this dynamic regression you must know, it is obvious, Pakistan has become a leading country to go away from. Our patriots are abroad. We despise and envy them. For the rest of us, our class, your family, we are in Hobbes's state of nature: insecure, frightened. We cling together out of necessity.' He became optimistic. 'We could be like Japan, a tragic oriental country that is now progressive, industrialized.' He laughed and then said, ambiguously: 'But only God keeps this country together. You must say this around the world: we are taking a great leap backwards.'

The bitterest blow for Rahman was the dancing. He liked to waltz and foxtrot. But now the expression of physical joy, of sensuality and rhythm, was banned. On TV you could see where it had been censored. When couples in Western programmes got up to dance there'd be a jerk in the film, and they'd be sitting down again. For Rahman it was inexplicable, an unnecessary cruelty that was almost more arbitrary than anything else.

Thus the despair of Rahman and my uncles' 'high and dry' generation. For them the new Islamization was the negation of their lives. It was a lament heard often; this was the story they told: Karachi was a goodish place in the sixties and seventies. Until about 1977 it was lively and vigorous. You could drink and dance in the Raj-style clubs (providing you were admitted) and the atmosphere was liberal—as long as you didn't meddle in politics, in which case you'd probably be imprisoned. Politically there was Bhutto: urbane, Oxford-educated, considering himself a poet and revolutionary, a veritable Chairman Mao of the subcontinent. He said he would fight obscurantism and illiteracy, ensure the equality of men and women, and increase access to education and medical care. The desert would bloom.

Later, in an attempt to save himself, appease the mullahs and rouse the dissatisfied masses behind him, he introduced various

Koranic injunctions into the constitution and banned alcohol, gambling, horse-racing. The Islamization had begun and was fervently continued after his execution.

Islamization built no hospitals, no schools, no houses; it cleaned no water and installed no electricity. But it was direction, identity. The country was to be in the hands of those who elected themselves to interpret the single divine purpose. Under the tyranny of the priesthood, with the co-operation of the army, Pakistan itself would embody Islam. There would now be no distinction between ethical and religious obligation; there would now be no areas in which it was possible to be wrong. The only possible incertitude was interpretation. The theory would be the eternal and universal principles which Allah created and made obligatory for men; the model would be the first three generations of Muslims; and the practice would be Pakistan.

This over-emphasis on dogma and punishment strengthened the repressive, militaristic and nationalistically aggressive state seen all over the world in the authoritarian eighties. With the added bonus that in Pakistan God was always on the side of the government.

But despite all the strident nationalism, as Rahman said, the patriots were abroad; people were going away: to the West, to Saudi Arabia, anywhere. Young people continually asked me about the possibility of getting into Britain and some thought of taking some smack with them to bankroll their establishment. They had what people called the Gulf Syndrome, a condition I recognized from my time living in the suburbs. It was a dangerous psychological cocktail consisting of ambition, suppressed excitement, bitterness and sexual longing.

Then a disturbing incident occurred which seemed to encapsulate the going-away fever. An eighteen-year-old girl from a village called Chakwal dreamed that the villagers walked across the Arabian Sea to Karbala, where they found work and money. Following this dream, people from the village set off one night for the beach, which happened to be near my uncle's house in fashionable Clifton. Here lived politicians and diplomats in LA-style white bungalows with sprinklers on the lawns, Mercedes in the drives and dogs and watchmen at the gates.

On the beach, the site of barbecues and late-night parties, the men of Chakwal packed their women and children into trunks and pushed them into the sea. Then they followed them into the water in the direction of Karbala. Soon all but twenty of the potential *émigrés* were drowned. The survivors were arrested and charged with illegal emigration.

It was the talk of Karachi. It caused much amusement but people like Rahman despaired of a society that could be so confused, so advanced in some aspects, so very naïve in others.

About twelve people lived permanently in my uncle's house, plus servants who slept in sheds at the back just behind the chickens and dogs. Relatives sometimes came to stay for months, and new bits had to be built onto the house. All day there were visitors, in the evenings crowds of people came over; they were welcomed and they ate and watched videos and talked for hours. People weren't so protective of their privacy.

Strangely, bourgeois-bohemian life in London, in Notting Hill and Islington and Fulham, was far more formal. It was frozen dinner parties and the division of social life into the meeting of couples with other couples to discuss the lives of other coupling couples.

In Pakistan there was the continuity of the various families' knowledge of each other. People were easy to place; your grandparents and theirs were friends. When I went to the bank and showed the teller my passport, it turned out he knew several of my uncles, so I didn't receive the usual perfunctory treatment.

I compared the collective hierarchy of the family and the permanence of my family circle with my feckless, rootless life in London, in what was called the 'inner city'. There I lived alone, and lacked any long connection with anything I'd hardly known anyone for more than eight years and certainly not their parents. People came and went. There was much false intimacy and forced friendship. People didn't take responsibility for each other. Many of my friends lived alone in London, especially the women. They wanted to be independent and to enter into relationships—as many as they liked, with whom they liked—out of choice. They didn't merely want to reproduce the old patterns of living. The future was to be determined by choice and reason, not by custom. The notions of duty and

145

obligation barely had positive meaning for my friends: they were loaded, Victorian words, redolent of constraint and grandfather clocks, the antithesis of generosity in love, the new hugging, and the transcendence of the family. The ideal of the new relationship was no longer the S and M of the old marriage—it was F and C, freedom plus commitment.

In the large old families of Pakistan where there was nothing but old patterns disturbed only occasionally by new ways, this would have seemed a contrivance, a sort of immaturity, a failure to understand and accept the determinacies that life necessarily involved. So there was much pressure to conform, especially on the women.

'Let these women be warned,' said a mullah to the dissenting women of Rawalpindi. 'We will tear them to pieces. We will give them such terrible punishments that no one in future will dare to raise a voice against Islam.'

I remember a woman saying to me at dinner one night: 'We know at least one thing. God will never dare to show his face in this country—the women will tear him apart!'

In the sixties of Enoch Powell and graffiti, the Black Muslims and Malcolm X gave needed strength to the descendants of slaves by 'taking the wraps off the white man'; Eldridge Cleaver was yet to be converted to Christianity and Huey P. Newton was toting his Army .45. A boy in a bedroom in a suburb, who had the King's Road constantly on his mind and who changed the pictures on his wall from week to week was unhappy, and separated from the sixties as by a thick glass wall against which he could only press his face. But bits of the sixties were still around in Pakistan: the liberation rhetoric, for example, the music, the clothes, the drugs, not as the way of life they were originally intended to be, but as appendages to another, stronger tradition.

As my friends and I went into the Bara Market near Peshawar, close to the border of Afghanistan, in a rattling motorized rickshaw, I became apprehensive. There were large signs by the road telling foreigners that the police couldn't take responsibility for them: beyond this point the police would not go. Apparently the Pathans there, who were mostly refugees from Afganistan, liked to kidnap foreigners. My friends, who were keen to buy opium which they'd give to the rickshaw driver to carry, told me everything was all right, because I wasn't a foreigner. I kept forgetting that.

The men of the north were tough, martial, insular and proud. They lived in mud houses and tin shacks built like forts for shooting from. Inevitably they were armed, with machine guns slung over their shoulders. In the street you wouldn't believe women existed here, except you knew they took care of the legions of young men in the area who'd fled from Afghanistan to avoid being conscripted by the Russians and sent to Moscow for re-education.

Ankle deep in mud, I went round the market. Pistols, knives, Russian-made rifles, hand grenades and large lumps of dope and opium were laid out on stalls like tomatoes and oranges. Everyone was selling heroin.

The Americans, who had much money invested in Pakistan, this compliant right-wing buffer-zone between Afghanistan and India, were furious that their children were being destroyed by an illegal industry in a country they financed. But the Americans sent to Pakistan could do little about it. The heroin trade went right through Pakistani society: the police, judiciary, the army, landlords, customs officials were all involved. After all, there was nothing in the Koran about heroin. I was even told that its export made ideological sense. Heroin was anti-Western; addiction in western children was what those godless societies with their moral vertigo deserved. It was a kind of colonial revenge. Reverse imperialism, the Karachi wits called it, inviting nemesis. The reverse imperialism was itself being reversed.

In a flat high above Karachi, an eighteen year old kid strung-out on heroin danced cheerfully around the room in front of me pointing to his erection, which he referred to as his Imran Khan, the name of the handsome Pakistan cricket captain. More and more of the so-called multi-national kids were taking heroin now. My friends who owned the flat, journalists on a weekly paper, were embarrassed.

But they always had dope to offer their friends. These laid-back people were mostly professionals: lawyers, an inspector in the police who smoked what he confiscated, a newspaper magnate and various other journalists. Heaven it was to smoke at midnight on the beach, as local fishermen, squatting respectfully behind you, fixed fat joints; the 'erotic politicians' themselves, The Doors, played from a portable

Hanif Kureishi

stereo while the Arabian Sea rolled onto the beach. Oddly, heroin and dope were both indigenous to the country, but it took the West to make them popular in the East.

The colonized inevitably aspire to be like their colonizers—you wouldn't catch anyone of my uncle's generation with a joint in their mouth. It was infra dig, for peasants. They shadowed the British, they drank whisky and read *The Times*; they praised others by calling them 'gentlemen'; and their eyes filled with tears at old Vera Lynn records.

But the kids discussed yoga, you'd catch them standing on their heads. They even meditated. Though one boy who worked at the airport said it was too much of a Hindu thing for Muslims to be doing; if his parents caught him chanting a mantra he'd get a backhander across the chops. Mostly the kids listened to the Stones, Van Morrison and Bowie as they flew over ruined roads to the beach in bright red and yellow Japanese cars with quadrophonic speakers, past camels and acres of wasteland.

I often walked from my uncle's house several miles down a road towards the beach. Here, all along a railway track, the poor and diseased and hungry lived in shacks and huts; the filthy poor gathered around rusty stand-pipes to fetch water; or ingeniously they resurrected wrecked cars, usually Morris Minors; and here they slept in huge sewer-pipes among buffalo, chickens and wild dogs. Here I met a policeman who I thought was on duty. But he lived here, and hanging on the wall of his falling-down shed was his spare white police uniform, which he'd had to buy himself.

A stout lawyer in his early thirties of immense charm—for him it was definitely the eighties, not the sixties. His father was a judge. He was intelligent, articulate and fiercely representative of the other 'new spirit' of Pakistan. He didn't drink, smoke or fuck. Out of choice. He prayed five times a day. He worked all the time. He was determined to be a good Muslim, since that was the whole point of the country existing at all. He wasn't indulgent, except religiously, and he lived in accordance with what he believed. I took to him immediately.

We had dinner in an expensive restaurant. It could have been in London or New York. The food was excellent, I said. The lawyer disagreed, with his mouth full, shaking his great head. It was

148

definitely no good, it was definitely meretricious rubbish. But for ideological reasons only, since he ate with relish. He was only in the restaurant because of me, he said. There was better food in the villages. The masses had virtue, they knew how to eat, how to live. Those desiccated others, the marginal men I associated with and liked so much, were a plague class with no values. Perhaps, he suggested, this was why I liked them, being English. Their education, their intellectual snobbery, made them un-Islamic. They didn't understand the masses and they spoke in English to cut themselves off from the people. Didn't the best jobs go to those with a foreign education? He was tired of these Westernized elders denigrating their country and its religious nature.

The lawyer and I went out into the street. It was busy. There were dancing camels and a Pakistan trade exhibition. The exhibition was full of Pakistani imitations of Western goods: bathrooms in chocolate and strawberry, TVs with stereos attached; fans, air-conditioners, heaters; and an arcade full of 'Space Invaders'. The lawyer got agitated.

These were Western things, of no use to the masses. The masses wanted Islam, not strawberry bathrooms or...or elections. Are elections a Western thing? I asked. Don't they have them in India too? No—they're a Western thing, the lawyer said. How could they be required under Islam? There need be only one party—the party of the righteous.

This energetic lawyer would have pleased and then disappointed Third World intellectuals and revolutionaries from an earlier era, people like Fanon and Guevara. This talk of liberation—at last the acknowledgement of the virtue of the toiling masses, the struggle against neo-colonialism, its bourgeois stooges, and American interference—the entire recognizable rhetoric of freedom and struggle ends in the lawyer's mind with the country on its knees, at prayer. Having started to look for itself it finds itself...in the eighth century.

I strode into a room in my uncle's house. Half-hidden by a curtain, on a verandah, was an aged woman servant wearing my cousin's old clothes, praying. I stopped and watched her. In the morning as I lay in bed, she swept the floor of my room with some twigs bound together. She was at least sixty. Now, on the shabby prayer mat, she was tiny and around her the universe was endless, immense, but God was above her. I felt she was acknowledging that which was larger than she, knowing and feeling her own insignificance. It was not empty ritual. I wished I could do it.

I went with the lawyer to the mosque in Lahore, the largest in the world. I took off my shoes, padded across the immense courtyard with the other man—women were not allowed—and got on my knees. I banged my forehead on the marble floor. Beside me a man in a similar posture gave a world-consuming yawn. I waited but could not lose myself in prayer. I could only travesty the woman's prayer, to whom it had a world of meaning.

Did she want a society in which her particular moral and religious beliefs were mirrored, and no others, instead of some plural, liberal *mélange*? A society in which her own cast of mind, her customs, way of life and obedience to God constituted authority? It wasn't as if anyone had asked her.

In Pakistan, England just wouldn't go away. Relics of the Raj were everywhere: buildings, monuments, Oxford accents, libraries full of English books, and newspapers. Many Pakistanis had relatives in England; thousands of Pakistani families depended on money sent from England. While visiting a village, a man told me that when his three grandchildren visited from Bradford, he had to hire an interpreter to speak to them. It was happening all the time—the closeness of the two societies, and the distance.

Although Pakistanis still wanted to escape to England, the old men in their clubs and the young eating their hamburgers took great pleasure in England's decline and decay. The great master was fallen. It was seen as strikebound, drug-ridden, riot-torn, inefficient, disunited, a society which had moved too suddenly from puritanism to hedonism and now loathed itself. And the Karachi wits liked to ask me when I thought the Americans would decide the British were ready for self-government.

Yet people like Rahman still clung to what they called British ideals, maintaining that it is a society's ideals, its conception of human progress, that define the level of its civilization. They regretted, under the Islamization, the repudiation of the values which they said were the only positive aspect of Britain's legacy to the subcontinent. These were: the idea of secular institutions based on reason, not revelation or scripture; the idea that there were no final solutions to human problems; and the idea that the health and vigour of a society was bound up with its ability to tolerate and express a plurality of views on all issues, and that these views would be welcomed.

The English misunderstood the Pakistanis because they saw only the poor people, those from the villages, the illiterates, the peasants, the Pakistanis who didn't know how to use toilets, how to eat with knives and forks because they were poor. If the British could only see *them,* the rich, the educated, the sophisticated, they wouldn't be so hostile. They'd know what civilized people the Pakistanis really were. And then they'd like them.

BOOKCLUB

51 Beak Street London W1R 3LF Telephone 01 437 2131

We offer our members new books at 25% off the published price.

AUTUMN BOOKS

ANITA BROOKNER
Family and Friends

ITALO CALVINO
Mr Palomar

JOHN FOWLES
A Maggot

MARY GORDON
Men and Angels

VASILY GROSSMAN
Life and Fate

HUMPHREY JENNINGS
Pandaemonium

NORMAN LEWIS
Jackdaw Cake

JAN MARSH
Pre-Raphaelite Sisterhood

MICHAEL MEYER
Strindberg

IRIS MURDOCH
The Good Apprentice

ADAM NICOLSON
Frontiers
From the Arctic to the Aegean

**CLAYRE PERCY
AND JANE RIDLEY**
The Letters of Edwin Lutyens
To his wife, Lady Emily

HEINRICH BÖLL
A LETTER TO MY
SONS:
WAR'S END

Dear René, dear Vincent,

If you should find in this the slightest trace of glorying in Germany's survival and reconstruction, cross it out, laugh at it, put it down to irony or anger; but believe me, I don't intend to fall into the tone of the older generation, always out to tell their young listeners what a hard time 'we' had of it, and how easy it really is for them and always will be. Oh, those plucky types with their sleeves rolled up: they've still got them rolled up, even now—as I write, the notorious Amnesty Bill is being pushed through Parliament by the most brazen of them—even now the crooks are busy rolling over the Federal Republic.*

No, it's no easier for you than it was for us: don't let them tell you otherwise. It was possible to survive the last war, and that's what I want to tell you about: our experience of *the end of the war.* 'Telling a story' is a risky business—in every story-teller there invariably lurks a braggart or a show-off; but in actual fact he's a true hero as well or at least a true sufferer. Even the Odyssey is full of boasting, and what I want to tell you about is like a little Odyssey. I've written enough about the war; read it with a forgiving eye, and if you detect—as you may here—anything accusatory in the tone, it's only the German Reich that I'm accusing, its leaders and its people, never the victorious powers, never the Soviet Union. I wouldn't have any grounds anyway on which to accuse the Soviet Union. I was ill there a few times, and I was wounded there, but that's war, and it was always clear to me: no one *asked* us over there. It just so happens that in a war you get shot at—they had those mortars, 'Stalin's organ pipes', and the like; and sometimes you had to eat and drink things that were unsafe or unfit for consumption. When you're half crazy with thirst (one lesson I will pass on to you—thirst is always worse than

---

*Heinrich Böll's letter to his two sons, René and Vincent, was written in May of last year. It is the last piece Böll was to write before he died. The controversial Amnesty Bill, proposed by Chancellor Kohl's Christian Democratic party, was intended to absolve all politicians who had accepted undeclared 'contributions' from large industrial corporations.

hunger!), you do drink from puddles and you forget all the warnings about germs and bacteria. You can tell I wasn't keen to fall into Soviet hands by the way that, from the autumn of 1944 onwards, I managed to keep to the west, although they would have liked to send me back eastwards. I did what I could. Anyway, soldiers—and I was one—shouldn't complain about the people they've been sent to fight against, only about those who sent them there.

For years I've been thinking about a little project I haven't yet found time for: 'The Soldier in Fairy-tales', including Grimms' *Märchen*. Kings and emperors and other commanders don't come out of them too well. All fairy-tales stress the callousness of superiors. The *Märchen* are far more realistic on this point than most war novels, which tend to ignore the callousness of most 'supreme commanders' and put the 'enemy'—whose enemy?—in the foreground. So when I have to come to the time when I was a prisoner of war, please remember that I'm not attacking or protesting about the British and American armies. After the war, after *that* war, I was expecting the worst: decades of forced labour in Siberia or somewhere. And it didn't turn out half as bad as I had thought: not bad at all when you think about the devastation caused by the war, and the fact that without the German army—to which I belonged—not one concentration camp could have existed for even a single year. You should know too that the incidence of death among Soviet prisoners of war in German camps was 57.8 percent—that's 3.3 million dead prisoners of war; the rate among German prisoners in the Soviet Union was between 35.2 and 37.4 percent—that's between 1.1 and 1.15 million. In the First World War the mortality rate for Russian prisoners of war in Germany was 5.4 percent, and even that was higher than the normal figure, which was about 3.5 percent. So the mortality rate for Soviet prisoners in the Second World War was over *ten times* higher. Do you see? It was *extermination,* and that was the main occupation of the Nazis. The *extermination* of the Soviet Union wasn't quite successful; there were a few surviviors, and a few houses for them to live in. Nor did they quite manage the *extermination* of Germany, where equally there were a few survivors, and a few houses left standing.

How do you survive *extermination* and *chaos* in an atmosphere in which anyone might be an informer (though fortunately not everyone was)? Read reports, statistics, accounts about the Soviet Union and the effects of the war, everything I can't enumerate here. Of the more than five million Poles who were killed, nine-tenths were civilians, while in Yugoslavia the ratio of civilian dead to military dead was three to one. Don't despise statistics, though they may sometimes be inaccurate or just 'rough'—who anyway could count every one of the dead?

When you can see the proportions, the figures take on a bewildering concreteness. I'll give you one last statistic: out of approximately fifty-five million dead in Europe, forty percent were citizens of the Soviet Union.

W here should I start what is not a 'story', but simply an account of how we experienced the *end of the war*? I suppose the best thing is to begin with my mother's death, on 3 November in Ahrweiler, while I was in hospital in Bad Neuenahr. I wasn't sick or wounded; I had been transferred from hospital in Ahrweiler to Dresden, then discharged from there and sent back to Ahrweiler. In order to get another spell in hospital after my leave had come to an end, I had once again helped Nature along a bit, with something I'd been given by a Cologne doctor who's still alive. After my mother's funeral we left the hotel in Ahrweiler, probably round the seventh or eighth November. Her death probably saved our lives. A few days after we moved out of the hotel, it was destroyed by a bomb with a direct hit. Our 'move'? No, I shan't describe it. It would turn out as an adventure story, and there are enough of those already. One important thing, though: the lorry-driver was a saint—patient, gentle, friendly. We billeted ourselves rather forcibly, although by invitation, on my relations: Maria, Alois, Marie-Theres, Franz and Gilbert in Marienfeld, where your little brother Christoph is buried. Our welcome in our new home was appropriate enough: a bomb, the first to be dropped on the village since the war began. Nothing from me here about food and living conditions; all that's been done often enough. Six adults and three children in temporary accommodation. My father was almost seventy-five, and still fond of cigars. The only reliable source of tobacco was a Polish prisoner of war who worked as a joiner in the house next door. His name was Toni, and he was a perfect gentleman in dress and demeanour.

157

We had one wish only: to live, not exactly for ever, but preferably a while longer, and without the Nazi pestilence.

How many novels would it take to describe the time between 3 November 1944 and April 1945? Remember that the Minister of the Interior was Himmler, and that after 20 July he was also the Commander-in-Chief of the reserve army: *my, our,* Commander-in-Chief. The internal terror that prevailed between 20 July and the end of the war has yet to be described.

We not only had the frivolous desire to survive this horror, we were hungry as well; there were nine, sometimes ten or eleven of us to be fed. Ask Annemarie, your mother, ask her about it when you get the chance: she knitted gloves that would have delighted any boutique, and in exchange she would get half a bucketful of potatoes, a few of them already starting to rot. The winter was a cold one, like all the winters of the war. Why do we remember them all as so cold? I don't know what an objective, meteorological view would be. What else could we do but beg and steal? The stealing was confined to firewood, which had to be chopped by the women in a little wood nearby, up to their knees in the snow, under the strict supervision of your grandfather. Later, in the temporary accommodation for the nine of us, he sawed up the wood expertly on the kitchen table, after first, equally expertly, sharpening the saw. Do you know the sound of a saw being sharpened, one tooth at a time, with a saw-file? The wood was wet, and paper scarce; how could your grandfather, who always insisted on doing it himself, get a fire going? Well, our accommodation was the former vestry, only reachable from the street by a ladder, and in the loft above were stored the posts that carry the banners on Corpus Christi Day and other processions. The wood was dry, and the thickness of the posts ideal. We called them 'pastors', because one of the banners in the procession at Corpus Christi read 'Bless Our Pastor'. Every so often one of the 'pastors' would have to be secretly got down from the loft under the cover of darkness and sawn up into stove-sized lengths. We often asked ourselves whether the 'pastors' would last us till the end of the war (later on in the prisoner-of-war camp, with the approach of Corpus Christi, I wondered what would happen when the villagers found out that their 'pastors' had disappeared!). But you can't light a fire just with dry wood and a little paper; you need matches or a lighter, and we had neither. And so your grandfather would position himself at the gate at six o'clock on dark winter mornings, and wait for someone whose lighter he could use to light a twist of paper. Neverthless he used to curse those farmers, who got up too late for his taste; he got up between five thirty and six all his life, to go to Mass.

Your uncle Alois, a 'sponti' before his time, had the understandable, if also dangerous, inclination to absent himself from his unit on repeated occasions, which could quite easily have been taken as desertion. Officially he 'served'—that is, did nothing—in the Hacketäuer barracks in Cologne-Mülheim-of-wretched-memory. He would borrow or somehow get hold of a bicycle and just turn up, usually exhausted and drenched in sweat, having cycled via Much to Marienfeld. We sometimes had visits from the military police (known as 'guard dogs'). The military police meant real danger, and not just for Alois, whom they could have shot, or strung up from the nearest tree—no, I too had reason to fear their visits, because I wasn't always able to keep my papers up to date, or have them properly falsified. Once I had to hide in the broom-cupboard, and the 'guard-dogs' luckily didn't look in there. The three children were useful for camouflage and distraction. Also we brothers had the good fortune to resemble each other, so that the neighbours could never be quite sure whether there was just one of us, or both, around at any time. That's why we couldn't go out and help with chopping wood in the daytime.

At this point, I must mention Johann Peters, the farmer from Berzbach near Much, who would not only give us two litres (!) of milk every day (!) in return for two worthless Kriegsmarks, but who would also—he was an amputee from the First World War, a Catholic and an anarchist—welcome a couple of German deserters to his stove, and give us the odd pipe of tobacco to smoke, which was worth considerably more than two Kriegsmarks. Milk soups of the winter of '44, maybe it's to you and farmer Johann Peters that we owe our lives! Two litres of milk a day in a winter in the war. Our evening milk soup was the only meal we could depend on. Fetching the milk by daylight became a dangerous business—sometimes Annemarie and Marie-Theres could escape the low-flying fighter planes only by leaping off the road into the ditch.

Fear and hunger, hunger and fear of the Germans. Perhaps now,

159

Heinrich Böll

Vincent and René, you'll understand a bit more what we so often tried to explain to you: why even today shopping for me is always panic-buying, why I always get too much bread, too much milk, eggs and butter, and cigarettes preferably by the carton; and maybe you'll understand why I'm continually astonished that I didn't spend the rest of my life sitting by the stove, reading with a few cigarettes to hand. After all, I was married to a secondary-school teacher, decently well-off, whose salary would, while modest, have been enough for us all. To sit by the stove and read; to be free for just a few hours from fear of the 'guard-dogs' and of Herr Himmler, the Minister of the Interior, and Herr Himmler, the Commander-in-Chief, and his laws and his emissaries: it'll help you understand also how the merest hint of Fascism throws me into a panic; why I always keep my car filled up with petrol, why I like to have enough money in my pocket to last at least a week, and why I live within reach of the Dutch and Belgian border. Crazy, I know, crazy. And perhaps you'll understand that only fear can make you brave—only the situation where the choice is between being courageous and being destroyed—and that it was this fear that gave me the courage to exist on faked papers, which I then boldly handed in at some army office for genuine ones, to be faked in their turn. Don't take this as a tip or advice from me, René and Vincent, just as a statement on my behaviour, which at the time felt 'historically correct', in view of the imminent *end of the war*—something historians will see entirely differently. If it should happen to you, it will happen quite differently. Advice isn't much use there.

The first time I falsified my papers was in the spring of '44, when I persuaded the girl who was making out my hospital discharge in a Hungarian hospital to leave a blank under the rubric 'Destination'. My fountain pen probably saved my life: in the toilet of the train, I wrote in '*Metz*', the westernmost point still in Nazi hands. Otherwise I would have had to report for a front-posting in Debrečen—and the chaos in the Balkan theatre of war in the autumn of '44 you can read about in any account. From Hungary via Ahrweiler to Metz, from Metz via Ahrweiler to Dresden, from Dresden via Ahrweiler and Bad Neuenahr to Marienfeld. I want to describe *one* moment from all that time. It must have been September or October '44, and I was coming from Munich or Vienna to change trains in Remagen. As I went down the subway stairs to the Ahrweiler platform, your mother was coming down the opposite steps into the same subway—and we met in the tunnel! Can you understand how even after forty years our hearts still quake when we travel through Remagen?

I had gone to Marienfeld with genuine papers, my discharge from hospital in Neuenahr. As the expiry date came nearer, I panicked and travelled to Siegburg, having again first 'doctored' myself, duly arrived there with a temperature, and got the document extended. The extension ran out, I changed the date; that date too elapsed and I presented myself, again with a temperature, to a civilian doctor in Much who extended the faked date, thereby making it almost 'official' again. I faked the 'officially' extended date, that too elapsed—and the scrap of paper became so tatty and so covered with typed-in corrections as to be unusable. Do I need to tell you that we weren't just longing for the Americans to get through, we used to pray, even curse them on their way? But they still didn't come. Do I have to describe our alarm when my brother Alois kept going on longer and crazier walkabouts away from his unit?

It occurred to me that I had one more card up my sleeve. After all, with three or four months in hospital and so many periods of illness at home I was still, in the German army's terms, a 'reconvalescent', and thus before they could send me back to the war again I was still entitled—what 'entitlements' did you have anyway, with Herr Himmler as Minister of the Interior and Commander-in-Chief?—to some 'convalescence leave'. With my utterly tattered bit of bumf, the best thing seemed to me to return to the bosom of my damned unit, called a 'reserve force', based in some miserable dump south of Mannheim. I went there. Yes, went. All the stations were like enormous caravanserais, swarming with exhausted, nervous, mostly filthy groups of people with their squalid baggage: civilians, 'ordinary' travellers, bombed-out refugees, soldiers, POWs, policemen of all species...then I get a few things mixed up; the chronology isn't quite there, so I'll give you just a few guaranteed absurd details.

The reserve unit was quartered in a tobacco-village in Baden, I've forgotten its name. A company usually numbered just over a hundred men, but there were 800 in mine, and they stood there on

161

parade, variously grumpy and cursing: some without an arm, others a leg, or both legs, or both legs and an arm, on crutches, with improvised artificial limbs, waiting for their pension-claims to be settled, decorated heroes queueing up for a dollop of dried vegetables. I suppose it was January or February, freezing cold, and you only got a coat if you put yourself down as 'fighting fit'. You slept in tobacco-sheds from which the tobacco had wisely been removed or confiscated. The false limbs were hung up at night from various hooks and nails on the wall; everything mouldy, foul coffee substitute, dry bread with a little jam. At least I'd got rid of my tatty, suspicious papers without any query and was legal again. I was cold and hungry, had to wait two days for my turn to eat. Evenings spent in farm-kitchens and the back-rooms of pubs, haggling over cigarettes; not a girl for miles, roll-calls barked out, shouting and swearing—oh, noble fatherland of mine, the way you treat your heroes, your crippled heroes (see *Märchen*!). Annemarie had lent me her wonderfully warm and light Turkish shawl for the trip and I'd created quite a stir with that, all draped in red. I straightaway got myself put down as 'fighting fit', got a coat and, just as important, some genuine papers. I was given a 'convalescence leave' note. Ask Annemarie about the years before that, the meeting in Remagen, the weeks in Metz, the Cologne apartments. Perhaps now you can understand what feelings and memories are set off in us by the stations at Remagen, Cologne, Bonn? When we visit the Kopelevs in Cologne, they live directly opposite the house in the Neuenhöfer Allee where we, newlyweds at the end of '42, experienced the worst of the bombing raids. One particular memory—the flat—surfaces irresistibly and unasked. I don't know how many times I stayed there, five or six or seven; the last was the night of 29 June 1943, when Cologne was almost totally demolished.

I can't locate the order given by Himmler in those last weeks of the war, allowing any soldier to shoot any other soldiers found 'out of earshot of battle'. That made every German into a potential summary court-martial for every other German—even though the one doing the finding would himself have to be 'out of earshot of battle'. The number of executions was enormous, running into tens of thousands. Now we know that Himmler gave this order shortly before he tried to arrange a separate peace through Count Bernadotte—of which

Hitler was of course unaware—to save his own skin. His honour was his fidelity. (The SS slogan!) The Commander-in-Chief tried to save himself while all around him tens of thousands of men were shot and hanged on *his* orders. Between 20 July 1944 and the *end of the war,* Germany was completely terrorized by Himmler, the Minister of the Interior. And on the radio, Goebbels's screeching. Let me tell you that the American army shot *one* deserter in Europe, just one, and his widow sued the Pentagon for years afterwards, for decades. No one knows how many German soldiers were executed; certainly upwards of 30,000. And was there one single German widow, fiancée, mother or sister who tried to sue the German Reich or its successors, or one of the surviving Field-Marshals under whose jurisdiction the shooting or hanging took place? Of course there's no way of knowing how many of those who were executed found their way into the statistics of 'war dead', and are possibly now immortalized on memorial plaques.

I didn't want to swell their numbers myself. Your uncle Alois nearly did on several occasions. He owes his survival not only to his fantastic good-fortune, but also to his wife Aunt Maria, to your mother Annemarie, and especially to your other aunt, my sister Mechtilde. Fortunately, the women had no idea of the sort of danger Alois was in, and they went with astonishing courage and almost inspired naïvety into the various lions' dens, to Cologne, or to Engelskirchen, to win time for him. To delay his execution, I'm tempted to say. His luck on his 'walkabouts' would take a novel in itself to describe. Finally it transpired that he had kidney trouble and belonged in hospital anyway, quite legitimately; from there he eventually came home, crossing the American lines disguised as a priest to avoid imprisonment. Once, in December 1944, both of us went illegally to Siegburg for the wedding of our brother Alfred to your aunt Cläre.

I knew one 'deserter' who was shot. It was in a village called Kaldauen near Siegburg, and he spoke to me briefly once when I was back with the army. He was an NCO with the unusual name of Schmitz, a quietly-spoken fellow, and he talked to me because he knew Maria and Alois. After the war I heard he'd been shot for desertion. He had left the front—Kaldauen is about three or four kilometres from the outskirts of Siegburg—to visit his parents, probably to have a cup of coffee with them, and one of those licensed

German murderers must have caught up with him, 'out of earshot' of the fighting. It wouldn't have taken long, and there was no fuss afterwards. A little later, in the early '50's, German women didn't oppose rearmament. I never understood that; maybe you can try.

Then things get a bit disorganized. I know for a fact that I was in Ludwigshafen at one stage. Why? What was I doing? Was I on the way to the tobacco-village in Baden? I suppose so.

I was also in Mainz, in February '45. As I hated hanging around in the gigantic mouldering station/caravanserais, I went into the town (yes, I can vouch for the truth of this 'story'!), saw the sign 'Area Command', went inside—don't ask me why—asked for the 'legal officer' of all people and, with my faked leave in my pocket, had my name sent in to him. Was I suicidal? No, I still wanted to live. The officer, a major, had me shown in and I told him a whole string of lies: how on the way back to my unit I had heard of my mother's death (she was already dead four or five months), and had to attend the funeral, and I'd also heard that our flat in Cologne had been bombed (which in fact had happened a year and a half before), and so I had to go to Cologne as well as to the funeral to rescue my library and my papers, which were absolutely vital for me as I was finishing a doctorate (my official designation was the highly ambiguous 'student', and of course the officer had no way of knowing or guessing, let alone checking, that I'd been called up during my first term at university). Well, this incredible man, a major or perhaps even a lieutenant-colonel, who looked terribly stern and Prussian, he *believed* me, or—this only occurred to me later—he pretended to believe me, because he knew the war was lost and wanted to save whatever lives he could. He allowed me a fortnight's leave, and there I was again with legitimate papers and time off. One thing you've experienced, perhaps, so you know it's not a boast, just a fact: I can be pretty cool-headed when I have to.

I know one other thing: it was this leave that expired on 2 March 1945, so it must have been mid-February that I found myself—for what reason I really couldn't say—in Mainz, *with* a coat.

A fortnight was generous, a fortnight was forever, and the Americans would have to get through some time. Those fourteen days, with a proper set of documents in my pocket, were just about carefree, except that I was afraid for my brother, who was in greater danger than the women of our family had realized. It was during that fortnight that I cycled to Cologne on Tilla's bicycle in order to check up on our flat and to buy some cigarettes on the black market. But after that, things get a bit confused again: I do know that on 2 March I stood on the Michaelsberg in Siegburg, and watched the gigantic clouds of dust that had once been Cologne roll over the plain towards Siegburg. Also, I'm absolutely certain that 2 March was the deadline of my very last legal leave, but did I alter this before Siegburg or after? Probably before, because in Siegburg that day I could easily have fallen into the hands of the *Heldenklau* (detachments which went around quite indiscriminately nabbing soldiers and taking them to the nearest fighting unit—that is, into the notorious 'earshot of battle'). My falsification this time was to type in a '5' after the '2', using my father's old office typewriter: the '5' turned out crooked, and it was in a different typeface. A fake like that wouldn't have helped me much if I'd fallen into the hands of a proper criminologist; then—I don't know, daren't think about it—some German moron could have shot me quite easily. I still don't know why I didn't type in a '9' after the '2'. I had gained twenty-three days, twenty-three eternities, but why not twenty-seven? Even unfaked, the papers weren't worth very much, because in this phase of the war no one was given five weeks' leave at a time. Perhaps we were just absolutely convinced that by then—at the very latest—the Americans, our liberators, would have got through.

Well, they hadn't reached us by the twenty-fifth, and yet they'd taken Cologne, and had crossed the Rhine at Remagen as far back as the seventh. Remagen! Can you imagine what that name meant to us? Not only our totally unexpected, fairy-tale meeting there, not only the Americans crossing the Rhine there, but also where, between July '43 and November '44, Annemarie used to change trains almost every day on her way from Ahrweiler to Cologne, usually accompanied by my father, who was looking after 'business' there (there was plenty—mending windows!). Annemarie travelled to Cologne to take her pupils into the air raid shelter. I don't know how many hundreds of air raids she experienced. It was insanity, daily worsening insanity.

At some time I can remember going around bombed-out Bonn

with Annemarie, probably to try and get into hospital again after 'doctoring' myself once more. This time it didn't work. And once—yes, this is all like 'Once upon a time'—once I was in Engelskirchen with my sister Mechtilde, where Tilla was arranging something again for Alois. It was the head-quarters of Field Marshal General Model, a feared murderer who at least had the decency to shoot himself in a wood between Duisburg and Düsseldorf, aged fifty-four—two years younger than his supreme commander and nine years older than Himmler (yes, in 1945 Himmler was just forty-five; when you have the time work out how many murders he committed for each minute of his life). Strafing raids, the roads crawling with soldiers, refugees, evacuees—if anyone wanted to make a film about this they would need hundreds of thousands of extras. Troops advancing, troops retreating: who could tell the front from the rear?

We knew of course from listening to foreign radio stations (punishable by death!) that the Americans had gone on down the *Autobahn* from Remagen as far as Hennef, and had reached the river Sieg, which was only twelve kilometres away from us. Well, they had other plans: they moved east as far as Kassel, and together with the British who had advanced from Arnheim, they formed a pocket in the Ruhr where they trapped a large part of the German army—but they didn't come to Marienfeld. So, the twenty-fifth came ever nearer, and this time there was nothing left to falsify and without valid papers and out of 'earshot of battle' I'd have been strung up pretty smartly. Sometimes I think the chaos during and after the Thirty Years War couldn't have been as great as it was in this one. The geographical area covered was much the same, but its population had increased many if not thousands of times over and the potential for chaos was far greater. Also, our enemies weren't the advancing British and Americans: our enemies were the great death-and-chaos-specialists, one of whom called himself the Führer and sat in his concrete ivory tower in Berlin, and the other the Minister of the Interior and Commander-in-Chief of the reserve army, Herr Himmler; and they had transmitted their mania for destruction to subordinate organizations composed of great sections of the population. You'll always be able to tell a German by whether he refers to the eighth of May as a day of defeat or a day of liberation. *We* awaited our 'enemies' as liberators. One of the surviving Field Marshal Generals wouldn't talk of 'defeat' but of 'lost victories'. Don't read this as an adventure story, even though a few adventurous elements are unavoidable: read it as a crime-thriller, though it can't be *that* exciting since the main issue—do they catch him?—is settled irrefutably by my own survival. The most exciting question you could ask would be: How did he manage not to get caught?

T he twenty-fifth March came and went without the Americans crossing the Sieg and liberating us; there was cold comfort in the fact that even a '9' after the '2' wouldn't have made much difference, since on the twenty-ninth they still hadn't.

There was nothing for it but to rejoin the German army. By now the question was: Where did you have a better chance of surviving, with the army or away from it? The answer we came up with, after giving it a great deal of thought, was with the army. Away from it, and without papers—that would have been dicing with death. But rejoining the army meant parting and further separation; a parting in wartime, and more especially in a *Nazi* war, could always be final, and it didn't help much that we were convinced it 'really couldn't last much longer now'. After all, it had gone on for two years after Stalingrad, and if they'd had the chance the Germans would have prolonged the famous 'five past midnight' to the break of day.

So, we prolonged our farewells. Annemarie accompanied me to the nearest army headquarters, which was a couple of kilometres away near a village called Bruchhausen. It turned out to be a staff headquarters: lots of people with red stripes on their trousers, a nervous staff who couldn't make anything of this private who had just turned up and who weren't able to give me legal papers in exchange for my ill-omened fakes. I was told to go on to a vil- lage called Birk on the way from Siegburg to Much, and was given some proper marching-rations: bread, sausage, margarine, cigarettes—and we extended our farewell further by sharing these together somewhere off the road between Bruchhausen and Marienfeld: we were both hungry, and your mother was pregnant. Annemarie walked with me as far as Much, a long downhill journey that she would have to make back uphill again later, and then we said goodbye at the crossroads down in the valley, with hordes of soldiers and civilians streaming past each other, sometimes into each other.

Germany was on the move, and I had those rotten documents in my pocket. Yes, goodbye. No descriptions. How should I describe fifty or even a hundred farewells? In Cologne, Ahrweiler, Marienfeld, Metz, Bitsch, St. Avold and elsewhere.

I trotted off towards Birk, with a wholly irregular walking-stick in my hand which caused an officer of the military police who was driving past to stop and give me a severe ticking-off for being turned out in a way unbefitting a German solider. I was too upset even to feign remorse, told him where I was going—and he ordered me to get into his car. He looked stern and punctilious, and I was afraid—he was after all a military police officer—that he would ask to see my papers, or even take me in immediately. He did neither, but dropped me without a word outside the unit's orderly room in Birk, waited for me to go in, and drove on. I gave my name to the duty sergeant and presented my papers, but before he could study them he was called away into the next room. I grabbed the wretched scraps of paper, my *corpus delicti*, and when he came back and asked where they were I said, 'But you took them with you.' He was surprised and confused, but left it at that; I was incorporated into the company, and was once more legal. That ill-fated leave-note must still be around somewhere among my untidied war-letters, that document which probably saved my life.

On with the thriller. I felt relieved and depressed at the same time: after half a year, I was once more separated from Annemarie and the others, back with the German army. The excursions to the tobacco-village, to Mainz and elsewhere, had been risky, but more calculable in their consequences. I was pretty miserable, especially not being able to phone, which had always been a comfort in the earlier years of the war. In the evening I went for a walk in Birk, despairing, but still toying with the idea of simply slipping away—only where to? Then, in the main street in Birk, I bumped into the daughter of a Cologne shopkeeper whom we had bought food from many times—and on tick for years. A nice girl, whom unfortunately I have never seen since. She took me 'home' with her: to temporary accommodation, where I met her father; they had left home just two days ago, fleeing to avoid being recruited into the *Volkssturm* territorials. We exchanged our news, and Herr Fog, as his name was, told me that he wanted to move nearer to the American lines to steer clear of the *Volkssturm*, and asked me whether he might hide for a day or two with my family in Marienfeld. I said of course, and he asked me if I would, as it were, book him in, and gave me as an advance a stout bag containing twenty-five pounds of sugar. Twenty-five pounds of sugar, at the end of March 1945! How could I get it to Marienfeld this late at night? Well, I was crazy, the girl lent me her bicycle, I jammed the sugar into the basket and set off. It was madness, and perhaps this sugar-transport, 'quitting my unit'—like a subsequent bicycle-ride under similar circumstances that I'll come to later—was my only act of 'heroism': sugar for Marienfeld! I cycled down minor roads; avoided dangerous crossroads where military police and the *Heldenklau* might be lurking, pushed sugar and bicycle up embankments, and finally reached Marienfeld bathed in sweat. That was some homecoming! A surprise, and yet still painful, and again the problem: whether to stay or go back. Finally, my 'sense of honour' prevailed: I had promised the girl I would return her bike, and in these times a bicycle was worth more than a fleet of cars. Bicycles played a big part in determining my destiny, to the good as it turned out. So I rode off in the middle of the night, returned the bicycle, and crept back into our sleeping-quarters. Legal again.

Now the last phase begins, which I don't want to write about in detail because it's stuff you can read up on in any war book. In Kaldauen, I met Corporal Schmitz whom they later shot a few hundred yards from his parents' home; then I was transferred to Niederauel, facing the town of Blankenberg across the river. We were positioned facing the Americans, separated only by the Sieg, so that we could see with our own eyes the white, white bread—it shone like the moon. There was no shooting: it was forbidden, so to speak, because if a single German shot fell whole barrages of American artillery would be sent over in return. Dissolution, mayhem, barely any normal rations, stealing, milking cows, contriving to spend the night in barns and animal-sheds for the warmth—you may wonder why I didn't go over to the Americans right away and surrender to that white, white bread. The answer is simple: not only did I want to survive, I wanted if possible to survive without being imprisoned—a really frivolous wish. Alois and I had decided that we would go and hide in the little loft at home in Marienfeld, among the remaining

'pastors', and 'await developments' there. I wanted to be with
Annemarie, at home, and besides I would have had to swim or ford
the cold Sieg. I waited. Open talk of desertion: some had tried
already—they had families living in American-occupied
territory—and climbed and crawled their way along a ruined
bridge—and were shot at, because they were taken for a
reconnaissance patrol. No, I waited, and once more a bicycle led me
into temptation.

Together with a few others I was ordered to escort our relief-
detachment, a company from a bicycle-corps of Cologne policemen,
from Allner back to Niederauel at night. It wasn't far from Allner to
Marienfeld—twelve, at most fifteen kilometres. I was able to
persuade one of the policemen to part with his bicycle. He must have
been a saint because, as I say, a bicycle was precious, and how could
you trust anyone in early April 1945, at the worst moment of
Germany's chaos? Well, he gave it to me (I don't know his name,
otherwise I'd put up a monument to him, like farmer Peters), and I
rode off into the night, as muddled and impulsive as I'd always
accused Alois of being, got to Marienfeld, saw Annemarie, took my
father a couple of cigars—and more discussion: should I go or stay?
Up into the loft with the 'pastors', or back to Allner, which was
tantamount to going back to the front? By now the poor people had
even had someone else 'billeted' on them in the 'temporary
accommodation'. My father had common sense and advised me to
take to the loft, but I could see the policeman's decent, honest face in
front of me. I'd promised to take the bicycle back to him, and so I set
off back to Allner, down side-roads in the dark night. Later on I
heard that the entire company of policemen and their bicycles had
been wiped out.

We, my unit, moved on, through the Bröl valley towards
Waldbröl: an utter rabble, dragging this way and that. Once, I recall,
we reached the edge of a village and saw white flags flying.
Somehow—I can't remember exactly how it happened—the whole
show broke up there and I set off home, until in the middle of
nowhere I ran into this lieutenant who literally held a pistol to my
head and forced me to join his own 'unit', which bore the insane name
'Garrison Brüchermühle': the tiny hamlet that gave its name to the
last German army unit I belonged to must be situated somewhere

between Denklingen and Waldbröl. I thought it best not to resist this madman, and so finally, after a few unpleasant days I came to be an American prisoner at Brüchermühle. Finally? I was surprised: we had begged, implored and cursed the Americans to come; it meant liberation, to be *finally rid of the Germans*—and yet, this was the surprise: I found it difficult to raise my hands. I found it difficult, but of course I did.

The rest doesn't matter so much now. A chilly night in an improvised camp in Rosbach on the Sieg, the Final Victory whisperings still going on. The thrilling drive through the Westerwald to Linz, across the Rhine to Sinzig, Namur, Attichy—a huge camp. Of course, it wasn't a rest home. I had feared the worst, but it really wasn't half so bad in the end. It had always been the Germans who were the real danger, holding trials and doing away with 'defeatists' in the latrines—and all this in April 1945, while the Soviet and American armies were fraternizing on the Elbe. No, no complaints. The important thing is that I was able—don't ask me how, it's a mini-thriller in itself—to refuse the inducement of better rations, and not to do physical work. I thought to myself, If you do physical work now (it was absurd 'work'), then you'll end up doing it for years, maybe decades into the future. Rather a few more months of hunger, I thought, than years of being a labourer somewhere. Perhaps that was the first occasion when I acted with 'historical awareness'. Still later, when the camp—200,000 men apparently— was broken up and handed over (sold) to the French, I was able, after a detailed test of suitability for work, to get categorized as 'unable to do the work for which he is qualified'. This was astonishing, as my occupation was 'student'. At this point, with about sixty out of 200,000 of us 'unable to work', the Americans showed their sometimes surprising common sense: we were split off from the others, fed separately, almost well, and even got our own medics who gave us washing things, until we were moved on, this time to a British camp near Waterloo. The British were very different, less obsessed with hygiene than the Americans, but there was proper food and lots of tea with milk and sugar, which the Germans despised. To begin with, I wasn't a tea-drinker either, but I soon became one, acquired a taste for that incomparable English tea, and kept what was left over of it in a one-litre Belgian beer bottle that became my most precious possession.

One last bicycle still has to be mentioned. It belonged to Hilde Merl in Siegburg, and she lent it to me the day I was released from British captivity by the Belgians. I reached Siegburg one day in October '45, too late to reach Nesshoven by curfew where Annemarie now had a room. I cycled as fast as I could up the road I had ridden down six months earlier with the bag of sugar, and got there before curfew, sweating and worn out. No one had expected me back so soon. There was great joy and surprise, but a few days later there was also sorrow: we had to bury your little brother Christoph.

I was there for six months, and you'll wonder what I did. I don't remember, but it wasn't much. There were too many people in the kitchen anyway, so sometimes when my papers were in order I would go looking for food. I waited for the Americans to come. I read. I read Kierkegaard's *Diaries*. Once, on Tilla's bicycle and with impeccable papers, I went into Cologne to rescue a few more 'valuables' and to buy some cigarettes. In some places in this report, you'll detect my familiar traits of cynicism and frivolity. Maybe they'll make you laugh. Go on and laugh: we survived, and of course we weren't gloomy all the time either. (Ask your mother about it, ask your aunt Maria and your cousin Marie-Theres, your cousins Franz and Gilbert, how *they* remember it all; differently from me, and differently also from the way Alois would have told it.)

Too many things come back to me, and I must stop, otherwise I'll write a whole novel, and start 'telling stories' and get into uncertain territory when I meant to stay on the 'solid ground' of 'true experience'. Perhaps some things will be clearer for you now: why we're quite incapable of throwing bread away, why we hate pouring away tea or coffee, why I take what's left over of those precious commodities with me into my study after breakfast, and why I can't stop smoking cigarettes. And you should know that on my wanderings from 1939 to 1945, no Circe was able to lure me onto her rocks. The squalid sexuality in and around stations and trains at that time never held any attraction for me. Penelope was at once herself *and* Circe. You should also know that in the American camp were men with both legs amputated at the thigh who had been captured fighting with grenade-launchers: last ditch desperadoes. And that when a train full of British soldiers on their way home stopped next to ours at a station on the Lower Rhine, they passed us their half-smoked cigarettes.

Maybe now you'll understand why characters like Filbinger and Kiesinger—who smoothly, smirkingly survived everything, in untroubled bourgeois complacency—infuriated us most of all. And you should know that Adenauer's celebrated move to release POWs concerned mainly the senior officers, the ones who thought in terms of 'lost victories' rather than 'defeat' or 'liberation', and who were useful in the rebuilding of the German army (now called the *Bundeswehr*) and who were a bigger drain on pension-money than some invalid or shot-up soldiers, because they lived longer.* Perhaps you'll understand better why our many trips abroad always had about them an element of running away, running away from types like Filbinger, who couldn't remember having participated in the execution of a man he'd sentenced to death. (Just imagine: he couldn't remember!) How many Germans there are who can't remember: not all of them judges, but all potential executioners, into whose hands I might have fallen. And what about 'German mothers', a much-lauded group—how many of them sent their fourteen- and seventeen-year-olds to their deaths, sacrificed to Hitler, without resistance, without undue grief, some even with enthusiasm? There was one called Ferdinand Schörner, one of Hitler's personal favourites—in March 1945, he promoted Schörner to Field-Marshal General—whose courts-martial were as notorious as Herr Model's; his soubriquet was 'Bloodhound', his 'disciplinary measures' the terror of his troops. He died not in 1945, like his beloved Führer, but

---

*Hans Filbinger, former Prime Minister of Baden-Württemburg, was discovered to have passed death sentences on sailors in the German Navy. Kurt-Georg Kiesinger, another prominent politician, worked in Nazi Foreign Ministry. Konrad Adenauer, Chancellor of West Germany after World War Two, secured the release of POWs still held in the Soviet Union ten years after the war.

Heinrich Böll

in the Year of German Grace 1973, in Munich. I think he was one of those whose release Adenauer secured.

Around sixteen years ago, dear Vincent, dear René, one of Rudolf Hess's sons wrote to me to ask if I would join the long list of those pleading for the release of Herr Hess. I couldn't do it. *My conscience wouldn't let me*; and even now that Hess is ninety, *my conscience doesn't let me.* As late as 1946, in Nuremberg, this peculiar dove of peace was insisting that Hitler was the greatest son that Germany's millennial history had brought forth. And I can't get that wheedling, fanatical racist's voice I heard on the radio as a sixteen-year-old out of my head, and I can't forget that face I saw in the cinema news: the piercing eyes that asked for sacrifice and obtained sacrifice. No, I wouldn't protest *against* his release, but I can't plead *for* it.

And you should know that I refused to participate in the clearing-up in Cologne, as was the declared duty of every returning man. I didn't lift a single *public* stone, but quietly and alone, knocking the plaster from every stone, I cleared the debris in my father's workshop on the Vondelstraße, which Alois was running then. Not one *public* stone.

I just want to remind you again of the four bicycles in this report.
One: Tilla's bicycle, on which I rode to Cologne around February 1945 to see to our flat in the Neuenhöfer Allee, to rescue jewellery and Annemarie's family's solid silver (which today, 1984, is still in its red case, unopened and unused), and to buy cigarettes on the black market.

Two: the bicycle of Anton Fog's daughter, on which, illegally and at night, I brought twenty-five pounds of sugar from Birk to Marienfeld on 25 March 1945.

Three: the bicycle of the unknown police officer from Cologne, on which I rode from Allner to Marienfeld, again at night, in April.

Four: Hilde Merl's bicycle, on which I rode from Siegburg to Nesshoven in October 1945 to see Annemarie before the curfew fell.

A few days ago, around mid-July, as I was finishing this report, SS General Karl Wolff died at the age of eighty-four. He was quite a spectacular Nazi, who in 1937 was already a

General in the SS, Himmler's personal chief-of-staff, but who by late February 1945 was nevertheless convinced that the war was lost (you may laugh: by late February!). After negotiations through intermediaries with Alan Dulles, the German army in Italy capitulated. Well, well. Later Wolff was sentenced to four years in a labour camp, of which he served *one week*. Accused subsequently of complicity in the deaths of 300,000 Jews, he denied all knowledge of the death camps (and this was Himmler's personal chief-of-staff!). He got fifteen years in prison, and was released after seven. Remission of sentence. And lived on another thirteen years afterwards! That isn't a joke, dear René, dear Vincent, that's what *happened.* That's German history.

Your Father

Translated from the German by
Michael Hofmann

Outstanding writing by women

The Secret Self
SHORT STORIES BY WOMEN
Selected and introduced by HERMIONE LEE

A richly enjoyable collection of 32 stories, all written this century, offering intriguing perspectives on the very different lives of women from Ahdaf Soueif's child-bride in patriarchal Egypt to Doris Lessing's middle-aged wife in colonial Africa, from the wise mother of Alice Walker's American South to Angela Carter's wild wolf-child.
£3.95

Let the Lion Eat Straw
ELLEASE SOUTHERLAND
Poor, black and illegitimate, Abeba Williams' life promised to be a hard one despite an exceptional musical talent. Raped by her uncle, her hardships multiply but she never loses her capacity for joy or her determination to fight for a decent life.

'This book is a miracle . . . As a debut it is astounding; as an achievement it is even more so.' Bernard Levin, *Sunday Times*
£2.95

in EVERYMAN FICTION EF. PAPERBACKS

175

KAZUO ISHIGURO
OCTOBER, 1948

Kazuo Ishiguro

I have never at any point in my life been very aware of my own social standing, and even now I am often surprised afresh when some event, or something someone may say, reminds me of the rather high esteem in which I am held. Just the other evening for instance I was down in our old pleasure district, drinking at Mrs Kawakami's place, where—as happens increasingly these days—Shintaro and I had found ourselves the only customers. We were as usual sitting up at the bar on our high stools, exchanging remarks with Mrs Kawakami, and as the hours had gone by, and no one else had come in, our exchanges had grown more intimate. At one point, Mrs Kawakami was talking about some relative of hers, complaining that the young man had been unable to find a job worthy of his abilities, when Shintaro suddenly exclaimed:

'You must send him to Sensei here, Obasan! A good word from Sensei in the right place, your relative will soon find a good post.'

'What are you saying, Shintaro?' I protested. 'I'm retired now. I have no connections these days.'

'A recommendation from a man of Sensei's standing will command respect from anyone,' Shintaro had persisted. 'Send the young man to Sensei, Obasan.'

I was at first a little taken aback by the conviction of Shintaro's assertions. But then I realized that he was remembering yet again that small deed I had performed for his younger brother all those years ago.

It must have been in 1935 or 1936, a very routine matter as I recall—a letter of recommendation to an acquaintance in the State Department, some such thing. I would have given the matter little further thought, but then one afternoon while I was relaxing at home, my wife announced there were visitors for me at the entryway.

'Please show them in,' I had said.

'But they insist they won't bother you by coming in.'

I went out to the entryway, and standing there were Shintaro and his younger brother—then no more than a youth. As soon as they saw me, they began bowing and giggling.

'Please step up,' I said, but they continued simply to bow and giggle. 'Shintaro, please. Step up to the tatami.'

'No, Sensei,' Shintaro said, all the time smiling and bowing. 'It

178

is the height of impertinence for us to come to your house like this.
The height of impertinence. But we could not remain at home any
longer without thanking you.'

'Come on inside. I believe Setsuko was just making some tea.'

'No, Sensei, it is the height of impertinence. Really.' Then
turning to his brother, Shintaro whispered quickly: 'Yoshio!
Yoshio!'

For the first time, the young man stopped bowing and looked up
at me nervously. Then he said: 'I will be grateful to you for the
remainder of my life. I will exert every particle of my being to be
worthy of your recommendation. I assure you, I will not let you
down. I will work hard, and strive to satisfy my superiors. And
however much I may be promoted in the future, I will never forget
the man who enabled me to start on my career.'

'Really, it was nothing. It's no more than you deserve.'

This brought frantic protests from both of them, then Shintaro
said to his brother: 'Yoshio, we have imposed enough on Sensei as
it is. But before we leave, take a good look again at the man who has
helped you. We are greatly privileged to have a benefactor of such
influence and generosity.'

'Indeed,' the youth muttered, and gazed up at me.

'Please, Shintaro, this is embarrassing. Please come in and we'll
celebrate with some sake.'

'No, Sensei, we must leave you now. It was the greatest
impertinence to come here like this and disturb your afternoon. But
we could not delay thanking you for one moment longer.'

This visit—I must admit it—left me with a certain feeling of
achievement. It was one of those moments, in the midst of a
busy career allowing little chance for stopping and taking
stock, which illuminate suddenly just how far one has come. For
true enough, I had almost unthinkingly started a young man on a
good career. A few years earlier, such a thing would have been
inconceivable and yet I had brought myself to such a position almost
without realizing it.

'Many things have changed since the old days, Shintaro,' I
pointed out the other night down at Mrs Kawakami's. 'I'm retired
now, I don't have so many connections.'

179

But then for all I know, Shintaro may not be so wrong in his assumptions. It may be that if I chose to put it to the test, I would again be surprised by the extent of my influence. As I say, I have never had a keen awareness of my own standing.

In any case, even if Shintaro may at times display *naïveté* about certain things, this is nothing to be disparaged, it being no easy thing now to come across someone so untainted by the cynicism and bitterness of our day. There is something reassuring about going into Mrs Kawakami's and finding Shintaro sitting up there at the bar, just as one may have found him on any evening for the past seventeen or so years, absent-mindedly turning his cap round and round on the counter in that old way of his. It really is as though nothing has changed for Shintaro. He will greet me very politely, as though he were still my pupil, and throughout the evening, however drunk he may get, he will continue to address me as 'Sensei' and maintain his most respectful manner towards me. Sometimes he will even ask me questions relating to technique or style with all the eagerness of a young apprentice—though the truth is, of course, Shintaro has long ceased to be concerned with any real art. For some years now, he has devoted his time to his book illustrations, and his present speciality, I gather, is fire-engines. He will work day after day up in that attic room of his, sketching out fire-engine after fire-engine. But I suppose in the evenings, after a few drinks, Shintaro likes to believe he is still the idealistic young artist I first took under my supervision.

This childlike aspect of Shintaro has frequently been a source of entertainment for Mrs Kawakami, who has a somewhat wicked side to her. One night recently, for instance, during a rainstorm, Shintaro had come running into the little bar and begun squeezing his cap out over the doormat.

'Really, Shintaro-san!' Mrs Kawakami had shouted at him. 'What terrible manners!'

At this, Shintaro had looked up in great distress, as though indeed he had committed an outrageous offence. He had then begun to apologize profusely, thus leading Mrs Kawakami on further.

'I've never seen such manners, Shintaro-san. You seem to have no respect for me at all.'

'Now stop this, Obasan,' I had appealed to her after a while. 'That's enough, tell him you're just joking.'

'Joking? I'm hardly joking. The height of bad manners.'

And so it had gone on, until Shintaro had become quite pitiful to watch. But then again, on other occasions, Shintaro will be convinced he is being teased when in fact he is being spoken to quite earnestly. There was the time he had put Mrs Kawakami in difficulties by declaring cheerfully of a general who had just been executed as a war criminal: 'I've always admired that man since I was a boy. I wonder what he's up to now. Retired, no doubt.'

Some new customers had been present that night and had looked at him disapprovingly. When Mrs Kawakami, concerned for her trade, had gone to him and told him quietly of the general's fate, Shintaro had burst out laughing.

'Really, Obasan,' he had said loudly. 'Some of your jokes are quite extreme.'

Shintaro's ignorance of such matters is often remarkable, but as I say, it is not something to disparage. One should be thankful there are still those uncontaminated by the current cynicism. In fact, it is probably this very quality of Shintaro's—this sense that he has remained somehow unscathed by things—which has led me to enjoy his company more and more over these recent years.

As for Mrs Kawakami, although she will do her best not to allow the current mood to affect her, there is no denying she has been greatly aged by the war years. Before the war, she may still have passed for a 'young woman', but since then something inside her seems to have broken and sagged. And when one remembers those she has lost in the war, it is hardly any wonder. Business too has become increasingly difficult for her; certainly, it must be hard for her to believe this is the same district where she first opened her little place those sixteen or seventeen years ago. For nothing really remains of our old pleasure district now; almost all her old competitors have closed up and left, and Mrs Kawakami must more than once have considered doing likewise.

But when her place first appeared, it was squeezed in amidst so many other bars and eating houses, I remember some people doubting if it could survive long. Indeed, you could hardly walk down those little streets without brushing against the numerous cloth banners pressing at you from all sides, leaning out at you from their shop fronts, each declaring the attractions of their establishment in boisterous lettering. But in those days, there was enough custom in the district to keep any number of such establishments thriving. On the warmer evenings particularly, the area would fill with people strolling unhurriedly from bar to bar, or just standing talking in the middle of the street. Cars had long ceased to venture through, and even a bicycle could only be pushed with difficulty past those throngs of uncaring pedestrians.

I say 'our pleasure district', but I suppose it was really nothing more than somewhere to drink, eat and talk. You would have had to go into the city centre for the real pleasure quarters—for the geisha houses and theatres. For myself though, our own district was always preferable. It drew a lively but respectable crowd, many of them people like us—artists and writers lured by the promise of noisy conversations continuing into the night. The establishment my own group frequented was called Migi-Hidari, and stood at a point where three side streets intersected to form a paved precinct. The Migi-Hidari, unlike any of its neighbours, was a large sprawling place with an upper floor and plenty of hostesses both in Western and traditional dress. I had played my own small part in the Migi-Hidari's coming to so dwarf its competitors, and in recognition of this, our group had been provided with a table in one corner for our sole use. Those who drank with me there were, in effect, the élite of my school: Kuroda, Murasaki, Tanaka—brilliant young men, already with growing reputations. They all of them relished conversation, and I remember many passionate arguments taking place around that table.

Shintaro, I should say, was never one of that select group. I would not myself have objected to his joining us, but there existed a strong sense of hierarchy amongst my pupils, and Shintaro was certainly not regarded as one of the first rank. In fact, I can recall one night, shortly after Shintaro and his brother had paid that visit to my house, my discussing that episode around our table. I remember the likes of Kuroda laughing at how grateful the brothers had been over 'a mere white-collar appointment;' but then they all listened solemnly as I recounted my view on how influence and status can creep up on someone who works busily, not pursuing these ends in themselves, but for the satisfaction of performing his tasks to the best of his ability. At this point, one of them—no doubt it was Kuroda—leaned forward and said:

'I have suspected for some time that Sensei was unaware of the high regard in which he is held by people in this city. Indeed, as the instance he has just related amply illustrates, his reputation has now spread beyond the world of art, to all walks of life. But how typical of Sensei's modest nature that he is unaware of this. How typical that he himself should be the most surprised by the esteem accorded to him. But to all of us here it comes as no surprise. In fact, it may be said that respected enormously as he is by the public at large, it is we here at this table who alone know the extent to which that respect still falls short. But I personally have no doubt. His reputation will become all the greater, and in years to come, our proudest honour will be to tell others that we were once the pupils of Masuji Ono.'

Now there was nothing remarkable in all this; it had become something of a habit that at some point in the evening, when we had all drunk a little, my protégés would take to making speeches of a loyal nature to me. And Kuroda in particular, being looked on as a sort of spokesman for them, gave a fair proportion of these. Of course, I usually ignored them, but on this particular occasion, as when Shintaro and his brother had stood bowing and giggling in my entryway, I experienced a warm glow of satisfaction.

But then it would not be accurate to suggest I only socialized with the best of my pupils. Indeed, the first time I ever stepped into Mrs Kawakami's, I believe I did so because I wished to spend the evening talking something over with Shintaro. Today, when I try to recall that evening, I find my memory of it merging with the sounds and images from all those other evenings; the lanterns hung above doorways, the laughter of people congregated outside the Migi-Hidari, the smell of deep-fried food, a bar hostess persuading someone to return to his wife—and echoing from every direction, the clicking of numerous wooden sandals on the concrete. I remember it being a warm summer's night, and not finding Shintaro in his usual haunts, I wandered around those tiny bars for some time. For all the competition there must have existed between those establishments, a neighbourly spirit reigned, and it was quite natural that on asking after Shintaro at one such bar that night, I should be advised by the hostess, without a trace of resentment, to try for him at the 'new place'.

No doubt Mrs Kawakami could point out numerous changes—her little 'improvements'—that she has made over the years. But my impression is that her little place looked much the same that first night as it does today. On entering, one tends to be struck by the contrast between the bar counter, lit up by warm, low-hung lights, and the rest of the room, which is in shadow. Most of her customers prefer to sit up at the bar within that pool of light, and this gives a cosy, intimate feel to the place. I remember looking around me with approval that first night, and today, for all the changes which have transformed the world around it, Mrs Kawakami's remains as pleasing as ever.

But little else has remained unchanged. Coming out of Mrs Kawakami's now, you could stand at her doorway and believe you have just been drinking at some outpost of civilization. All around, there is nothing but a desert of demolished rubble. Only the backs of several buildings far in the distance will remind you that you are not so far from the city centre. 'War damage,' Mrs Kawakami calls it. But I remember walking around the district shortly after the surrender and many of those buildings were still standing. The Migi-Hidari was still there, the windows all blown out, part of the roof fallen in. And I remember wondering to myself as I walked past those shattered buildings if they would ever again come back to life. Then I came by one morning and the bulldozers had pulled down everything.

So now that side of the street is nothing but rubble. No doubt the authorities have their plans, but it has been that way for three years. The rain collects in small puddles and grows stagnant amidst the broken brick. As a consequence, Mrs Kawakami has been obliged to put up mosquito wiring on her windows—not an effect she thinks will attract customers.

The buildings on Mrs Kawakami's own side of the street have remained standing, but many are unoccupied; the properties on either side of her, for instance, have been vacant for some time, a situation which makes her uncomfortable. If she became suddenly rich, she often tells us, she would buy up those properties and expand. In the meantime, she waits for someone to move into them; she would not mind if they became bars just like hers, anything provided she no longer had to live in the midst of a graveyard.

If you were to come out of Mrs Kawakami's as the darkness was setting in, you may feel compelled to pause a moment and gaze at that wasted expanse before you. You may still be able to make out through the gloom those heaps of broken brick and timber, and perhaps here and there, pieces of piping protruding from the ground like weeds. Then as you walked on past more heaps of rubble, numerous small puddles would gleam a moment as they caught the lamplight.

And if on reaching the foot of the hill which climbs up to my house, you pause at the Bridge of Hesitation and look back towards the remains of our old pleasure district, if the sun has not yet set completely, you may see the line of old telegraph poles—still without wires to connect them—disappearing into the gloom down the route you have just come. And you may be able to make out the dark clusters of birds perched uncomfortably on the tops of the poles, as though awaiting the wires along which they once lined the sky.

One evening not so long ago, I was standing on that little wooden bridge and saw away in the distance two columns of smoke rising from the rubble. Perhaps it was government workers continuing some interminably slow programme; or perhaps children indulging in some delinquent game. But the sight of those columns against the sky put me in a melancholy mood. They were like pyres at some abandoned funeral. A graveyard, Mrs Kawakami says, and when one remembers all those people who once frequented the area, one cannot help see it that way.

Are you one of us?

If you want to do work you adore and keep doing it long after others retire; if you threw out the old conventions on sex, sex roles and love, and are still creating your new ones; and if you want a politics that relies less on bureaucracy and more on people—then, chances are, you're one of us.

Why not find out? Take a look at the next issue of MOTHER JONES—for free.

MOTHER JONES is irreverent, bright, and bold. Like you, we haven't given up our dreams born in the 60's. But we know it takes innovative thinking and passionate commitment to translate them during the 80's.

Like you, we're on the prowl for new ideas. We find them, and we print them.

MOTHER JONES is your early warning system. We told you about Bendectin and birth defects, years before the drug companies took it off the market . . . why there are steroids in your steak but not in Ronald Reagan's . . . the latest DES tragedy, DES sons . . . how laboratories that test your products have falsified or covered up data for years . . . the true story behind the Grenada invasion.

MOTHER JONES brings you people. After Tom Brokaw gave us a personal interview, he got into hot water with his boss at NBC . . . we profiled Geraldine Ferraro before she was nominated for Vice-President . . . In a MOTHER JONES interview Benigno Aquino assessed his chances of being assassinated just before he left on his fatal plane trip to the Philippines . . . Plus we've brought you West German peace activist Petra Kelly, science fiction writer Ursula LeGuin, Atlanta Mayor Andrew Young, the lost love letter of Emma Goldman, an interview with Yoko Ono.

"Perhaps a glass of water to wash down that incredible bunch of lies."

MOTHER JONES is on the cutting edge. We printed excerpts from The Color Purple, by Alice Walker, long before the book won a Pulitzer Prize . . . we've brought you Maxine Hong Kingston, Studs Terkel, Alice Adams, Kurt Vonnegut, Grace Paley, Edmund White. MOTHER JONES' award-winning, gutsy graphics have included works by Brad Holland, Sue Coe, Marshall Arisman, and international photographers like Sue Meisalas.

Bring MOTHER JONES into your life—the magazine that's as imaginative, as unpredictable and as bright as its readers.

ALICE MUNRO
A QUEER STREAK
PART ONE:
ANONYMOUS
LETTERS

Alice Munro

V iolet's mother—Aunt Ivie—had three little boys, three baby
boys, and she lost them. Then she had the three girls. Perhaps
to console herself for the bad luck she had already suffered,
on a rocky farm in a back corner of Turnberry Township—or
perhaps to make up, ahead of time, for a lack of motherly
feelings—she gave the girls the fanciest names she could think of:
Opal Violet, Dawn Rose, and Bonnie Hope. She may not have
thought of those names as anything but temporary decorations.
Violet wondered—did her mother ever picture her daughters having
to drag such names around sixty or seventy years later, when they
were heavy, faded women? She may have thought her girls were going
to die, too.

Lost meant that somebody died. She lost them, meant, they died.
Violet knew that. Nevertheless she imagined Aunt Ivie her mother
wandering into a swampy field, which was the waste ground on the
far side of the barn, a twilight place full of coarse grass and alder
bushes. There Aunt Ivie, in the mournful light, mislaid her baby
children. Violet would slip down the edge of the barnyard to the waste
ground, then cautiously enter it. She would stand hidden by the red-
stemmed alder and nameless thorn-bushes (it always seemed to be
some damp desolate time of year when she did this—late fall or early
spring) and she would let the cold water cover the toes of her rubber
boots. She would contemplate getting lost. Lost babies. The water
welled up through the tough grass. Further in, there were ponds and
sink-holes. She had been warned. She shuffled on, watching the water
creep up on her boots. She never told them. They never knew where
she went. Lost.

The parlour was the other place that she could sneak to by
herself. The window-blinds were down to the sills, the air had a
weight and thickness, as if it was cut in a block that exactly filled the
room. In certain fixed places could be found the flushed, spiky shell
with the roar of the sea caught inside it, the figure of the little kilted
Scotsman holding a glass of amber liquid which would tilt but never
spill, a fan made entirely out of glossy black feathers, a plate which
was a souvenir of Niagara Falls and showed the same picture as the
Shredded Wheat box. And a framed picture on the wall which
affected Violet so intensely that she couldn't look at it when she first
came into the room. She had to work her way around to it, keeping it

always in a corner of her vision. It showed a king with his crown on, and three tall, queenly-looking ladies in dark dresses. The king was asleep, or dead. They were all on the shore of the sea, with the boat waiting, and there was something coming out of this picture into the room—a smooth, dark wave of unbearable sweetness and sorrow. That seemed a promise to Violet, it was connected with her future, her own life, in a way she couldn't explain or think about. She couldn't even look at the picture if there was anybody else in the room. But in that room there seldom was anybody else.

Violet's father was called King Billy, King Billy Thoms, though William was not in his name. There was also a horse called King Billy, a dapple-grey horse that was their driver, hitched to the cutter in winter-time and the buggy in summer. (They didn't own a car until Violet was grown up, and bought one, in the 1930s.)

The name King Billy was usually connected with the Parade, the Orange Walk, on the Twelfth of July. A man chosen to be King Billy, wearing a cardboard crown and a raggedy purple cloak, would ride at the head of the Parade. He was supposed to ride a white horse, but sometimes a dapple-grey was the best that could be found. Violet never knew if the horse, or her father, or both, had figured in this parade, either separately or together. Confusion abounded, in the world as she knew it, and adults as often as not resented being asked to set it straight.

But she did know that her father, at one time in his life, had worked on a train up north, that ran through the wild bush where bears were. Loggers would ride this train on the weekends, coming out of the bush to get drunk, and if they got too rambunctious on the way back, King Billy would stop the train and kick them off. No matter where the train was at the time. In the middle of the wilderness—no matter. He kicked them off. He was a fighter. He had got that job because he was a fighter.

Another story, from further back in his life. He had gone to a dance, when he was a young man, up near Hespeler where he came from. Some other young fellows who were there had insulted him, and he had to take their insults, because he did not know a thing about fighting. But after that he got some lessons, from an old prize-fighter, a real one, who was living in Owen Sound. Another night, another dance—the same thing as before. The same kind of insults. Except that this time King Billy lit into them and cleaned up on them, one by one.

Lit into them and cleaned up on them, one by one.

No more insults of that kind, anywhere up in that country.

(The insults had to do with being a bastard. He didn't say so, but Violet figured it out from her mother's muttering. 'Your daddy didn't have *no people*,' Aunt Ivie said, in her dark, puzzled, grudging way. 'He never did. He just didn't have *no people* at all.')

Violet was five years older than her sister Dawn Rose, and six years older than Bonnie Hope. Those two were thick as thieves, but mainly docile. They were redheads, like King Billy. Dawn Rose was chubby and ruddy and broad-faced. Bonnie Hope was small-boned and big-headed, with hair that grew at first in wisps and patches, so that she looked like a wobbly young bird. Violet was dark-haired and tall for her age, and strong like her mother. She had a long handsome face and dark blue eyes that looked at first to be black. Later on, when Trevor Auston was in love with her, he had some nice things to say about the colour of her eyes matching up with her name.

Violet's mother as well her father had an odd name, being called Aunt Ivie most of the time even by her own children. That was because she was the youngest of a large family. She had plenty of people, though they didn't often come to see her. All the old or precious things in the house—those things in the parlour, and a certain hump-backed trunk, and some tarnished spoons—came from Aunt Ivie's family, who had a farm on the shores of Arran Lake. Aunt Ivie had stayed there so long, unmarried, that her nieces' and nephews' name for her became everybody's name, and her daughters too chose it over Mama.

Nobody ever thought she would marry. She said so herself. And when she did marry the little bold red-headed man who looked so odd beside her, people said she didn't seem to stand the change too well. She lost those first boy babies, and she didn't take too happily to the responsibility of running a house. She liked to work outside, hoeing in the garden or splitting wood, as she had always done at home. She milked the cows and cleaned out the stable and took care of the hens. It was Violet, getting older, who took over the housework.

By the time she was ten years old, Violet had become quite

house-proud and dictatorial, in a sporadic way. She would spend all Saturday scouring and waxing, then yell and throw herself on the couch and grind her teeth in a rage when people tracked in mud and manure on their shoes.

'That girl will grow up, and she won't have nothing but stumps in her mouth, and serve her right for her temper,' Aunt Ivie said—as if she was talking about some neighbour child.

Aunt Ivie was usually the one who had tracked in the mud and ruined the floor.

Another Saturday there would be baking, and making up recipes. One whole summer Violet was trying to invent a drink like Coca-Cola, which would be famous and delicious and make them a fortune. She tried out on herself and her sisters all sorts of combinations of berry juice, vanilla, bottled fruit essences and spices. Sometimes they were all off in the long grass in the orchard, throwing up. The younger girls usually did what Violet told them to, and believed what she said. One day the butcher's man arrived to buy the young calves, and Violet told Dawn Rose and Bonnie Hope that sometimes the butcher's man was not satisfied with the meat on the calves, and went after juicy little children, to make them into steaks and chops and sausages. She told this out of the blue and for her own amusement, as far as she could recall later on when she told these things as stories. The little girls tried to hide themselves in the hay-mow and King Billy heard their commotion and chased them out. They told what Violet had said and King Billy said they should be smacked for swallowing such nonsense. He said he was a man with a mule for a wife and a hooligan daughter running his house. Dawn Rose and Bonnie Hope ran to confront Violet.

'Liar, liar! Butchers don't chop up children! You told a lie, liar!'

Violet, who was cleaning out the stove at the time, said nothing. She picked up a pan of ashes—warm but fortunately not hot—and dumped it on their heads. They knew enough not to tell a second time. They ran outside and rolled in the grass and shook themselves like dogs,trying to get the ashes out of their hair and ears and eyes and underwear. Down in a corner of the orchard they started their own playhouse, with pulled grass heaped up for seats and bits of broken china for dishes. They vowed not to tell Violet about it.

But they couldn't keep away from her. She put their hair up in rags to curl it, she dressed them in costumes made from old curtains, she painted their faces, using concoctions of berry juice and flour and stove polish. She found out about the playhouse and had ideas for furnishing it that were superior to theirs. Even on the days when she had no time for them at all, they had to watch what she was doing. She was painting a design of red roses on the black and threadbare kitchen linoleum. She was cutting a scalloped edge on all the old green window-blinds, for elegance.

It did seem as if ordinary family life had been turned upside-down at their place. At other farms it would usually be the children you would see first, as you came up the lane—children playing, or doing some chore. The mother would be hidden in the house. Here, it was Aunt Ivie you would see, pulling up the potatoes or just prowling around the yard or the chicken-run, wearing rubber boots and a man's felt hat and a dingy assortment of sweaters, skirt, droopy slip and apron, and wrinkled, spattered stockings. It was Violet who ruled in the house, Violet who decided when and if to pass out the pieces of bread and butter and corn syrup. It was as if King Billy and Aunt Ivie had not quite understood how to go about making an ordinary life, even if they had meant to.

But the family got along. They milked the cows and sold the milk to the cheese factory and raised the calves for the butcher and cut the hay. They were members of the Anglican Church, though they didn't often attend, owing to the problems of getting Aunt Ivie cleaned up. They did go sometimes to the card parties in the schoolhouse. Aunt Ivie could play cards, and she would remove her apron and felt hat to do so, though she wouldn't change her boots. King Billy had some reputation as a singer, and after the card-playing people would try to get him to entertain. He liked to sing songs he had learned from the loggers, that were never written down. He sang with his fists clenched and his eyes closed, resolutely.

'On the Opeongo Line I drove a span of bays,
One summer once upon a time for Hooligan and Hayes,
Now that them bays is dead and gone and grim old age is mine,
I'm dreamin' that I'm teamin',' on the Opeongo Line.'

Who was Hooligan? Who was Hayes?
'Some outfit,' said King Billy, expansive from the singing.

Violet went to high school in town, and after that to teachers' college in Stratford. People wondered where King Billy got the money. If he still had some put by from his railway pay, that meant he had got some money from Aunt Ivie's family, when he took her off their hands and bought the farm. King Billy said he didn't grudge Violet an education, he thought being a teacher would suit her. But he didn't have anything extra for her. Before she started at high school she went across the fields to the next farm, carrying a piece of Roman-striped crêpe she had found in the trunk. She wanted to learn to use the sewing-machine, so that she could make herself a dress. And so she did, though the neighbour woman said it was the oddest-looking outfit for a schoolgirl that she ever hoped to see.

Violet came home every weekend when she was at high school, and told her sisters about Latin and basketball, and looked after the house as before. But when she went away to Stratford, she stayed until Christmas. Dawn Rose and Bonnie Hope were big enough by then to take care of the house, but whether they did or not was another matter. Dawn Rose was actually big enough to be starting high school, but she had failed her last year at the local school and was repeating it. She and Bonnie Hope were in the same class.

When Violet did come home, in the Christmas holidays, she had changed a great deal. But she thought it was everything and everybody else that had changed.

She wanted to know if they had always talked this way. What way? With an accent. Weren't they doing it on purpose, to sound funny? Weren't they saying 'youse' on purpose, to sound funny?

She had forgotten where some things were kept, and was astonished to find the frying-pan under the stove. She took a dislike to the dog, Tigger, who was allowed to stay in the house now that he was getting old. She said he smelled, and that the couch-blanket was full of dog-hairs.

She said the parlour smelled mouldy and the walls needed papering.

But it was her sisters themselves who got the full force of her surprise and displeasure. They had grown since the summer. Dawn Rose was a big stout girl now, with loose breasts jiggling inside her dress, and a broad red face whose childish expression of secretiveness had changed to a look that seemed stupid and stubborn. She had developed womanly smells, and she did not wash. Bonnie Hope was still childish in body, but her frizzy red hair was never combed out properly and she was covered with flea-bites that she got from playing with the barn cats.

Violet hardly knew how to go about cleaning these two up. The worst was that they had become rebellious, looked at each other and snickered when she talked to them, avoided her, were mulish and silent. They acted as if they had some idiotic secret.

And so they did, they had a secret, but it did not come out until quite a while later, not until after the events of the next summer, and then indirectly, with Bonnie Hope telling some girls who told another who told another, and mothers getting to hear about it, then a neighbour woman, who finally told Violet.

In the late fall of that year—the year Violet went away to teachers' college—Dawn Rose had begun to menstruate. She was so affronted by this development that she went down to the creek and sat in the cold water, resolved to get the bleeding stopped. She took off her shoes and stockings and underpants and sat there in the shallow, icy water. She washed the blood out of her underpants and wrung them out and put them on wet. She didn't catch cold, she didn't get sick, and she didn't menstruate again all year. The neighbour woman said that such a procedure could have affected her brain. 'Driving all that bad blood back into her system, it could have.'

Violet's only pleasure that Christmas was in talking about her boy-friend, whose name was Trevor Auston. She showed her sisters his picture.

It was cut from a newspaper. He wore his clerical collar.

'He looks like a minister,' said Dawn Rose, snickering.

'He is. That picture's from when he was ordained. Don't you think he's handsome?'

Trevor Auston was handsome. He was a dark-haired young man with narrowed eyes and a perfect nose, a chin flung up in the air and a thin-lipped, confident, even gracious smile.

Bonnie Hope said, 'He must be old, to be a minister.'

'He just got to be a minister,' said Violet. 'He's twenty-six. He isn't an Anglican minister, he's a United Church minister,' she said, as if that made a difference. And to her, it did. Violet had changed churches in Stratford. She said that at the United Church there was a lot more going on. There was a badminton club—both she and Trevor played—and a drama club, as well as skating parties, tobogganing parties, hayrides, socials. It was at a Hallowe'en social in the church basement, bobbing for apples, that Violet and Trevor first met. Or first talked, because Violet of course had noticed him before in church, where he was the assistant minister. He said that he had noticed her, too. And she thought that maybe he had. A group of girls from the teachers' college all went to that church together, partly on Trevor's account, and they played a game, trying to catch his eye. When everybody was standing up singing the hymns they stared at him, and if he looked back they dropped their eyes at once. Waves of giggles would spread along the row. But Violet sang right back at him as if her eyes had just lit on him by accident.

Rise up oh men of God
And gird your armour on—

Locked eyes, during the hymn-singing. The virile hymns of the old Methodists, the scourging psalms of the Presbyterians, had come together in this new United Church. The ministry then, in that church, attracted vigorous young men intent on power, not too unlike the young men who went into politics. A fine voice and a good profile did no harm.

Locked eyes. Kisses at the door of Violet's boarding-house. The cool, nicely shaved, but still slightly bristling and foreign male cheek, the decent but promising smell of talc and shaving-lotion. Soon enough they were slipping into the shadows beside the doorway, pressing together through their winter clothing. They had to have serious talks about self-control, and these talks were in themselves inflammatory. They became more and more convinced that if they were married, they would be having the kind of pleasures that nearly make you faint when you think about them.

Soon after Violet got back from her Christmas holidays, they became engaged.

Then they had other things to think about and look forward to, besides sex. A responsible and important sort of life lay ahead of them. They were asked to dinner as an engaged couple by older ministers and rich and powerful members of the congregation. Violet had made herself one good dress, a cranberry wool serge with box

195

pleats—a great improvement over the Roman-striped crêpe creation.

At those dinners, they had tomato juice to start with. Pitchers of iced water sat on the tables. No one in that church could touch alcoholic beverages. Even their communion wine was grape juice. But there were great roasts of beef or pork, or turkeys, on silver platters, roasted potatoes and onions and slatherings of gravy, then rich cakes and pies and divinely moulded puddings with whipped cream. Eating was not a sin. Card-playing was a sin, except for a specially created Methodist card-game called Lost Heir, dancing was a sin for some, and movie-going was a sin for some, and going to any kind of entertainment, except a concert of sacred music for which one did not pay was a sin for all on Sundays.

This was a change for Violet, after the easy-going Anglicanism of her childhood, and the rules—if there were any rules—at home. She wondered what Trevor would say, if he could see King Billy downing his tot of whisky every morning, before he started out to do the chores. Trevor had spoken of going home with her to meet her family, but she had been able to put him off. They could not go on Sunday because of his church services, and they could not go during the week because of her classes. She tried to push the idea of home out of her mind for now.

The strictness of the United Church might have been something to get used to, but the feeling of purpose and importance there was about it, the briskness and energy, were very agreeable to Violet. It was as if the ministers and top parishioners all had jobs in some thriving and important company. The role of a minister's wife she could see as hard and challenging, but that did not discourage her. She could see herself teaching Sunday school, raising money for missions, leading in prayer, sitting nicely dressed in the front pew listening to Trevor, tirelessly pouring tea out of a silver pot.

She didn't plan to spend the summer at home. She would visit for a week, once her exams were over, then work for the summer in the church office in Stratford. She had applied for a teaching job in Sebringville, close by. She meant to teach for one year, then get married.

The week before exams were due to start, she got a letter from home. It was not from King Billy or Aunt Ivie—they didn't write letters—but from the woman on the next farm, the owner of the sewing-machine. Her name was Annabelle Wrioley and she took some interest in Violet. She had no daughter of her own. She used to think that Violet was a terror, but now she thought she was a go-getter.

Annabelle said she was sorry to bother Violet at this time, but thought she should be told. There was trouble at home. What the trouble was she didn't like to say in a letter. If Violet could see her way to coming home on the train, she could go to town and meet her. She and her husband had a car now.

So Violet came home on the train.

'I have to tell you straight out,' said Annabelle. 'It's your father. He's in danger.'

Violet thought she meant that King Billy was sick, but it wasn't that.

He had been getting strange letters. Terrible letters. They were threats on his life.

What was in those letters, Annabelle said, was disgusting beyond belief.

Out at home, it looked as if all daily life had been suspended. The whole family was frightened. They were afraid to go to the back pasture to get the cows, afraid to go to the far end of the cellar, or to the well or the toilet after dark. King Billy was a man willing even now to get into a fight, but he was unnerved by the idea of an unknown enemy, waiting to pounce. He could not walk from the house to the barn without whirling around to see if there was anybody behind him. When he milked the cows he turned them around in their stalls so that he could be in a corner, where nobody could sneak up on him. Aunt Ivie did the same.

Aunt Ivie went around the house with a stick, beating on cupboard doors and the tops of chests and trunks and saying, 'If you're in there, you better stay in there until you suffocate to death! You murderer!'

The murderer would have to be a midget, Violet said, to be hiding in any of those places.

Dawn Rose and Bonnie Hope were staying home from school, although it was the time of year when they should have been preparing to write the entrance examinations. They were afraid to get undressed at night, and their clothes were all wrinkled and sour-smelling.

Meals were not being cooked. But the neighbours brought food. There seemed to be always some visitor sitting at the kitchen table, a neighbour, or even someone not well-known to the family, who had heard about their trouble and come from a distance. The dishes were being washed in cold water if they were washed at all, and the dog was the only one interested in cleaning up the floor.

King Billy had been sitting up all night to keep watch. Aunt Ivie barricaded herself behind the bedroom door.

Violet asked about the letters. They were brought out, spread for her inspection on the oilcloth of the table, as they had been spread before all the neighbours and visitors.

Here was the letter that had come first, in the regular mail. Then the one that came second, also through the mail. After that the notes were found in different places around the farm.

On top of a cream can in the stable.

Tacked to the barn door.

Wrapped around the handle of the milk pail that King Billy used every day.

Some argument started up as to just which note was found in which place.

'What about the postmark?' Violet cut in. 'Where are the envelopes of the ones that came in the mail?'

They didn't know. They didn't know where the envelopes had got to.

'I want to see where they were posted from,' said Violet.

'Don't make no difference where it was posted from seeing he knows right where to find us,' Aunt Ivie said. 'Anyway he don't post them now, he sneaks up here after dark and leaves them. Sneaks right around here after dark and leaves them, he knows where to find us.'

'What about Tigger?' said Violet. 'Didn't he bark?'

No. But Tigger was getting too old now to be much of a watch-dog. And with all the visitors coming and going he had practically given up barking altogether.

'He likely wouldn't bark if he seen all the hosts of hell coming in at the gate,' King Billy said.

The first note told King Billy that he might as well sell off all his cows. He was a marked man. He would never live to cut the hay. He was as good as dead.

That had sent King Billy to the doctor. He took it that there might be something wrong with him, that could be read in his face. But the doctor thumped him and listened to his heart and shone a light in his eyes and charged him two dollars and told him he was sound.

'What a fool ignoramus you were to go to the doctor,' the next letter said.

You could have saved your two-dollar bill to wipe your dirty old arse. I never told you that you were going to die of any disease. You are going to be killed. That is what is going to happen to you. You aren't safe no matter how good your health is. I can come in your house at night and slit your throat. I can shoot you from behind a tree. I can sneak up from behind and throw a rope around you and strangle you and you will never even see my face, so what do you think of that?

So it wasn't a fortune-teller or somebody who could read the future. It was an enemy, who planned to do the job himself.

I wouldn't mind killing your ugly wife and your stupid kids while I'm at it. You ought to be thrown down the toilet-hole head first. You bow-legged stupid rotten pig. You ought to have your thing cut off with a razor-blade. You are a liar too. All those fights you said you won are a lie. I could stick a knife in you and catch your blood in a bowl and make a blood pudding. I would feed it to the pigs. How would you like a red-hot poker in your eye?

When she finished reading, Violet said, 'The thing to do is to show these to the police.'

She had forgotten that the police did not exist out here in that abstract, official way. There was a policeman, but he was in town, and furthermore King Billy had had a run-in with him last winter. According to King Billy's story a car driven by Lawyer Boot Lomax had skidded into King Billy's cutter at a junction, and Lomax had summoned the policeman.

'Arrest that man for failing to stop at an intersection!' shouted

Boot Lomax (drunk), waving his hand in its big fur-lined glove.

King Billy jumped up on the hard heaped-up snow and readied his fists.

'Ain't no brass buttons going to put the cuffs on me!'

It was all talked out in the end, but just the same it would be bad policy to go to that policeman.

'He's going to have it in for me, no matter. Could be even him is writing them.'

But Aunt Ivie said it was that tramp. She remembered a bad-looking tramp who had come to the door years ago, and when she gave him a piece of bread he didn't say thank-you. He said, 'Haven't you got any baloney?'

King Billy thought more likely it could be a man he had hired once to help with the hay. The man quit after a day and a half because he couldn't stand working in the mow. He said he had nearly choked to death up there on the dust and the hayseeds and he wanted fifty cents extra for the damage to his lungs.

'I'll give you fifty cents!' King Billy yelled at him. He jabbed at the air with a pitchfork. 'Come over here and you'll get your fifty cents!'

Or could it be somebody settling an old score, one of those fellows he had kicked off the train long ago? One of those fellows from further back than that, that he had cleaned up on at the dance?

Aunt Ivie recalled a boy who had thought the world of her when she was young. He had gone out west but might have come back, and just heard that she was married.

'After all this time to come ragin' after you?' King Billy said. 'That's not what I'd call likely!'

'He thought the world of me, just the same.'

Violet was studying the notes. They were printed, in pencil, on cheap lined paper. The pencil strokes were dark, as if the writer kept bearing down hard. There was no rubbing-out or problem with the spelling—for instance of a word like 'ignoramus'. There was an understanding of sentences and capital letters. But how much could that tell you?

The door was bolted at night. The blinds were drawn down to the sills. King Billy laid the shotgun on the table and set a glass of whisky beside it.

Violet dashed the whisky into the slop-pail.

'You don't need that,' she said.

King Billy raised his hand to her—though he was not a man to strike his wife or his children.

Violet backed off but went on talking.

'You don't need to stay awake. I'll stay awake. I'm fresh and you're tired. Go on, Papa. You need to sleep, not drink.'

After some arguing this was agreed on. King Billy made Violet show him that she knew how to use the shotgun. Then he went off to sleep in the parlour, on the hard couch there. Aunt Ivie had already pushed the dresser against the bedroom door and it would take too much yelling and explaining to get her to push it away.

Violet turned up the lamp and got the ink-bottle from the shelf and started writing to Trevor, to tell him what the trouble was. Without boasting, just telling what was happening, she let him see how she was taking over and calming people down, how she was prepared to defend her family. She even told about throwing out the whisky—explaining that it was due to the strain on his nerves that her father had thought of resorting to whisky in the first place. She did not say that she was afraid. She described the stillness, darkness and loneliness of the early summer night. And to someone who had been living in a town or city, it was very dark and lonely—but not so still, after all. Not if you were listening for something. It was full of faint noises, distant and nearby, of trees lifting and stirring and animals shifting and feeding. Lying outside the door, Tigger made the noise once or twice that meant he was dreaming about barking.

Violet signed her letter 'your loving and longing future wife,' then added, 'with all my heart.' She turned the lamp down and raised a window-blind and sat there, keeping watch. In her letter she had said that the countryside looked lovely now with the buttercups blooming along the roads, but as she sat watching to see if any moving shape detached itself from the bulging shadows in the yard, and listening for soft footsteps, she thought that she really hated the country. Parks were nicer for grass and flowers, and the trees along the streets in Stratford were as fine as you could ask for. Order

201

prevailed there, and some sort of intelligence. Out here was emptiness, rumour and absurdity. What would the people who had asked her to dinner think, if they could see her sitting here with a shotgun in front of her?

Suppose the intruder, the murderer, did come up the steps? She would have to shoot at him. Any wound from a shotgun would be terrible, that close. There would be a court case and her picture would in the papers. HILLBILLY SQUABBLE.

If she didn't hit him it would be worse.

When she heard a thump she was on her feet, with her heart pounding. Instead of picking up the gun she had pushed it away. She had thought the sound was on the porch, but when she heard it again she knew it was upstairs. She knew too that she had been asleep.

It was only her sisters. Bonnie Hope had to go outside to the toilet.

Violet lit the lantern for them.

'You didn't need to both get up,' she said. 'I could have gone with you.'

Bonnie Hope shook her head and pulled on Dawn Rose's hand. 'I want her,' she said.

This fright seemed to be making them into near-imbeciles. They would not look at Violet. Could they even remember the days when they had trusted her, and she had instructed and spoiled them, and tried to make them pretty?

'Why can't you wear your nightgowns?' Violet said sadly, and unbolted the door. She sat by the gun until they came back and went to bed.

She lit the coal-oil stove to boil water for coffee, because she was afraid of falling asleep again.

When she saw the sky getting light, she opened the door. The dog stood up, shivered all over, and went to drink from the old rag-plugged dishpan by the pump. The yard was surrounded by white mist. Between the house and the barn was a rocky hump of land, and the rocks were dark with the dampness of night. What was their farm but a few pockets of shallow soil scattered in among rubbly hills and swamp? What a place to think you could settle in, and live a life, and raise a family.

On the top step was an out-of-place object—a neat, glistening bun of horse-manure. Violet looked for a stick to push it off with—then saw the folded paper underneath.

Don't think your stuck-up slut of a daughter can help you. I see you all the time and I hate her and you. How would you like to get this rammed down your throat?

He must have put it here during the last hour of the night, while she was drinking her coffee at the kitchen table. He could have looked in through the window, and seen her. She ran to wake her sisters to ask if they had seen anything when they went out, and they said no, nothing. They had gone down those steps and back up with the lantern, and there was nothing. He had put it there since.

One thing this told Violet, that she was glad of. Aunt Ivie could have had nothing to do with it. Aunt Ivie had been shut up in her room all night. Not that Violet really thought that her mother was spiteful enough or crazy enough to do such a thing. But she knew what people said. She knew there would be people now, saying they were not too surprised about what was going on here. They would not be blaming Aunt Ivie, they wouldn't go that far. They would just be saying that certain people attract peculiar troubles, that in the vicinity of certain people things are more likely to happen.

Violet worked all day at cleaning up. Her letter to Trevor lay on the dresser. She never got down to the mailbox with it. People dropped in, and it was the same as yesterday—the same talk, the same suspicions and speculations. The only difference was that there was the new note to show.

Annabelle brought them fresh bread. She read the note and said, 'It just makes me sick to my stomach. So close, too. You could've almost heard him breathing, Violet. Your nerves must be about shot.'

'There's not nobody can realize it,' said Aunt Ivie proudly. 'What us up here are going through.'

'Anybody even steps on this place after dark,' King Billy said, 'from now one he's likely to get shot. And that's all I've got to say.'

After they had eaten supper, and milked and turned out the cows, Violet took her letter down to the mailbox for the mailman to pick up in the morning. She set the pennies on top of it for the stamp. She climbed up on the bank behind the mailbox, and sat down.

203

Nobody went by on the road. The days were at their longest now, the sun was just going down. A killdeer went cheeping by with a wing dragging, trying to get her to follow. Its eggs must be somewhere close by. Killdeers laid their eggs practically on the road, right on the gravel, then had to spend their time trying to lure people away.

She was getting as bad as King Billy, thinking she sensed somebody behind her. She tried not to look around, but couldn't stop herself. She jumped up and turned, all at once, and saw a streak of red hair caught by the low sun, behind a juniper bush.

It was Dawn Rose and Bonnie Hope.

'What are you doing there, trying to scare me?' Violet said bitterly. 'Aren't all of us scared enough already? I can see you! What do you think you're doing?'

They came out, and showed her what they had been doing—picking the wild strawberries.

Between the time she first saw the streak of red hair, and the time she saw the red strawberries in their hands, Violet knew.

But she would never get it out of them unless she coaxed and pleaded, and seemed to admire and sympathize. Maybe not even then.

'Can't I have a berry?' she said. 'Are you mad at me? I know your secret.'

'I know,' said Violet. 'I know who wrote those letters. I know it was you. You played a good trick on them, didn't you?'

Bonnie Hope's face started twitching. She clamped her teeth down on her bottom lip. Dawn Rose's face didn't change at all. But Violet saw her fist close on the berries she had picked. Red juice oozed out between Dawn Rose's fingers. Then she seemed to decide that Violet was on her side—or that she didn't care—and she smiled. This smile, or grin, was one that Violet thought she would never forget. It was innocent and evil, like the smile of some trusted person turned, or revealed to be, an enemy, in a dream. It was the smile of chubby little Dawn Rose, her sister, and the grin of a cold, sly, full-grown, slatternly, bad-hearted stranger.

It was all Dawn Rose's doing. That came out. It all came out, now. Dawn Rose had written all the letters and figured out where to put them, and Bonnie Hope had not done anything but stand by and keep her mouth shut. The first two letters were posted from town. The

204

first time was when Dawn Rose had been taken to town to see the doctor for her earache. The second was when they had gone along with Annabelle for the ride. (Annabelle found a reason to go to town almost every day, now that she had the car.) Both times it had been easy to get to the Post Office. Then Dawn Rose had started putting the notes in other places.

Bonnie Hope was giggling faintly. Then she started to hiccup, and to sob.

'Be quiet!' said Violet. 'It wasn't you!'

Dawn Rose did not show any such signs of fright or remorse. She cupped her hands to her face to eat the squashed berries. She didn't even ask if Violet was going to tell. And Violet didn't ask her why she had done it. Violet thought that if she did ask, point-blank, Dawn Rose would probably say that she had done it for a joke. That would be bad enough. But what if she didn't say anything?

After her sisters had gone upstairs that night, Violet told King Billy that he wouldn't have to sit up any more.

'Why's that?'

'Get Mother out here and I'll tell you.'

She was conscious of saying 'Mother' instead of 'Aunt Ivie' or even 'Mama'.

King Billy banged on the bedroom door.

'Move that stuff away and get out here! Violet wants you!'

Violet let up the window-blinds and unbolted and opened the door. She stood the shotgun in the corner.

Her news took a long time to sink in. Both parents sat with their shoulders slumped and their hands on their knees and looks of deprivation and bewilderment on their faces. King Billy seemed to comprehend first.

'What's she got against me?' he said.

That was all he kept saying, and all he ever could say when he thought about it.

'What do you think she could've had against me?'

Aunt Ivie got up, and put on her hat. She felt the night air coming in through the screen-door.

'People get their laugh on us, now,' she said.

'Don't tell them,' said Violet. (As if that would be possible). 'Don't tell them anything. Let it die down.'

Aunt Ivie rocked herself on the couch, in her felt hat and dismal night-gown and rubber boots. 'They'll say we got a queer streak in this family now, for sure.'

Violet told her parents to go to bed, and they went, as if they were the children. Though she hadn't been to bed last night, and her eyes felt as if they had been rubbed with sandpaper, she was sure she could never sleep herself. She got down all the letters that Dawn Rose had written from their place behind the clock, and folded them without looking at them and put them in an envelope. She wrote a note and put it in with them, and addressed the envelope to Trevor.

'We have found out who wrote these,' her note said. 'It was my sister. She is fourteen years old. I don't know if she is crazy, or what. I don't know what I should do. I want you to come and get me and take me away. I hate it here. You can see what her mind is like. I can't sleep here. Please if you love me come and get me and take me away.'

She took this envelope down to the mailbox in the dark, and put in the pennies for the stamp. She had actually forgotten the other letter and the pennies already there. It seemed as if that letter had gone off days before.

She lay down on the hard parlour couch. In the dark she couldn't see that picture that she used to think so powerful, so magical. She tried to remember the feeling it had given her. She fell asleep very soon.

Why did Violet do this, why did she send those ugly letters to Trevor, and put such a note in with them? Did she really want to be rescued, told what to do? Did she want his help with the problem of Dawn Rose, his prayers even? (Since this whole thing began Violet hadn't given a thought to praying, or involving God in any way.)

She would never know why she had done it. She was sleepless and strung-up and her better judgement had deserted her. That was all.

The day after those letters were collected, Violet herself was standing by the mailbox in the morning. She wanted to get a ride into town with the mailman, so that she could catch the one o'clock train to Stratford.

'You folks got some bad business going on?' the mailman said.

'Some bad business with your daddy?'

'That's all right,' said Violet. 'That's all over.'

She knew that mail posted here was delivered in Stratford the next day. There were two deliveries, one in the morning and one in the afternoon. If Trevor was out all day—and he usually was—his letters would be left waiting for him on the hall table of the house where he boarded, the house of a minister's widow. The front door was usually left unlocked. Violet could get to the letters before he did.

T revor was at home. He had a bad summer cold. He was sitting in his study with a white scarf wrapped like a bandage around his throat.

'Don't come near me, I'm full of germs,' he said, as Violet crossed the room towards him.

From his tone of voice, you would have thought she was.

'You forgot to leave the door open,' he said.

The door of the study had to be left open when Violet was in there, so that the minister's widow would not be scandalized.

Spread out on his desk, among his books and sermon notes, were all the smudged, creased, disgraceful letters that Dawn Rose had written.

'Sit down,' said Trevor, in a tired, croaking voice, 'Sit down, Violet.'

So she had to sit in front of his desk like some unhappy parishioner, some poor young woman who had got into trouble.

He said that he was not surprised to see her. He had thought she might show up. Those were his words. *Show up.*

'You were going to tear them up if you got here first,' he said.

Yes. Exactly.

'So I would never have known,' he said.

'I would have told you someday.'

'I doubt it,' said Trevor in his miserable croaking voice. Then he cleared his throat and repeated, 'I doubt it,' in an attempt to be kinder, more patient.

They talked from mid-afternoon until dark. Trevor talked. He rubbed the outside of his throat to keep his voice going. He talked until his throat was quite raw, stopped for a rest, and talked again. He didn't say a single thing that Violet couldn't have predicted, from the

207

moment when he first raised his eyes to her. From the moment when
he said, 'Don't come near me.'

And in the letter which she received from him, a few days
later—in which he said the final things he couldn't quite bring himself
to say to her face—there was also not one word she didn't know
ahead of time. She could have written it for him. (All the letters
written by Dawn Rose were enclosed.) A minister, unfortunately, is
never quite free to love and choose for himself. A minister's wife must
be someone who doesn't bring with her any problem which might
distract her husband and deflect him from serving God and his
congregation. A minister's wife also must not have anything in her
background or connections which would ever give rise to gossip or
cause a scandal. Her life is often difficult, and it is necessary that she
should have the very best of physical and mental health, with no
hereditary taint or weakness, in order to undertake it.

All this came out with a great deal of repetition and enlargement
and side-tracking, and in the middle of it they had some sort of
wrangle about bringing Dawn Rose to see some doctors here, getting
her put away somewhere.

Trevor said that Dawn Rose was obviously a very deranged sort
of person.

But instead of feeling that she wanted the problem of Dawn Rose
solved for her, by Trevor, Violet now seemed to feel that she had to
protect Dawn Rose against him.

'Couldn't we ask God to cure her?' she said.

She knew by his look that he thought she was being insolent. It
was up to him to mention God, not her. But he said calmly that it was
through doctors and treatment that God cured people. Through
doctors and treatment and laws and institutions. That was how God
worked.

'There is a kind of female insanity that strikes at that age,' he
said. 'You know what I mean. She hates men. She blames them.
That's obvious. She has an insane hatred of men.'

Later, Violet wondered if he had been trying to keep a door open
for her then. If she had agreed to Dawn Rose's banishment, would he
have broken off their engagement? Perhaps not. Though he tried to
sound so superior and sensible, he too was probably feeling
desperate.

Several times he had to say the same thing to her.
'I won't talk to you, I can't talk to you, unless you stop crying.'
The minister's widow came in and asked if they wanted supper.
They said no, and she went away, disapproving. Trevor said he
couldn't swallow. When it was getting dark, they went out. They
walked down the street to a drugstore and ordered two milkshakes,
and a chicken sandwich for Violet. The chicken felt like bits of wood
in her mouth. They walked on to the YWCA where she could get a
room for the night. (The room at her boarding-house was being held
for her, but she couldn't face going there.) She said she would catch
the early-morning train.

'You don't have to do that,' said Trevor. 'We could have
breakfast. My voice is gone now.'

It was. He was whispering.

'I'll pick you up,' he whispered. 'I'll pick you up at eight-thirty.'

But never touched, again, his mouth or his cool cheek to hers.

The early train left at ten to eight, and Violet was on it. She
planned to write to the woman at the boarding-house and to
the church office where she had meant to work. She would not
write her examinations. She could not stay in Stratford another day.
Her head ached horribly in the morning sunlight. This time she really
had not closed her eyes all night. When the train began to move it was
as if Trevor was being pulled away from her. More than Trevor. Her
whole life was being pulled away from her—her future, her love, her
luck and her hopes. All that was being pulled off like skin, and hurt as
much, and left her raw and stinging.

Did she despise him, then? If she did, she didn't know it. That
wasn't something she could know about. If he had come after her, she
would have gone back to him—gladly, gladly. Until the last minute
she hoped that he would come running on to the station platform. He
knew when the early train left. He might wake up, and know what she
was doing, and come after her. If he had done that she would have
given in about Dawn Rose, she would have done anything he wanted.

But he hadn't come after her, he hadn't come, no face was his,
she couldn't bear to look at anybody.

At moments like this, thought Violet, it must be at moments like
this that people do the things you hear about, and read about in the

newspapers. The things you try to imagine, or try not to imagine. She could imagine it, she could feel what it would be like. The quick sunny flight, then the smack of the gravelly bank. Drowning yourself would be pleasanter, but would require a firmer purpose. You'd have to keep wanting it, still wanting it, hugging the water, gulping it down.

Unless you jumped from a bridge.

Could this be Violet, could she be the person thinking these thoughts, reduced to such possibilities, her life turned upside down? She felt as if she was watching a play, and yet she was inside it, inside the play, she was in crazy danger. She closed her eyes and prayed rapidly—that too part of the play, but real: the first time in her life, she thought, that she had really prayed.

Deliver me. Deliver me. Restore me to my rightful mind. Please. Please hurry. Please.

And what she afterwards believed that she learned, on this train trip which took less than two hours altogether, was that prayers are answered. Desperate prayers are answered. She would believe that she had never had an inkling before of what prayers could be, or the answers could be. Now something settled in her in the train, and bound her. Words settled on her, and were like cool, cool cloths, binding her.

It was not your purpose to marry him.

It was not the purpose of your life.

Not to marry Trevor. Not the purpose of your life.

Your life has a purpose. and you know what it is.

To look after them. All of them, all of your family, and Dawn Rose in particular. To look after all of them, and Dawn Rose in particular.

She was looking out of the window, understanding this. The sun shone on the feathery June grass and the buttercups and toadflax and all the raggedy countryside that she would never care for, and the word that came into her mind was, *golden.*

A golden opportunity.

What for?

You know what for. To give in. To give up. Care for them. Live for others.

That was the way Violet saw to leave her pain behind. A weight gone off her. If she would bow down and leave her old self behind as

210

well, and all her ideas of what her life should be. The weight, the pain, the humiliation would all go, magically. And she could still be chosen. She could be like the June grass that the morning light passed through, and lit up like pink feathers or streaks of sunrise cloud.

People said that King Billy was never the same after his scare. Never really. They said that he got old, withered visibly. But he had been old, fairly old, when it all happened. He was a man who hadn't married till he was over forty.

He went on milking the cows, getting back and forth to the barn, through a few more hard winters, then died of pneumonia.

Dawn Rose and Bonnie Hope had gone to live in town by that time. They didn't go to high school. They got jobs in the shoe factory. Bonnie Hope became reasonably pretty and sociable, and she caught the eye of a salesman named Collard. They were married, and moved to Edmonton. Bonnie Hope had three daughters. She wrote proper letters home.

Dawn Rose's looks and manners improved, too. She was known in the shoe factory as a hard worker, a person not to be crossed, and one who could tell some good jokes if she was in the mood for it. She married, too—a farmer named Kemp, from the southern part of the county. No strange behaviour, or queerness, or craziness ever surfaced in her again. She was said to have a blunt way with her—that was all. She had a son.

Violet went on living with Aunt Ivie on the farm. She had a job in the Municipal Telephone Office. She bought a car, so that she could drive back and forth to work. Couldn't she have managed to write her teacher's examinations another year? Perhaps so. Perhaps not. When she gave up, she gave up. She didn't believe in trying to get back. She was good at her job.

Aunt Ivie still prowled the yard and the orchard, looking for where some hens might have hidden their eggs. She wore her hat and her boots. She tried to remember to scrape her boots off at the door, so that Violet wouldn't throw a tantrum.

But Violet never did that any more.

Alice Munro

One afternoon when she was off work, Violet drove over to see Dawn Rose. They were friendly, Dawn Rose's husband liked Violet, there was no reason not to arrive unexpectedly. She found the doors of the house open. It was a warm summer day. Dawn Rose, who was very stout now, but gentler and more cheerful-looking, came out on the porch and said that it wasn't a good day for visiting, she was varnishing the floors. And indeed this was so—Violet could smell the varnish. Dawn Rose didn't offer lemonade or ask Violet to sit down on the porch. Just that day she was too busy.

Her little timid-looking fat son, who had the odd name of Dane, came up and clung to her legs. He usually liked Violet, but today he made strange.

Violet drove away. She didn't know, of course, that in a year Dawn Rose would be dead, of a blood clot resulting from chronic phlebitis. It wasn't Dawn Rose she was thinking of, but herself, as she drove along a low stretch of road with trees and thick brush on either side, and heard a voice say, 'Her life is tragic.'

'Her life is tragic,' the voice said clearly and without any special emotion, and Violet, as if blinded, ran the car right off the road. There wasn't much of a ditch at all, but the ground there was boggy, she couldn't get out of it. She walked around and looked at where her wheels were, then stood by the car, waiting for somebody to come along and give her a shove.

But when she did hear a car coming, she knew she didn't want to be found. She couldn't bear to be. She ran from the road into the woods, into the brush, and she was caught. She was caught, then, by berry-bushes, little hawthorns. Held fast. Hiding because she didn't want to be seen, if her life was tragic.

MARIANNE WIGGINS
HERSELF IN LOVE

Marianne Wiggins

H ere's what women say, they say: 'I loved him for his way with words, I loved the skin around his eyes.' They subdivide their men, they apportion to them grassy knolls on which to loll, they make swamp bogs (the things they cannot love) and bottomlands (the areas with margin for improvement). They make mental lists: his nails, his teeth, his nose hairs. They think of men not so much as objects of their love but as a toy that comes wrapped at Christmas, unassembled. His gentleness with dishes. His 'visions'. His wretched socks. The way he tells a joke, the way he shifts the Datsun. The way he lifts his head from kisses on our breasts and gives us back a breath of our perfume. His *naïveté* in face of doom. His stomach muscles and the sweep of his long back.

A man is something which is nothing like the full sum of its parts—the way a snow crystal is not. A little dust, a little air, a little water at high altitude do not freeze the mind in wondrous contemplation of the universe until, in combination, catching on a random tuft of crimson scarf, a snowflake, fluidizing, breaks a woman's heart.

'Tis love.

What women say, they say: 'He hit me like a ton of bricks. He took my breath away. He unhinged me and I started shaking. He undid me. He has done me in.' They turn tin ears on the music of the spheres and talk about his *skin* his *smile* his *tender failings*. No enigma equals why a woman tries to justify her love. Love is not a theft; or is it. Love is not a treason, is it. Love is not a perjury, or crime. It cannot kill, or can it. It will not test the morals of a race, or raze civilization. It won't annihilate the native vegetation. It may not even exist. As God might not. Why bother with it.

But women say, they say: 'I can't go on without him. I think about him night and day. He turns me inside-out.' They say, 'He has *spaces* between his fingers. He has *fine hairs* along his shoulders. He has *toes*.' It's as though discovery of the other sex, the sense of parts apart, discloses brand new meaning on existence. I never knew who *I* was '*till*,' they say, he kissed me or he touched me or he closed his eyes and laid his head down and said 'thank you'.

H erself had had that kind of bliss, and 'You can keep it' was her attitude. Herself had said 'No more.' No more love for her. No more staring pie-eyed at the farthest wall, no more starving, no more feasting, no more fast breaks from routine. The work at hand was far too arduous *a menos de amor.* The work at hand was Being. Thinking. Living. One. Surviving.

In walked Killebrew.

Killebrew that bastard couldn't put two things together without causing one of them to break out in a rash. Herself was decent, ordered, sedulous, just. Killebrew was seepage. 'Oh God, it's Killebrew,' herself might say in much the same way as, 'Oh God, the sink is leaking.' Killebrew appeared from time to time like water on the floor inside a house. Unwanted news.

You'd think if love were going to strike there'd be a sign, some *frissonnement,* the birds gone suddenly, scaremongeringly, *mute.* But nothing outside the mere ordinary graced the day, a Thursday, garbage pick-up day, when Killebrew accumulated like a puddle on her side of the road.

'Hey, Killebrew,' she acknowledged.

'How's herself?' he said.

'Not bad. How's yours?'

'The same. I've been ringing your credenza there for half an hour.'

He pointed toward the door. *Credenza* in this case might signify her doorbell. Or it might not. With Killebrew one never knew.

'So what's up?' she asked, while surveying him: motley mouldy workpants with perhaps no zipper in the fly; workboots; several tattered layers of several tattered shirts topped with a red hooded sweatshirt bunched and tied around his face so he resembled Rumpelstiltskin in a baby bunting.

'Use your phone,' he said.

'Sure. Wander in, you'll find it.' She started walking up the driveway towards the backyard garbage bin. He fell in beside her.

'What are you up to this morning?' he asked. He seemed to have forgotten his request to use her phone. 'You like my sweatshirt?' he asked. He pulled two little peaks of it out from his topography and read the chest logo out loud as though he'd just discovered it: '"N.O.A.A." Know what that stands for?'

215

'Nope.'

'Me neither,' he admitted.

'National Organization of Another Annoyance?' she guessed.

'Yep, that's me.'

'I guess you'll want a cup of coffee, too,' she guessed again.

'Oh, no, just the bill will do, thank you...'

Inside her house he wandered through the downstairs till he found the phone. It was an old house and the phone had been installed in a small front room by some windows. When herself had claimed its tenancy she'd left the phone where she had found it. It seemed inordinately housewifely to have a phone moved to the kitchen. As though a caller might expect to find her there. Battering fried chicken.

'Fred?' she heard him say. 'Is Fred there? Fred is *out?* Well when's he due? No. Fine. No problem. I'll call back.'

Killebrew came back into the kitchen, took his sweatshirt off, and sat down on the blue stool by the stove. Then he stood up, took a coffee cup from her cabinet and poured himself a cup of coffee. 'Murphy's out, the dumb mullah,' he announced. 'Lucky thing I didn't go up there on time.' Then he sat down.

'You want milk?' she asked.

He shook his head.

She leaned against the dishwasher and stared at him and thought this would be as good a time as any to start baking the rum and raisin cake for Christmas. 'Mind if I go about my chores?' she said.

'No, go right ahead. You like my sweater?'

There had been a sweater underneath the sweatshirt.

'It's very nice,' she said.

He made the same gesture he had made before, lifting out the fabric with his thumb and forefinger.

'Did you get it at the thrift shop?' she asked, conversationally.

'It's brand new!' he protested. 'Cosmic knitted it, my birthday was last week.'

'"Cosmic?"'

'And she never knitted anything before.'

'Well, it's very nice. It will keep you very warm.' It looked like vacuum cleaner fuzz, she thought. 'Who's "Cosmic?"' And because she didn't really care, she read the recipe: '"Put the raisins in a bowl and add the rum. Let stand overnight. Stir occasionally." Now *that's* real comic writing...'

'You don't know about The Cosmic and myself? Been going on about four months. Call her The Cosmic Korean. After my divorce I took the pledge, you know: no more white women.'

He looked at her.

'Yeah, they say whole wheat's a whole lot better for you,' she said, pointedly.

'Definitely. Or rye,' he answered. She heard it 'wry'.

He got up, left the kitchen, made another phone call and came back.

'One third cup dark rum to one cup raisins seems like a lot of rum to me,' she said. She measured out the rum and poured it on the raisins. She looked worried. Killebrew came over and peered inside the bowl. 'Those babies will sop it up in no time,' he maintained. He lifted the rum bottle by its neck and took a large swallow of it. He lit a cigarette. He walked into the pantry, stared at all her plates and came back into the kitchen with an ashtray. He sat down.

'"Sift together"... Right, I did that. "A quarter teaspoon salt," it says, "*if desired*"...'

'Don't use it,' he said, emphatically.

She looked at him. 'No?'

'No salt.'

'Sometimes salt, though, brings out sweetness. Heightens it...'

He was staring at her. He stood up, walked to the sink, put his cigarette out with running water and lit another. He left the room to make another call. She heard him say, 'Fred? Killebrew. I'm socked in here in town so I'll be running late. A little late. How late? It won't be *days*, all right?' She thought, This is ridiculous—I don't want to bake this *cake*. I want him to *leave*. He came back into the kitchen and she thought, Ten minutes more and then you're finished, Killebrew.

They talked about a movie they had both just seen. They talked about a book or two, while he poured himself another cup of coffee and smoked another cigarette. She set aside the dry ingredients, chopped the walnuts, watched the clock. '"Freshly grated nutmeg,"' she read; 'Give me a break.' She crossed the kitchen to the spice cabinet. 'That's the sort of instruction we ignore, right? Like "Whip to strong peaks over ice"—' She turned to smile at him and he was

leaning at the counter, bent a little, both hands on his heart.
'John, what the hell—?'
He stared at her.
'For God's sake, are you all right?'
'No. What? I'm with you.'
He began to pace.
'Are you having an attack?'
'What? No.'
'Are you in pain?'
'Pain? No. Yes. I don't know. My heart was beating very fast.'
'Are you having palpitations?'
'No.'
'Sit down.'
'No. Fine. I'm fine. It's going to pass.'
'For God's sake, it's the coffee. I put in these espresso beans, not everyone can—'
'Not the coffee.'
'Plus two cigarettes.'
'Not the cigarettes.'
'And rum.'
'Oh, lady, lots of rum.'
'Anxiety attack. Or stress. You're late for that appointment...'
'No.'
'Do you have to do something today that you don't want to do? That could be the cause of the anxiety.'
'I don't have to do a single thing today that I don't want to do. In fact, I don't have to do a thing, if I don't want to.'
'Well then, Killebrew, it's cigarettes.'
She turned back to the recipe and its freshly grated rinds of lemons.
'In fact,' he said, 'it is anxiety.'
He came to stand quite near her, then moved away.
'It *is* anxiety. It's anxiety over not being able to know how to start to begin to say what I'm going to say.'
She smiled at him, as an encouragement, and walked over to the refrigerator and took out two lemons. He stopped. She looked at him. 'Do I have to be over there,' she joked, pointing to where he stood, 'for you to say it?'

"Yes, ma'am."
She returned.
With the lemons.
He sat down at the table a foot or so from where she was working. The scene smelled of rum, the open jar of nutmeg and, now as she was grating it, tart lemon. 'I wanted to say, what I didn't know if I was going to be able to say was how really nice it is, it's really nice, to come around and sit and drink your coffee and just talk to you...'

She looked up and smiled and tilted her head and said, 'Why, thank you, Killebrew.'

'...And then the other thing, when I was sitting over there,'—he pointed to the blue stool by the stove; she grated—'I was sitting over there and I was thinking why am I sitting here when I really want to walk over there'—he pointed to where she was standing—'and just kiss your face.'

For what seemed a long time she stared at the lemon in her left hand and its odd grater in the other. Then she laid the lemon and the grater down. It seemed to her that some response was necessary and it seemed to her that anything that she could say would be an insult to his sensibility and that the only thing that she could do with any rightness would be bend to him and give him a sweet kiss right on his cheek and when she did that he very gently turned her lips to his and they were kissing. Soon, somehow, they were standing, too, and kissing and the aroma of the lemon from her hands encompassed them. 'I want you,' he whispered. 'I've always wanted to make love to you. I've always acted like a gentleman.'

'We would make very tenderhearted love,' she heard herself observe.

After a while he murmured, 'Let's go upstairs.' She held her breath and considered the idea. 'Oh, no,' he said. 'Oh, no, don't frown.' He placed his lips between her eyebrows where years had traced a worry line. 'I'll leave, if that's what you think I should do,' he suggested, but he didn't budge.

She heard herself admit, 'If we don't do it now, we'll never do it.'
'Then let's do it.'
She sighed. 'Well, all right, John.'
He started to lead her to the stairs. 'You sound so enthusiastic about it. You'll see. This is a great idea.'

219

'It's not a *great* idea, John,' she said, climbing the stairs in front of him.

'You'll see. It's a good idea.'

'It's not the best idea I've ever heard...'

'Oh, no, you're right. Print this on the front page of the *Times* and people won't say *that's* the best idea I've ever heard, but you'll see. It's a good idea...'

Better than most.

In a little while, he was getting dressed again. 'Are you leaving?' she asked. It was a stupid question.

He sat down on the bed next to where she lay and tied his shoes. 'I wasn't even thinking about this when I woke up this morning,' he explained. 'You weren't even on my mind—I guess you were. Yeah, I think you were. I think I thought about you late last night. I was writing a letter to this girl named Connie that I knew once in the third grade back in Buffalo and I was trying to explain my life and this letter just kept going on and going on and I thought, Jesus, who could I ever show this to and I thought of you. I wasn't even writing it to Connie, after a while. I don't know *who* I was writing it to. To whom.' He took her hand. 'Then, I swear to God, I just stopped by your house to use your phone and my heart started pounding. I've never had that happen. Once. One time before. And I thought, John, boy, you've got to say something to her, or you've got to get your coat on and get out the door.'

'You weren't wearing a coat, John.'

'It's allegorical.' He kissed her. 'See me out?'

'No.'

'*No?*'

'I'm staying in bed.' She pulled a pillow close to her. 'I'm somewhere close to being in a dream state...'

'Well, you're right there. That says it.' He looked at her and said, 'This whole thing's put me on "Stun"...'

Friday she didn't run into him in town; nor Saturday. On Sunday she ran into him on Main Street when she went to buy her Sunday papers. He was with a group of other men, dressed for heavy weather, autumn water; scallopers. He looked guilty of contrition and a mite confused.

'Hey, Killebrew,' she acknowledged.

'How's herself?' he asked. The other men were watching carefully to see if something dropped.

'I'm well,' she nodded. 'And how's *your* health, John?' His eyes revealed a clear understanding of her frame of reference, and a tinge of panic that accompanies proximity to an incendiary substance. She slipped her hand inside her coat and laid her palm across one breast so everyone could see and said, 'No more heart palpitations?'

'No, ma'am,' he said, smiling, walking backwards. 'Got that matter well in hand. I saw a specialist.'

'Well, good. You must be real glad it didn't keep me on my back for long—'

She coloured furiously.

She'd meant to say, *you* on *your* back.

Monday came and went and Tuesday morning around ten o'clock she was unloading from her car some kindling she had gathered, when Killebrew pulled up. He sat staring at her from the cab of his truck until she walked over to him. 'Hey, Killebrew,' she said. She thought she ought to be really angry with him but instead she started noticing the skin around his eyes, the different colours intermingling in his beard.

'This is for you,' he said. He handed her a file folder with a few typed pages in it. 'It's the letter I started writing to that girl I used to know in the third grade back in Buffalo. Connie. She and I and her kid brother and my brother Rick grew up together. Long time ago.' He touched a piece of tree bark where it had caught in the loose weave on the cuff of her sweater. 'You shouldn't stand out in the rain,' he told her. She hadn't even noticed it was raining.

She said, 'Can I give you a cup of coffee?'

He held up a chipped mug of coffee and said, 'I have mine,' but he got out of the truck anyway. They walked up the front porch steps and he said, 'Is it after ten o'clock? I promised this old geezer on Hines Point I'd drop off my sander by ten o'clock. He's got the whole day planned around my sander...'

They were in the kitchen and she had taken down a clean cup from the cabinet for herself and gone to the refrigerator for the quart of milk and instead of letting the refrigerator door close automatically, she slammed it. They stared at one another.

'Can I kiss you?' she asked. That part of her that was always squaring edges, crossing out, correcting, justifying, thought 'Can?' *Can* I kiss you? Almost imperceptibly he nodded, yes. In less than a minute they were starting up the stairs, Killebrew shedding his sweater as he went and four minutes later he was lacing up his boots on his way down.

She thought her clock had stopped.

'What are we calling this—"The Phantom Strikes"?' she asked.

'I'm really sorry. No kidding. I wasn't going to come here. Swear to God. This geezer on Hines Point is such a nice old guy...'

John was leaving, half undressed.

She, herself, was in her bare feet, T-shirt and her underwear. He had got up as if the house had been on fire and she had followed right along with him.

'If you can find some time to read my letter I'll appreciate it. It won't take you long to read. It won't take up too much of your time.'

'John, nothing could take less time than this—'

He put his arms around her and held her securely and kissed her. 'Thank you,' he told her.

'For God's sake, Killebrew, you don't say "thank you" to a lover.'

'Right. You're right there. I'll go home and look that up in *Webster's* and it'll say "Not said to a lover"...'

The letter was workmanlike enough in its beginning: Dear Connie, comma. He'd moved away, he'd got married, he'd dodged the draft, he'd had a son. He'd lived in Arizona where his marriage fell apart. He'd worked his trade and made a living, moved around; then finally followed his estranged wife and their son back east to this small fishing village on the bay. That seemed to sum it up, he wrote, except that it suggested a black vacuum at the centre of his life into which his past, his present and his future seemed to float. And maybe that was why he was sitting down to try to write these things. To try to find out where the emptiness came from. Why it existed. When it had begun. Most people didn't understand what he did for a living, he wrote. Or what it meant to him. He was a carpenter. A good one. Most people thought of that profession as being 'in the trades.' And it was true, sometimes to pay his way he had to take the nothing job, nail-banging job. But what he loved to do was finework. Beading a moulding with a ninteenth-century Stanley number forty-five jack plane. Working wood: wood working. 'I've seen men sign the top tread of a gooseneck staircase before fastening it in place,' he wrote. 'I've seen descriptions of the weather of the day on the back of mouldings applied sixty-five years ago, as well as a sequential signing of men who have removed the same moulding. Five names in sixty-five years. Names of extinct millhouses, newspapers—a crew of mine wrote a fifty-chapter novel describing the exploits of, the building of, a house on its framing, to be covered for years to come by wallboard. I personally have taken to putting Latin epigrams and the latest barometric pressure on the back or bottom of piecework as an encouragement to those anonymous artisans, for whom the work is always more important than their names. I admire the ability of those,' the letter ended, 'who could spend fifteen or twenty years building a cathedral. I guess I'm sorry that I'll never get that chance.'

She thought, Love is a Revelation, like a religion, some religions; like Islam. She thought about the tile-cutters, the tile-layers, the mosaicists of mosques. She thought about cathedral spires and pagodas. She thought about the artist's handprint on the cave wall at Lascaux. She thought about what sets humans apart—their art, their fossilizing edifices, love, and their devotion to their sense of time. But time is bogus. Time does not exist in any universal way. It's not the thread that twines through heaven—like gravity, the condition time imposes is exact, but not eternal. The act of even thinking of eternity is a captive act of sitting in time's trap. Without time, what is there? Days of staring pie-eyed at the farthest wall. Minutes leaning on a rake. Hours lost in random conversation.

Nights on 'Stun.'

'It's after one.'

'It isn't.'

'Yes.'

'It can't be.'

'Right you are. You're right there. In Vladivostok, it's not one. But around here, vampires are thinking about lunch...'

223

They had been talking for five hours—making love, and talking. The candles had burned down on her bedside tables and her bedroom seemed a berth inside a floating ship. They had talked about their families and their pasts. Or, *he* had talked and she had listened. It seemed a natural balance, effortless, the way he talked; she listened. His way with words. They'd been lovers ten days, not that she was counting. A week from now, a month, a year: what then? Maybe they would dash their manic clever selves off cliffs into black water.

Here's what women think, they think: Forever.

'Tell me about Connie,' she said.

'Connie. *Consuelo*,' he breathed. He settled down against the pillow and wrapped her in his arms. 'She and I and her kid brother and my brother Rick were trouble on a stick in the third grade. Wasn't anything that could hold still between us. We were thick as thieves. Called ourselves the Chicken Eaters. I was Chicken John. Rick was Chicken Rick. Joe was Chicken Joe. And Con was Chicken Con. Then one day we were running chicken drills, training chickens down by the river. We were standing in this burned-out rubble field by the Niagara and we all, together, got to feeling really weird. Chicken Con, she was a real tomboy and I never saw her do a single thing that anyone could classify as sissy, but she took hold of my hand. They were diverting the water from the American Fall so they could measure its erosion. Whole bunch of geodesic gnomes from the Army Corps of Engineers. Big programme. And us kids were standing down there by the river and this wall of water starts coming through the plain, this enormous wall, water backed up all over itself and the *sound* it makes is just amazing, it must have been, well, I don't know because we were all just kids, it must have been three or four storeys high. And Chicken Con, she got this mean determined look on not to be too scared and she takes hold of my hand. Then, the next thing that you know, it's come and gone. It was all over in a minute. There was nothing we could do but stand right there and stare at it. The most amazing thing. So that's who Connie is.'

She wanted to say, 'I love you, John.'

She lay against him as if she were his shore, and she wanted to say, 'I love you, John,' but something told her he would turn to her and tell her 'thank you' so she lay there, watching him, for what may have passed as hours as he turned in sleep and rolled, inexorably, towards dreaming.

DORIS LESSING
MY MOTHER'S LIFE
(PART TWO)

In the twenties, and even more in the thirties, young middle class people fled from Britain, where they could not get work, to make a life in the colonies. Often they had no money, but knew they would be given land and loans. They struggled, and very often failed. If their families at home sent them their return fares, they went back to what they had left—genteel poverty—and, one presumes, to be rescued by World War Two. How many of them were there? A great many, I think, for the turnover of white people, certainly in Southern Rhodesia, was always large. There is no way now of finding out about them. What a story! What stories! Recently I read two of them, for I was sent a couple of manuscripts by women, memoirs of their lives as white settlers, one in Kenya, one in southern Rhodesia. These people, without any psychological or practical training, found themselves in the bush, usually without an acre cleared for planting, in some kind of shack, coping with floods, droughts, fires, wild animals and black labour which, forced out to work by a Poll Tax imposed for precisely that reason, were sullen, angry, inefficient. Not the least of the ironies was that the whites saw themselves as pitifully poor, and the blacks saw the whites as unreachably rich. Both were right. What comes through most strongly in these accounts is that it seemed—once these unsatisfactory members of the family had left Britain—that Britain was out of sight, out of mind. The most frequent note struck is how small sums of money—fifty pounds, twenty-five pounds—would often have saved a situation, but money was never forthcoming. That the middle classes tend to be mean to their own is well-known, but never have I seen it shown so painfully. Perhaps their families did not have any money to help out with? There was no money to help my parents: all our relatives were just surviving.

These memoirs forced me to think about the differences between my parents and those settlers who would never have left home if only they could have found what my father loathed so bitterly and left: a good, safe, respectable job. There were two kinds of immigrants: those who could not make it in Britain, and those who could, but who would not conform to 'British respectability'. My father was one of the misfits who peopled the landscape of my growing-up, colourful characters whose eccentricities, suppressed in Britain, had plenty of room to expand in Africa.

Above all, it was my mother who was defined by these women's

227

memoirs: reminiscences of failure, incapacity, incompetence, muddle. They could not cope with floods and fires and snakes, or having to cook bread in ant heaps when the kitchen burned down, or making furniture from paraffin boxes, or curtains and dresses from flour sacks. They could not do more than just suffer what was happening to them, and of course they despised and feared the blacks. With what wails of self-pity and misery did they struggle to impose respectability on the veld, their main drive being to remain what they were—middle class; their fear being that they could become poor whites, on the level of the blacks, just as at home their nightmare was that they might be forced into the working class. 'This continent of Africa,' Denys Finch Hatton, says watching the little villas of surburbia marching across the magnificent wildness of the N'gong Hills towards Nairobi, 'has a very fine sense of sarcasm' (from Karen Blixen's *Out of Africa*).

But the fear was real enough. Very often I heard my parents say in the troubled, grieved voice we used for those whose fate may easily be ours, 'So-and-so's gone bust, he's got a job as storekeeper at the mine, she's going to be a matron'—or governess or housekeeper—'and God help those kids.'

Far from wailing and wincing, my mother enjoyed all the contriving and making-do. They complained, 'No decent fruit here, no vegetables, our chickens die . . .' Her vegetable garden could have fed a village, and she had fruit trees, chickens, rabbits. She made cheese, and the store-hut was always full of preserves. She was endlessly adaptable and inventive. She had too much energy, capacity, for her situation. Her fate should have been to run a large organization, hospital or even an industry. On the farm she burned herself out.

Five years after we arrived on the farm, land had been cleared, more and different crops were being grown, but we were much in debt to the Land Bank. The house, built to last two years, was going to have to stand much longer. Verandahs and additions of all kinds had been made. My brother, aged eight, was still being taught at home, but like all the boys of the district he spent most of his time in the bush. I, after a couple of bad choices in the way of schools, was in a convent in Salisbury. Convents are more ladylike than other schools. If my mother had known what went on there, she would have removed me at once, but children do not tell parents about school. She knew only that I was homesick—a symptom seen these days of something very wrong at home, but in those unsophisticated times she saw it as an expression of proper and gratifying affection. She did not feel it shocking to send a child of seven to boarding-school. At that age, children were sent home from India to board; in England boys wee sent at seven to boarding schools: what else could she have done? All the farmers' children went to school in the towns.

Her husband, not her children, was her main worry. It is hard for the competent—and for those who have all their will behind what they do—to understand people who simply cannot make things work. My father's dreams of getting rich in five years had become a brave family joke. Besides, the slump had begun. Long past were the days when farmers made sudden fortunes out of maize; still in the future were the fortunes made out of tobacco. Everywhere, farmers were just holding on, nursing their debts to the Government, running up bills at the grocer and the butcher, taking small risks on crops like sunflower, cotton, peanuts, sunhemp. Things were against my father, but his own nature was worse. He did not really care, and I think she never understood that. War had only intensified what he was, and—from her point of view—that had been bad enough, though she might have remembered that his father, married to an ambitious and forceful woman, had been happy as a bank clerk, spending every free moment playing the organ in the village church. Left to himself, my father would dream his life away, content, contemplating the African night sky, sunsets, ants at work in a log, fires burning their slow way across the mountains in the dry season, the changing colours of the veld—but a good way behind Nature—and the fascinating improbabilities of human behaviour, white and black.

My mother pushed and nagged and made plans. Her aims were simple. Enough money must be made to pay off the debts, and then we must sell the farm and return to England where real life was waiting for her. Talk about life in London went on all my childhood and was referred to by my brother and myself as 'getting-off-the-farm'. It was simply too remote, this talk

229

of good schools and nice houses, of housemaids and buses, theatres and parks.

But my father didn't want to get off the farm. If he reached England, what then? He loathed the bank, where he might not get a job now. And she could not return easily to nursing, with two children. How would they live? Never mind! All that would sort itself out once they had got off the farm.

The pressures from my mother to do better caused my father not to become a successful farmer, but to take a step sideways into the old dream of finding gold.

It sounds absurd, but it wasn't. The district is called Banket, after a certain type of gold-bearing reef on the Rand, identified by some early prospector. All that country is full of gold-bearing reefs and outcrops. My brother and I continually came on old trenches dug by some gold-seeker, or rocks where you could see the prospector had chipped off a sample to pan. There were two gold mines not far from the farm. We could hear the mine-stamps going day and night from the mine just over the ridge. Prospectors came through all the time with guns, pans, hammers, corners of sacks of maizemeal and blankets. They came more often as the slump deepened. There were many men living off the bush in those days— it cost nothing—while their wives rode out the bad time as housekeepers some place where they could also have the children in the holidays. Gold was all about us, in the earth, in talk, in the history of the Rand, which was full of old diggings when the first explorers and missionaries came in. It was said that the old diggings had been made by the Arabs.

When my father took a hammer and brought back samples of rock, then crushed them in the mortar and panned them, he did no more than most farmers did when they came on a likely bit of reef. But very soon it became an obsession. Supervising farm work took second place to gold-seeking. He was spending hours every day stomping over the veld on his wooden leg, and the car always came back loaded with rocks. A man was taken off farm work to dig trenches round a likely reef, pound samples, and take them into the Assay Office in Salisbury. On mail days, as we waited for the results, the tension was painful.

Soon it was not trenches but shafts that were being dug, and not one labourer but two or three were permanently at work. My mother protested that if the same effort were put into the farm work, then . . . But it wouldn't have been enough to change anything in slump-time. Farmers were going bankrupt, their land was being bought by more successful farmers, or by combines. This was the beginning of the creation of enormous units of land, hundreds of thousands of acres large, that would shortly grow not food but tobacco, making the fortunes of the 'tobacco barons'.

And then, it was not just prospecting but divining. My father had discovered he was successful divining for water. And if he could divine for water, why not divine for gold? If he could, it wouldn't just be a question of finding gold on our farm (and that was only a matter of time), but of becoming someone to whom big mining companies from all over the world would come rushing, demanding his services. And then he could train others, and he could start a school of divining . . .

While all this went on, my mother was trying to maintain what to her was normality. I am sure it never occurred to her that a lively social life was something one could do without. All her best memories of girlhood, her years as a nurse and her early marriage in Persia, were of visits and parties and musical evenings and jolly times. Among *nice people*. The people who farmed around us had all been working class or lower middle class, most of them Scots. While we visited them, and they us, and while she performed all the neighbourly functions, exchanging farm produce and helping during times of crisis, these people were not the sort she had in mind. My brother and I did not understand why so much effort had to go into keeping up friendships with people living so many miles away, why this was so important to her. We would 'spend the day' with whatever family it was, on their farm, or they would come to us. Some lived beyond rivers which might be impassable when the rains were heavy.

We would start off early, so as to arrive for morning tea. The men talked farming, and the women hungrily talked—and talked and talked. There was lunch. Then tea. All the people in the district ate five meals a day, a custom they brought from home (the Africans called the whites 'the people who never stop eating'). In between these meals, the children went climbing kopjes or exploring the bush, looking for baboon troops or wild pigs. After supper we drove home through the bush where all kinds of animals appeared in the headlights: the different kinds of buck, from little duiker to the big eland and koodoo, wild cats, porcupines, monkeys. My brother and I fought to stay awake.

These nice people had one thing in common that I didn't see then. They were survivors of World War I. The men had artifical arms or legs or eye-patches. They would discuss the whereabouts of various bits of shrapnel that were forever travelling about their bodies out of sight, but sometimes emerging from healthy tissue to tinkle into a shaving mug or onto a plate. One woman had four sons and a husband killed in the trenches, and farmed with her remaining son. She was dignified, stoical, and her house was filled with photographs of dead men. Another family had two boys whom we played with, but photographs of a third dominated the house and the talk of the parents: he had drowned in a torpedoed ship. There was a man with a steel plate which kept his brains in, and another rumoured to have a steel plate holding in his bowels. They talked about the war, both men and women—the war, the war, the war— and we children escaped from it into the bush.

At home, my brother and I tried to shut our ears against what my father came to call, sarcastically, the Great Unmentionable: 'I don't want to bore you with with the Great Unmentionable, God forbid that you should waste your time on anything so unimportant.' There we might be, the four of us, at the breakfast table. My father of course was thousands of miles away in immagination, probably in the trenches, or at some conference of scientists, all of them hanging on his every syllable. We, the children, sitting on either side of the table, would regard our mother with expressions of embarrassed impatience, while we fidgeted to be off into the bush. 'Do listen,' she would say, 'no, just this once, *listen*. One of these days, when we get off the farm, you'll have to live with nice people, just like everybody else, you won't be racketing around with every kind of person as you do here. Michael— you talk to them! Tell them to listen to me, just this once—*Michael!*'

'What is it?' he would say. 'Oh yes, now then you kids, listen to your mother.' But he would already be up and reaching for his divining rod, and we went as fast as we could after him, trying not to see the hurt, wistful look on her face.

This business of gold meant that the visiting and being visited were always threatened. My father would grumble for days at the prospect of having to go off to this or that family: 'Oh *Lord*, do I have to? Oh very well, but it'll have to be Sunday, when the boys are off.' Or: 'Sorry, impossible, we'll be starting the planting, now the rains have begun.' But he thought nothing of driving thirty miles on a workday to visit some little mine to test out a theory on a reef. He knew beforehand exactly how the reef ran underground, where it petered out, what minerals and rock composed it, how much gold it carried. And there my father was, all day in the punishing sun, a shabby but urgent figure walking back and forth, while my mother sat politely talking with a woman she was sure she had nothing in common with.

And then we drove back through the starlight, the night air scented from the grasses, but chilled, so that we had to wrap up well after the long hot day. My mother, sitting there in her smart hat with her gloves and bag on her lap would say: 'Well, Michael, was it worth it?'

'What, old girl? Yes, I think so.'

'We've been there all day,' she would persist, in the small unhappy voice she used when she felt that it was her duty to be stubborn, 'and there was no one keeping an eye on the farm . . .'

It was not their style to shout or raise their voices, accuse or sulk. I cannot remember this ever happening. But I can remember lying awake at night listening to them arguing. Their voices came easily through the cracking and loosening mud walls. My mother's voice was patient, persistent—the voice of reason. He stood his ground, but it was a very different one from hers. Her facts and figures were all small sober possibilities. His talk was of great sums of money and gold-bearing reefs like glittering rivers.

In 1935, ten years after my parents arrived in the colony, our house was still upright, a shambling old wreck, its thatch continually being repaired, the mud walls lumpy and patched. The roof leaked, and a bad storm sent water down in a dozen places into pails, buckets, basins. I will remember for ever an exquisite hammered copper basin from Persia standing in the middle of the floor on a shabby but glowing Persian rug, a picture from a fairy tale. Water fell into it from the thatch, bringing down beetles and ants that clung to the straws and laboured their way over the edge of the basin, down onto the rug, across the floor to the walls and so back onto the roof.

At the windows, the Liberty curtains still hung, pretty but threadbare. In a trunk behind the curtain a dozen evening dresses bought for the fascinating social life my mother had expected to find here lay in their folds of tissue paper with mothballs, when they were not being used for 'dressing up'. My father's dress clothes lay there too, unregretted.

My father had been talked into doing a couple of seasons of tobacco, and there were two tobacco barns to prove it. Barns were expensive, but they were standing empty. Getting up at night to check temperatures and the steamy air of the curing process (Virginia, not Turkish) had been too much for him. By now he had sugar diabetes as well. If he had got the disease a year before, he would probably have died, for he had it very badly and insulin had only just been discovered. He was supposed to eat only lean meat and lettuce and dry biscuits—but my mother rebelled and said he would die of starvation before he died of diabetes. She took command and worked out with him a variety of foods. She was with every day more of a nurse again. My father, like many diabetics, had become a hypochondriac. The man who had once disdained to make allowances for his wooden leg, climbing trees, riding horses, and going down mine-shafts in dangerous buckets, now talked of his symptoms with the intensity he still put into gold and divining. From resenting gold-fever my mother now became grateful to it, for it kept my father out every day divining, and then he wasn't thinking about his rapidly worsening health.

By now he saw the divining as a new science, which he was founding. He used iron rods and steel rods and twigs of various woods from the bush. He 'neutralized' the gold in the reefs far under his feet with gold rings held in his hands with the ends of the rods. He tried out silver rings, nuts and bolts from the plough, brass curtain rings, or dipped the rods in water, or in solutions of various chemicals and minerals. He worked at it most of the day, and dreamed of it at night. I wrote about my father, disguised, in a tale called 'Eldorado' describing the painful passion for gold. But gold, the lust and itch for it, had long since become secondary. He was lost in this 'science' of his. He believed he was creating a new method for finding any mineral. Gold only one of them. He was alone in the world as he saw it, with no one to talk to, though when they were not at school his children did listen, did try out the rods, and walked with him along the trenches tracking elusive reefs. Only the occasional water diviner who came wandering through the farms, hoping to pick up a five pound note for finding a well, listened to him with understanding, but would start to look quizzical when he began talking about gold and minerals. He wondered where the other people were who must be pursuing this line of thought? Perhaps he could advertise in the newspapers of the world, and make contact with them?

'No, you can *not*', said my mother, 'we can't afford it.' Prophets are never appreciated by their nearest and dearest.

But what could my mother do? Her common sense continually outraged, she suffered and rebelled, but mostly in silence, for she too was alone, with no one to listen to her. She herself had all kinds of symptoms, particularly bad headaches. She knew her heart was weak, but no one took this seriously, not even the doctors. She could sleep only when full of sedatives.

She had got her son into the only school in the country that could be compared with 'real' schools in England, a prep school run along English lines. Of course we could not afford it. She had used all her abilities to pull strings and get grants. But what would happen to him afterwards? Nothing like an English public school was available, and there was the question of his career. No money to set him up, no future! She wanted him to go into the Navy, and spend his life with nice people. But when she talked about it he looked vague, and went off into the bush with his rifle alone, or with a black boy.

Recently my brother came from Africa to visit, and we talked about our childhood in the old thatched mud house in the bush. A miracle of good luck! We had been on land never before farmed, and the bush was still unspoiled by white or by black idiots. We were surrounded by every kind of wild animal and bird, free to wander as we wanted over thousands of acres, solitude the most precious of our gifts . . . but our mother lay awake at night, ill with grief because her children were deprived, because they were not good middle class children in some London suburb.

235

If her son's future was an anxiety, then what could she say about her daughter!

I was always ill at school, and not only with homesickness. I did have a couple of real illnesses, malaria and dysentery, but with my mother's connivance I acquired vague ailments that were always taking me into the convent sickroom with the need to be cossetted. My mother would make her reluctant husband rush her the seventy miles into town, although the word 'rush' here is relative—in our ancient Overland the trip took hours. There she would inform the nuns and the doctor that I must have this or that kind of treatment: *she* knew best, she had been trained at the Royal Free, in London. When I was actually in the classroom, I did well enough, but I was trying to escape from my mother's intense need that I should be cleverer than anyone else. Her schemes for my future had the illusory, poisoned glow of the gold mining talk, to which by then I refused to listen. The music lessons I took must end on concert platforms, because she could have been a concert pianist. If I hummed a tune, grand opera was waiting for me. Talk of great painters accompanied my attempts at drawing. All this was in English terms. It was inconceivable that I, or any other white child, should learn Shona, or try to understand the lives of Africans. (It is impossible to believe now, but a man who travelled around making recordings of African music was considered a Kaffir-lover and a traitor to the whites. A poet who lived in the bush, befriending Africans and liked by them, was hated by the whites, who responded to any mention of him with that loud, uneasy, derisive laughter.)

I also wrote little pieces. But I hid these attempts from her because I felt that they weren't mine, but hers, for she took possession of them, talking about them to everyone.

When I was fourteen I finally slid out of school on a pretext and stayed on the farm, where I lay on my bed reading, or went about the bush with my rifle. I was supposedly ill with 'low fever'. Perhaps I did have it. I certainly had a permanent low temperature, lacked energy, and was dosed with quantities of quinine I am amazed didn't kill me. But there came a rescue. I was sent on a two months' holiday to another part of the country by a charitable organization. There I saw certain things very clearly. One was that there was nothing wrong with me. I knew I had to escape from that house where both parents were ill, obsessed with illness. When I went home I told my mother that I was very well, and said 'It's no good trying to make me ill, ever again.' She did not know what I meant; she believed that I was, as always, cruel and unfair. I think now that she was a bit crazy with the menopause. These days she would be given a few pills and remain her normal, humorous, moderate self.

She was obsessed. With the deficiencies of her black servants, for one thing. Like nearly all the white housewives then (and now, it goes on still in South Africa) she spoke to them in a nagging voice full of dislike, much to the distress of my father. 'What's the point of making people just out of their villages fuss about teaspoons and cups and saucers that match?' Most of the time she listened, but now she cried: 'I suppose you want me to lower my standards!' And she was obsessed with me: my brother was at school and safely out of the way. Everything I was, and did, shocked her. She wanted me to remain a little girl, in a country where girls grew up early. And because she therefore insisted that I wear childish clothes, I defied her and earned money by shooting guineafowl and doves for the local butcher to buy material and make my own clothes: grown-up clothes that she hated. I was reading books that I found for myself, no longer the classics and the 'good' children's books she ordered for me. I was critical about what I saw around me, the poverty of the blacks, the attitudes of the whites, but in a confused, uninstructed way, and this left me vulnerable to her. But what was really making her ill was that she needed to project all her energies and talents into her daughter, who would live, for her, the life she had been prevented from living. But the girl had become a sullen, angry wall of rejection, usually silent, then cracking into rudeness and derision.

'Why do you hate me so much?' she would cry, while I complained to my father, 'Why does she hate me? She has always hated me.'

Now I understand her state of mind very well. She was afflicted by that common disease of middle life, feeling that everything was slipping through her fingers; she could not grasp hold of or retain anything. Or as if she were juggling far too many balls in the air, and knew that if she dropped one they would all come clattering down.

I put an end to the awfulness of being at home with her by going off to Salisbury and becoming what is now known as an *au pair*. (This used to mean rich families in different countries exchanging daughters so that they could learn the language and the customs.) I did this in two different families for eighteen months. It was boring, not too bad; the people were pleasant, everyone got on. But it was a waste of time, and my mother was desperate because her daughter was a nursemaid. Her rage and misery reached me wherever I was in very long letters full of improbable threats, such as that I was bound to end up in the brothels of Beira. I had no defence against a mother I could not recognize, except to become cold and indifferent. I went back to the farm to write a novel. I was the apotheosis of a difficult adolescent. Now I am appalled at how I treated them both—though I could not have done differently. For them it must have been intolerable. For me it was intolerable. I finished and tore up two bad novels and went into Salisbury, and got a job in the Central Telephone Exchange. My mother experienced this as a final defeat: her daughter was a common telephone operator. The life she was leading (not that she told her parents anything, it was necessary to go into Salisbury and make enquiries) was 'fast', cheap and nasty.

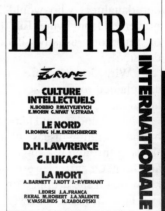

JOHN UPDIKE
ITALO CALVINO

The sudden death of Italo Calvino, scarcely into his sixties, deprives the world of one of its few master artists, a constantly inventive and experimental writer who nevertheless brought to his work a traditional elegance, polish and completeness of design. Twenty years ago, he was little known in the United States; it was John Barth, himself an avant-garde writer with a strong admixture of aesthetic conservatism, who first mentioned him to me, as someone urged upon him by his own writing students. These students had met him, primarily, in the science fiction of *Cosmicomics* and *t zero*. I began to read Calvino, with wonder and delight, and had the pleasure of reviewing at length his beautiful *Invisible Cities,* which was published in English in 1972. What struck me, along with the rigour of the book's intricate scheme and the inventiveness that filled out the scheme with a playful shimmering plenitude, was the tenderness of the civic concern that showed in his fantasy of many cities. The modern writer has often taken a mordant and hostile attitude towards human institutions; Calvino by contrast was a respectful sociologist, an amused and willing student of things as they are.

He was willing, in his basic reverence towards the human honeycomb, to submerge himself for years in his massive anthology *Italian Folktales,* whose pattern of numerous interwoven tales influenced the form of *The Castle of Crossed Destinies* and, to a lesser extent, that of *If on a Winter's Night a Traveller.* Plurality became the method of his fiction, most recently reflected in the twenty-seven symmetrical facets of *Mr Palomar.* This taste for complex patterns of little tales perhaps prevented his acceptance by that large public which likes the long and involving sweep of the novel, and which took Umberto Eco's *The Name of the Rose* to its bosom. But nevertheless within the last twenty years Calvino had become, at least in American academic circles, the best-known living Italian writer, whose name, along with those of Nabokov and Borges and Günter Grass, figured in the inventories of any who tried to compile the 'post-modernist' masters. Post-modernism, if it can be said to exist at all, had in Calvino its most seductive showman—an artist in whom the intellectual and revolutionary passions of the modernists had been transmuted to a marvellously knowing if relatively detached meditation upon the oddities and bemusements of the post-war world.

John Updike

Born in Cuba of agronomist parents, Calvino grew up in San Remo and fought with the Italian partisans as a young man. His war stories written in the late forties are like little else he wrote, in that the material outweighs, in interest, the form. His first novel, *The Path to the Spiders' Nest,* deals, from a boy's point of view, with the same material. Calvino began his literary career as a member of the Communist Party and of the neo-realist movement, but by the fifties had withdrawn from both and worked, as he would for the rest of his life, as an editor for the Turin publishing house of Einaudi. A state of metaphysical and political co-existence seems to be declared in his good-humoured, exquisitely imagined fables. The ancient sense of the tale-teller as an enchanter and verbal magician to an extent lived again in Calvino. Speaking at Columbia University in New York a few years ago, he described the Italian writer's need for finish, for elaborate schemata, as a way of coping with the quicksand upon which he stands. Certainly no fiction writer of his time was more fine-spun in the designs he perpetrated.

With all due homage to the insights and harmonies of his later work, the trilogy of early fanciful novels with parallel titles (collected in English as *Our Ancestors*) remains in my mind as perhaps the liveliest and blithest item of his production. All three begin with premises that seem impossible—a knight who is non-existent, a mere empty suit of armour; a viscount who is half a man, with one eye, arm and leg; and a baron who decides to live among the trees, vowing never to set foot on the ground. Calvino's inexhaustible fancy and great literary tact breathes life into these grotesques, and uses them to illustrate not only metaphysical and psychological ideas but to illumine various historical epochs. The learning behind his flights of fancy was always solid and extensive; his make-believe was spun from the real straw of scholarship. Of the three novels, the most extended and the most charming is *The Baron in the Trees,* which serves as a metaphor for the Enlightenment and for the life of the mind. Moving from limb to limb like a bird, concocting for himself many ingenious arboreal amenities, Cosimo avoids the earth even in death, when the dying old man sails skyward in a balloon. Calvino, too, seemed to live well off the ground—though of course the trees he so nimbly explored were firmly rooted in our earth. The son of scientists, he is never loose or vague in his inventions, even when they have the luxuriance of

242

tropical plants. His creative impulse, if a single one can be discerned behind an *oeuvre* so variously antic, so tirelessly eclectic and bookish, was a curiosity concerning how men live, with each other and in this crowded and paved-over world that they have made. His death removes from the global literary scene its most urbane star, its most civilized voice.

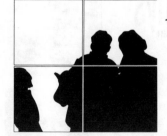

The role of women in society has been
redefined in the twentieth century – a
handful have led the way . . .

LIVES OF MODERN WOMEN

A major new Penguin series

General Editor: Emma Tennant

Freya Stark
CAROLINE MOOREHEAD

Rebecca West
FAY WELDON

Jean Rhys
CAROLE ANGIER

Bessie Smith
ELAINE FEINSTEIN

All £2.95
Also available in Viking hardback

NOTES FROM ABROAD

Israel
Amos Oz

My intention is to write one or two things about contemporary Hebrew literature, but as a matter of fact I already have second thoughts about my subject. It's the word 'contemporary' that baffles me. It occurs to me, really, that I should tell you some of the story of modern Hebrew literature, rather than pretend to sum it up for you and squeeze it into definitions and formulae: I am a story-teller, not a scholar. And stories of course are never 'contemporary', not even if they are set in the present time or told in the present tense. A story is bound, almost by. definition, to relate the past. Story-tellers are cripples, monsters really, born with their necks and faces turned backwards. So, although you may expect a report about the present, hoping perhaps to get a glimpse of the future of Israel and its literature as well, I am here to sell you nothing but old hats.

But just how far into the past do I go? Where does my story properly begin?

I could describe a number of significant recent Hebrew books—that would be the easiest thing to do—along with some plot summaries, and then put them all in a familiar context: so I could tell you who exactly is Israel's Saul Bellow, who is García Márquez, who resembles Günter Grass, who are the Frosts, the Ted Hugheses or the Solzhenitsyns in our little Israeli village. This is tempting and could be fun. In fact, I sometimes amuse people faintly familiar with Israel's literary scene by telling them that it is much like a continuing earthquake, with various geological strata exposed that have to be watched simultaneously: if you hit the right café in Tel Aviv at the right time of day you would see—at least until a few years ago—the John Donne and the Lord Byron of Hebrew poetry, and the Walt Whitman and the T.S. Eliot sitting together at the same table with the local Allen Ginsberg, all of them alive (and kicking hard), all of them on speaking—or rather on screaming—terms with each other. All this results from the fact that literary developments that occurred in English and other European literary traditions over centuries have taken place within decades in Hebrew.

I could go even further along the same line by pointing out that modern Hebrew has several features in common with Elizabethan English: our language is still like melting lava, an erupting volcano; it's bubbling still with steam and with fumes and with fury. A poet or a writer of modern Hebrew is still in a position to 'legislate' within the language, to force or seduce the language into 'having it his or her way'. I dare say that by comparison, modern English is a respectable elderly person with whom you do not dare take wild liberties so easily. (Admittedly Faulkner and Joyce and some other raving poets did just that to English.) But Hebrew nevertheless seems to encourage such practices: she still is a character of easy virtue.

The truth is, however, that despite some striking similarities and despite the strong influence of literature from eastern and western Europe, the basic context of Hebrew literature has always been Hebrew and Jewish and, recently, Zionist. Which makes my task much harder than it could have been if I thought that the context was basically European.

So where, at last, do I begin my story? I could start with the madmen, the desperados, those Hebrew poets and writers who emerged from the ghettos of Eastern Europe at the turn of this century: Mendele and Berdichevsky, Bialik and Brenner and Gnesin, the figures of 'The Great Generation'. I refer to them as madmen and desperados because they were writing in Hebrew for an audience that hardly existed, with little hope of future generations of readers. For many years they wrote in Hebrew to be read mainly by their fellow Hebrew writers and by very few others. Some of them died without ever dreaming that their words would be taught in school or that streets and kibbutzim would be named after them. In fact, at least some of them felt that they were the very end of Hebrew. They regarded themselves as authors of a tragic epilogue for an ancient drama that had begun millennia earlier and that was now, as they saw it, dying in the gutters.

So why didn't they simply quit? They were, after all, excellent writers in other languages. All of them could easily write in Yiddish—still the language of millions and, incidentally, the native tongue of them all. Some of them could have gone very far in this world by switching to Russian or German or Polish. Who, at the turn of the century, really cared to read Hebrew? Whom did they have in mind? There was a further complication: Bialik and Brenner and Berdichevsky knew only too well that there were millions of Jews at the turn of this century who could read Hebrew but only in their holy books, and not—Heaven forbid!—in secular ones. While at the same time there were already more and more Jews ready and eager to read stories and poems, but would rather read them in Russian or German or Polish. So for whom did those members of 'The Great Generation' write their Hebrew, whom did they have in mind? I happen to believe that at least a touch of the same madness and despair is still present in every significant contemporary Hebrew work, just as it is still secretly feeding the true Zionism (not the distorted Zionism—I refer to despair and zeal not insanity and fanaticism).

Where on earth do I begin? With Peretz Smolenskin perhaps, or with Mendele, who struggled to compose mimetic Hebrew prose à la Charles Dickens or à la Balzac and Victor Hugo, many years before any man in the world had ever said to a woman, 'I love you,' in modern Hebrew? Or do I start with Hayyim Nahman Bialik, who loved and hated and demolished, and who at the same time preserved and reconstructed in his Hebrew verse a Jewish world which in his days was still alive (in Yiddish) and still creative and vivacious (in Yiddish) and still blossoming (in Yiddish) with its last pulses of vigour? Oh, those sons and lovers and killers and undertakers and monument-builders and museum-keepers of the great shadow-state of the Jews in Eastern Europe, why and how did they do all this in Hebrew? After all, those writers, as well as their heroes, used to laugh and to weep and talk and dream and make love in languages other than Hebrew, which at the time was almost as dead as ancient Greek or Latin. Why on earth did they do it?

I suspect a deep sense of despair was behind all this. A terrible premonition of doom. Perhaps they sensed somehow that all was lost anyway, that soon there would be no more Jews, no more Yiddish or Hebrew. Perhaps it really was like a homecoming of a dying man. At least of Bialik, Berdichevsky and Brenner I suspect in fact that sometimes they wrote not for the living, not for any future generations of readers, but precisely for the ancient dead. Or was there, after all, some secret hope beyond hope? I do not know. All I know is that all of us write or talk to the dead in moments of great despair.

So where does my story begin? Perhaps at 48 Mile End Road, Whitechapel, London, in the year 1906, with twenty-six-year-old Yosef Hayyim Brenner who lived there, a wretched Jewish refugee from Russia, in a miserable rented room. He worked as a typesetter and lived on cabbage and potatoes, yet he was putting together nothing less than a fresh and modern and non-conformist Hebrew literary magazine. He printed it with his own hands and bound it with cheap glue and carried it in a sack on his back to the Post Office to be mailed to his 212 subscribers, scattered in eight or nine countries (hardly a handful of them in London itself), just a bunch of lunatics like himself who had not abandoned Hebrew, but were nonetheless bitterly divided into half a dozen rival literary 'movements'.

Not that Brenner had much faith in what he was doing. On the contrary. Just like his wistful characters, and just like his raving opponents, Brenner felt that it was all over and doomed: Zionism and Hebrew, as well as the world of Jewish Eastern Europe. Many of his characters, Tolstoyans who stepped right out of a Dostoevsky novel, were desperate people who maintained that the Jewish people was dying of an incurable, malignant, inherited disease. Nevertheless, something ought to be done to survive and even recover, no matter how pathetic or useless this 'something' might be. Brenner made his characters speak Hebrew; he made them pronounce in it thoughts that were, if anything, existentialist long before existentialism. His stories suggest that all of us are left alone in the world and it's up to us to struggle against odds, that we are bound to lose the battle and yet we ought to fight it. Brenner made his lone heroes say all this in Hebrew, perhaps as a kind of metaphysical protest: Hebrew was, after all, the language of the non-existing God; so with a complaint that God would never hear, let Him not hear it in Hebrew.

It would be unthinkable to call those writers of 'The Great Generation' *orthodox* in any sense, but then it would be equally wrong to call them *secular*. Even the raving atheists among them were obsessed with theology. Even those who denied God along with Judaism altogether were obsessed by the absence of God, and agonized over the stagnation of Judaism. Sceptics like Berdichevsky were nonetheless intrigued by believers. Rebels like Bialik and Brenner were nonetheless writing with a mixture of loathing, anger and envy about faith and redemption. Brenner himself even went so far on occasion as to create his own kind of theology for a Godless world.

Brenner, it has been pointed out many times, hated Jews. One Jew he hated in particular: himself. He called his collection of miserable characters—those dropouts and self-educated little refugees from Eastern Europe without guts or purpose—'Dead Souls'. There are, however, a few stunning exceptions in his stories. But most of them—including even his characters of pioneers in Palestine, where he himself settled in 1909 and where, in 1921, he was murdered in Arab riots—are, as he described them, 'Living Ghosts'. Hopeless Puritans, endlessly talking of sensual liberation; intellectuals chatting day and night about manual work and about 'going back to the land'. Little politicians using big words. Eternal wanderers, uprooted forever, exchanging phrases on 'roots'; atheists, sweating with guilt and shame whenever they dare to dream about a shadow of a woman. Would-be world reformers who cannot even tie their own shoelaces. Oh, he hated their guts. Yet let me tell you something: with an enemy like Brenner, who needs friends? Read *Breakdown and Bereavement* and see for yourself the desperate compassion he had after all for his characters, of whom he sometimes wrote like the worst of all anti-Semites. He made them look sick and phony and pompous, or at best pathetic and hopeless. That's what Brenner did, and that is what many other members of 'The Great

Generation' of modern Hebrew literature did, if not as vehemently. And this is the real context of even the most contemporary Hebrew literature: the soul-searching self-hatred mingled with compassion, wrath, irony and a sense of 'unrealness': about the people, the time, the place and the language.

What then happened when Brenner's own characters, his own models in real life, read his stories? Something that is, I believe, unique in the history of world literature: once the characters had read about themselves in the stories by Brenner and his fellow writers, they were deeply hurt, insulted, humiliated and shocked. In fact they grew very angry, not with Brenner (after all, they had all been through Dostoevsky before) but with themselves and with the entire air of decline and decomposition of Diaspora Jewish life, traditional and 'modernized' alike. So Bialik and Berdichevsky and Brenner and the others, without really meaning to, started the fire and the zeal of those few hundreds and eventually thousands of 'desperados' who created the foundations for modern Israel. Our grandparents. My own family. In a strange, paradoxical way they burned with desire to show Brenner just how wrong he was. So they stepped right out of his stories and indeed right out of their own skin just to show him that they were not at all what they really were. I realize that, with characters suddenly leaping out of the pages to demolish their author, this may sound like some wild detective story, but that's how it worked: a literature meant ultimately to commemorate a dying world ignited a revolution beyond its authors' wildest hopes. And so, eventually, Brenner's own characters made his stories sound wrong and cruel and hateful and shortsighted: his heroes became his refuters. Which is exactly what he might have wished in his heart of hearts.

Now, what has this to do with present-day Israeli literature? When, if ever, am I going to get to the point and discuss Natan Zach, Yehuda Amihai, Dan Pagis and Dahlia Ravikovitch? And what about Aharon Appelfeld and Abraham B. Yehoshua and Amalia Kahana-Carmon and their more recent successors?

Apparently, what is happening in the free state of Israel belongs to a brand-new story. Apparently, gone are the days of a ghost language used by desperate writers to mourn a dying world. Can't we just let the dead bury their dead and go about our own business? Indeed, such a mood prevailed over so-called 'Sabra Literature' for about one decade, just before and just after independence was achieved. Books seemed to convey a lot of heroism, and to celebrate the Gentile-Jew type, the new heroic, Jewish John Wayne, toiling over the land all day, fighting Arab attackers at dusk, then making wild love to the kibbutz girls all night. There was a combination of glee and machismo, perhaps a touch of Hemingway at his worst, and a touch of enthusiastic, Soviet-inspired Social Realism. But let me stress that even for those euphoric late-forties and fifties, my description is unfair to some major writers and poets like S. Yizhar, Amir Golboa and Haim Guri in his better poems. In fact my description refers just to the general widespread literary mood in those years. The pulses of dread and of guilt, of unreality and of neurosis had never disappeared completely from the literary scene.

Since the sixties, roughly, one can decipher a significant revival of themes and tunes and melodies and even techniques which used to be identified with 'The Great Generation'. It is the basic Hebrew context which reappears in the last two decades: the persistent fear of approaching disaster. Time and place feel suddenly unreal. There are longings for far-away places. Scepticism, irony and even self-hatred. Political siege is conceived as emotional siege. There are persistent, tormented moral ambiguities. And ultimately: the effort, which used to be so typical of 'The Great Generation', to seize within a fluid language a fluid, transitory reality.

The lasting conflict with the Arabs, sixty-five years of bloodshed and five full-scale wars, has not turned our literature into either a patriotic battle-cry or else a shallow, whining pacifist manifesto. The conflict has been conceived in Israeli literature as a Greek tragedy, a clash between right and right, rather than as a Wild West film. The sufferings of the Palestinian Arabs are often confronted, in a tragic way, with the historical ordeal of the Jews.

Arab fanaticism and ruthlessness is mirrored in several recent novels by the new Israeli arrogance and short-sightedness. Very much in the footsteps of Brenner and his fellow writers of 'The Great Generation', contemporary poets and story-tellers tend to fuse the private, personal experience with public, political and historical dimensions of reality. To many Israelis, history is a biographical experience, and biography is soaked with history.

As I was gathering material for my recent book, *In The Land of Israel,* I was fascinated to discover to what extent the person in the street in Israel is obsessed with public affairs; to what extent the entire Israeli nation is but a passionate seminar on politics, on ideology, on metaphysics, on 'the real purpose of God': a fiery collection of arguments, rather than a country or a nation. In a street café in a small town called Bet Shemesh, I found myself surrounded by an angry mob of observant, right-wing, hawkish, Oriental Jews, almost all of them sworn Beginites. They screamed at me that I ought to be hanged, drawn and quartered for being secular, a social-democrat and a dove. Yet those people were showering me with loving kindness and with warm, Oriental hospitality, insisting on paying for my coffee and lighting my cigarettes for me. They treated me as a stray lamb, a confused and embarrassing member of their own family. Rather than hang me, they actually strove to save my soul. Which is exactly what I tried to do with them.

Every queue by a bus stop in Israel is likely to catch a spark and turn into a soul-searching, theological session (with its participants, while speculating on 'the real significance of Jewish history' and about the secret divine scheme, nonetheless elbowing their way to the front of the queue). If you promise to take it with a pinch of salt, I will tell you that this nation of four million citizens is really an uneasy coalition of four million prime ministers, if not four million self-appointed prophets and messiahs.

The current literature reflects this vividly. You are not likely to find an Israeli novel about an academic writer unable to produce his next book, dashing to see his analyst, and ending up writing yet another bloodless novel about an author who went to discuss his writer's block with his psychotherapist. Rather, you will find in our current literature family stories reflecting a general social crisis, or a public crisis that becomes the background for a family tale. The political tends to turn metaphysical. An intimate pain begets a theological quest. A struggle between parent and child reflects a gap between the magnitude of the initial dreams and visions and the dreariness of petit-bourgeois realities. Nostalgia is not the right term here; it is a perpetual yearning for what *could have been,* rather than for any past 'finest hour'. There is in almost every current work of Israeli literature a secret pulse of messianic yearning.

If there is any common denominator for writers as different from each other as, say, Amihai and Amalia Kahana-Carmon, it is the following: the language is stretched to contain a gushing river of an unsettled reality. It is still the widespread feeling in today's Israeli literature that whatever looks real and permanent today has not been there yesterday and might be gone tomorrow; or else that tonight's dreams, nightmares or horrid memories might become real life next morning.

Israeli readers do not really enjoy their literature. They read it as if obsessed. They often complain that present-day writers and poets endanger the 'national morale' and damage Israel's self-image and reputation in the outside world. So, it may be that one day we, too, are going to irritate our readers to the point that they throw away our books and curse us and are moved to do something far-fetched and angry.

If and when this happens, it will turn contemporary Israeli literature, even though *post eventum,* into a political literature in the broadest sense of the word. Our readers may then become our refuters. If and when this happens, we may deserve to share the same bookshelf with Brenner and other members of 'The Great Generation'. And finally: you must have seen for yourselves that the story of modern Hebrew is characterized by despair and longing and incredible obstinacy along with a tremendous will for life. Indeed, it's a story full of sound and fury. Maybe it takes an idiot to try and squeeze some of it into a piece like this.

PICADOR
OUTSTANDING
INTERNATIONAL
WRITING

PICADOR

THOMAS PYNCHON

SLOW LEARNER

Slow Learner

The Early Stories

Thomas Pynchon

Five stories from this notoriously elusive writer, dating from 1959 to 1964, four of them written while Pynchon was still at college. Also included is a 20-page Introduction in which Pynchon paints a remarkably frank portrait of himself as a young man trying to develop a style of his own.

'Anything from the most monstrous talent in the post-war West should be pursued in earnest. I've eaten two copies already' *Time Out*
Paperback £2.95

PICADOR

STORIES BY BOB SHACOCHIS

EASY IN THE ISLANDS

Easy in the Islands

Bob Shacochis

Uncomprisingly realistic stories about Americans who have fled to the Caribbean in the hope of finding an easy-going life. Instead, they are confronted with a more complicated, extreme and passionate world than the one they left, in which intrigue, romance, politics, weird humour, poverty and extravagance are inextricably mixed.

'The stories in *Easy in the Islands* are well observed, witty, the work of a sure hand' *Robert Stone, author of A Flag for Sunrise*
Paperback £2.95 Hardback £8.95

PICADOR **JULIAN BARNES**

FLAUBERT'S PARROT

Flaubert's Parrot

Julian Barnes

'An intricate and delightful novel'
Graham Greene

'Endless food for thought, beautifully written . . . A tour de force'
Germaine Greer

'Delightful and enriching . . . A book to revel in!'
Joseph Heller

'A delight . . . Handsomely the best novel published in England in 1984' *John Fowles*
Paperback £2.95 Published: 8 November

A

BOOK

OF

ONE'S

OWN *PEOPLE AND THEIR DIARIES*

THOMAS

MALLON

PICADOR

A Book of One's Own

Thomas Mallon

A Book of One's Own is a deliciously witty and wide-ranging exploration of the art and history of diary writing. It is a guide to the great diaries – from Samuel Pepy's to Anais Nin's – and to the private chronicles of the famous, the infamous and the anonymous.

' . . . Reading it is like screening other people's dreams – at once intriguing and familiar' *Time*
Paperback £3.50 Published: 8 November

Notes on Contributors

An anthology of pieces from *Night and Day* of which **Graham Greene** was co-editor from July to December 1937, is available from Chatto and Windus in Britain. **Teresa Toranska** left Poland in the spring of this year, and is currently living in Paris. As this issue goes to press, she is preparing her book, *They,* for foreign publication. **Patrick Marnham** is the author of *So Far from God: A Journey through Central America.* His work has appeared in *Granta* 9 and 10, 'Travel Writing'. **Milan Kundera** lives in Paris and is currently working on a new novel. He is a regular contributor to *Granta.* **Bruce Chatwin** is the author of *In Patagonia, On the Black Hill,* and *The Viceroy of Ouidah.* He was in Benin in 1977. **Nadine Gordimer**'s essay 'The Essential Gesture: Writers and Responsibility' was published in *Granta* 15. **David Goldblatt** lives in Johannesburg. He and Nadine Gordimer are currently preparing *Lifetimes: Under Apartheid,* book of David Goldblatt's photographs and excerpts from Nadine Gordimer's fiction. **Hanif Kureishi**'s first film, *My Beautiful Laundrette,* opened in New York in February. 'A Letter to my Sons' is the last piece **Heinrich Böll** wrote before he died in July of this year. 'October, 1948' is from **Kazuo Ishiguro**'s second novel, *An Artist of the Floating World,* which Faber publish on 17 March. Part Two of **Alice Munro**'s 'A Queer Streak' will be published in *Granta* 18. It will also be included in her next collection of stories, *Progress of Love,* to be published in Britain in a year's time by Chatto and Windus. **Marianne Wiggins** is the author of three novels, including *Separate Checks.* **Doris Lessing**'s most recent novel is *The Good Terrorist.* The first part of her autobiographical account of her mother appeared in *Granta* 14, 'Autobiography'. **John Updike**'s most recent novel is *The Witches of Eastwick.* **Amos Oz**'s most recent book is *A Perfect Peace.* His piece is extracted from the William Jovanovich Lecture he gave at Colorado College.